John Stoughton

Lights and Shadows of Church Life

John Stoughton

Lights and Shadows of Church Life

ISBN/EAN: 9783337253745

Printed in Europe, USA, Canada, Australia, Japan

Cover: Foto ©Lupo / pixelio.de

More available books at www.hansebooks.com

LIGHTS AND SHADOWS
OF CHURCH LIFE

BY
JOHN STOUGHTON, D.D.

NEW YORK
A. S. BARNES & CO.
56, EAST 10TH STREET
1895

PREFACE

A FEW years ago I printed for private circulation a small volume on the lights and shadows of primitive Christendom, confining my view to the first three centuries, when the Church was unconnected with the State. Copies of the book were forwarded to several clergymen, including some distinguished scholars whom it was my privilege to know, and a number of Nonconformist brethren, including College professors and others of acknowledged learning. They asked me why I did not *publish* what I had written. Their kindly commendations encouraged me to review and revise the essay; and I saw it was advisable, if I did so, to continue my review down to the end of the sixth century, when the Church appeared under a new aspect, as protected and patronised by the State.

The approval of Episcopalian friends I took as

a recognition of the unsectarian purport of what I had written. The same spirit I had manifested in the first part of what I wrote I have endeavoured to maintain in the second My intention has been to present certain salient points in the constitution and proceedings of early Christendom, rather than to cover the whole ground which belongs to what is called "a history of the Church." Much is by me passed over which belongs to such a work as that title indicates, and subjects on the following pages are introduced not usually noticed by ecclesiastical historians. My aim is to point out on the one hand Christian excellences, and on the other religious defects.

If we confine attention to what corroborates our own beliefs, and decline referring to what opposes them, we take the place, not of historians, but of advocates, probably at the expense of historical justice, and certainly we miss the opportunity of affording warnings and cautions to those who stand in need of them. Also, if we pay exclusive or principal attention to the shady side of our subject, and shut out or obscure what illustrates genuine principles and examples not adopted by ourselves, we sacrifice benefits which can be gained only by a study of the entire subject.

Illustrations of faith and holiness, in those from whom more or less we differ, should be to us inspiring no less than grateful; and traces of error, superstition, and worldliness seen in those who have set us a good example in other respects should be used as warnings, helpful in the resistance of temptations besetting people in the nineteenth century as they did those of the first six.

Christendom and Christianity are not the same. Christianity pure and simple is the source of real goodness; but Christendom produces what is no part of Christianity. A system of doctrine and discipline exists in Revelation as a planetary system exists in the starry skies; and as in nature, so in Revelation, Divine guidance should be sought in daily life. Astronomical schemes have been contrived contrary to the original order published long ago and stereotyped; in like manner schemes of religious faith and ecclesiastical polity have been proposed in Christendom very different from inspired statutes in the Old and New Testaments.

The rise and progress of innovations in beliefs and practice it is our duty to trace to their real sources—some obvious, others difficult to discover.

Such discovery is the business of students in ecclesiastical history, and help in this direction is an object designed and desired by the author of the present volume.

Our judgment of principles and persons should not be guided by the same rules. Principles are not affected by times and circumstances; they remain unalterable age after age, and what was taught by inspired Apostles remains the same yesterday, to-day, and for ever. The forgetfulness of this has caused more mischief in Christendom than historians have discovered. But individual character is influenced to a wonderful extent by the age in which our lots are cast. Christians of the first six centuries are not to be judged in the same way as Christians of the nineteenth.

There is a passage in the Second Epistle of Peter where the writer speaks of being diligent in the Christian life, by adding to godliness brotherly kindness, and to brotherly kindness *charity*. A beautiful addition is that to our professed Christianity, for it is adapted to conciliate and bring over to Christ's side and service those who, at present, stand aloof. I believe nothing can be more winning on the Church's side than to gather up and reflect lights which the Divine Lord kindled long ago, and keeps shining in Christian literature still. Brotherly kindness and charity will effect what nothing else can accomplish. "Charity suffereth long, and is kind; charity envieth not; charity vaunteth not itself, is not puffed up, doth not behave itself unseemly, seeketh not her own, is not easily provoked, thinketh no evil; rejoiceth not in iniquity, but rejoiceth in the truth; beareth all things, believeth all things, hopeth all things, endureth all things." The extent to which this charity is absent accounts for still existing shadows in contemporary Christendom.

The great lights in literature have not always been charitably regarded. For instance, amongst primitive Fathers Origen of Alexandria has often been regarded simply as an example of theological self-sufficiency, making human reason the supreme test of truth and righteousness, and obstinately refusing to come under the yoke of Divine Revelation. On the other hand, Augustine of Hippo is regarded as self-bound on the chain of an eternal predestination, without any freedom of human activity and human choice. Some critics regard opinions, thus apprehended, as the sum and substance of specimens in patristic teaching. Thus wrong has been done to both. Even where "brotherly kindness" has been shown to these authors, as men of genius, charity has been denied to them as Christian teachers, and they have been unsparingly condemned. In other quarters such authors have been discriminatively treated, and what in them is true has been sifted out of what is erroneous. Such a course is what reason and justice demand.

It is such an ideal course that I have endeavoured to pursue in the following pages; but I fear not with the success desired.

NOTE.—Owing to imperfection of sight at my advanced age (87), I have been mainly dependent on my dear daughter, Mrs. Lewis, for corrections of the press; her assistance in many other ways has been of essential service in preparing this volume for publication.

CONTENTS

PART I

CHAPTER I
PAGE
INSPIRED RECORDS AND OTHER CHRISTIAN WRITINGS 1

CHAPTER II
RELIGIOUS NOVELS . . 14

CHAPTER III
LANDMARKS OF EARLY ECCLESIASTICISM . . 25

CHAPTER IV
LEADERS AND SCHOOLS OF THOUGHT . . . 49

CHAPTER V
DIFFUSION OF CHRISTIANITY . . . 90

CHAPTER VI
PERSECUTION AND HEROISM . 108

PART II

CHAPTER I
CHURCH AND STATE UNDER CONSTANTINE . . 129

CHAPTER II
SUBSEQUENT EMPERORS . . . 148

CHAPTER III
POST-NICENE COUNCILS . . 162

CHAPTER IV
EASTERN SEES, BISHOPS, AND FAMILIES 182

CHAPTER V
AFRICAN CHURCHES . . 211

CHAPTER VI
WESTERN BISHOPS 226

CHAPTER VII
EPISCOPAL ROME AND ITS CATACOMBS . 239

CHAPTER VIII
LATIN DIVINITY.   259

CHAPTER IX
RELIGIOUS WORSHIP   . 280

CHAPTER X
INCIPIENT EUROPEAN NATIONALISM   289

CHAPTER XI
MONKS AND MISSIONS 312

CHAPTER XII
ECCLESIASTICAL REVENUE AND OUTSIDE HELP .   . 332

CHAPTER XIII
SEPARATION BETWEEN EASTERN AND WESTERN CHRISTENDOM 341

CHAPTER XIV
THE BORDERLAND OF CHRISTENDOM   . . 351

CHAPTER XV
THE DIVINE LAWBOOK OF THE CHURCH . . . 359

CHAPTER XVI

HOLY CATHOLIC COMMUNION . . . 372

CHAPTER XVII

ON THE EDGE OF THE DARK AGES   381

INDEX .   389

PART I

CHAPTER I

INSPIRED RECORDS AND OTHER CHRISTIAN WRITINGS

NO one can study the origin of Christianity as we find it in Scripture, without being struck with the large information afforded on the subject. Buddhism, Brahmanism, Parseeism, are indistinct, as to origin and early progress. But in the New Testament we are face to face with the Divine Founder of our faith, and His disciples. In the four Gospels, with the Acts and the Epistles, we learn the foundation of Christianity; in the Acts of the Apostles we discover the beginnings of Christendom.

The four Gospels reveal the history of our Lord; and as old painters sometimes put their initials in the corner of their pictures, so the first Evangelist introduces his name in an early part of his narrative: "And as Jesus passed by, He saw a man, named

Matthew, sitting at the receipt of custom; and He saith unto him, Follow Me. And he arose and followed Him."[1] Sharp-sighted, clear-headed, honest-hearted, with a divinely given mastery of his subject, he wrote down what he had seen and heard, while following the Lord. At the beginning of his Gospel he reports the Sermon on the Mount; and at the close, a prophetic discourse touching the world's end, and the division of mankind into two companies, as "the shepherd divideth his sheep from the goats."

The second historian is Mark—to a large extent the amanuensis of Peter, who refers to him in his First Epistle, saying, "The Church that is at Babylon, elected together with you, saluteth you; and so doth *Marcus my son*."[2] This connection of the two, Mark and Peter, in authorship, gives special interest to the second Gospel, imparting a touch of inimitable tenderness to the angelic message after the resurrection, "Go, tell His disciples and *Peter* that He goeth before you into Galilee."[3] Justin Martyr calls Mark's Gospel "The Reminiscences of Peter." Tertullian says the Gospel is named after Mark, because "Mark edited the Gospel of Peter"; Irenæus adds, "Mark

---

[1] Matt. ix. 9. [2] 1 Peter v. 13. [3] Mark xvi. 7.

wrote it after the *Exodus* of Peter." Jerome describes it as "Peter's narration, and Mark's penmanship."[1] With these testimonies still preserved, we can scarcely doubt Peter's share in the composition of the second Gospel. It is remarkable that sections, peculiar to Matthew and Luke, have no corresponding passages in Mark.

The third historian, Luke, like Mark, was not a personal witness of the Saviour's words and deeds. The author tells us the way in which he produced his history: "Forasmuch as many have taken in hand to set forth in order a declaration of those things which are most surely believed among us, even as they delivered them unto us, which from the beginning were eye-witnesses, and ministers of the Word [*i.e.* the Apostles]; it seemed good to me also, having had perfect understanding of all things from the very first, to write unto thee in order, most excellent Theophilus, that thou mightest know the certainty of those things, wherein thou hast been instructed."[2] Luke was the companion of Paul, and as a principal authority for some facts and words

---

[1] Justin Martyr, *Dialogue with Trypho the Jew*, 106; Tertullian, *Marc*, 4, 5; Irenæus, *Hær.*, iii., 1; Jerome, *Catal.*
[2] Luke i. 1-4.

employed in the third narrative, Luke was, doubtless, indebted to the Apostle Paul, who had seen the glory of the Lord, not in the days of His pilgrimage on earth, but in the midday sky after His enthronement in heaven.

For the credibility of these three Gospels, then, we have the highest historical evidence, and if any one rejects that evidence, so great in its amount, the whole history of the world, down to that period, must to him, if consistent, be in a doubtful condition.

We come to the fourth Gospel. A theory has been invented that it did not appear till about the middle of the second century. But if internal proof carries with it authority, this wonderful book carries credentials sufficient to satisfy all unprejudiced inquirers. It is surprising how any critic, acquainted with second-century literature, can attempt to account for such an exception as this to productions of that period. We shall have occasion, presently, to notice narratives written then, and it will be plainly seen what a contrast the fourth evangelical narrative presents to traditional stories and to obvious fictions written at that time. The comparison demonstrates the difference between them and the fourth Gospel. Long discourses and minutely detailed conversations are rehearsed in that Gospel, which, if correctly given without supernatural aid, or if preserved only by tradition, must appear such a literary marvel, that it is far easier even on rationalistic grounds to accept it at once as a Divine record of what took place. The enlightenment of the Holy Spirit alone explains the origin of this unique production. Inspiration alone accounts for the origin of the Gospel according to St. John. So it was accepted by those who lived soon afterward. Modern scholarship has gone patiently into this question touching the origin of Christianity and the Church, and the evidence supporting the fourth Gospel.[1]

In the Acts of the Apostles we read of marvels on the day of Pentecost, the cloven tongues of fire on the heads of the Apostles, their speaking in languages they had never learnt, as the Spirit gave them utterance. " And the same day there were added unto them about three thousand souls." These were so many miraculous lights to shine on a dark world. That Whitsuntide was the birth-

---

[1] To enter at large upon controversies touching the fourth Gospel is impossible within the limits of this work. I must refer the reader to what has been written on the subject by Westcott and others.

day of Christendom, but shadows soon overcast the Church's sky.

In the same book we are told that certain men came down to Antioch from Judæa, and taught the brethren, saying, "Except ye be circumcised after the custom of Moses, ye cannot be saved."[1] We are not surprised that sons of Abraham imagined the rite of circumcision to be binding on Gentiles, saved by faith like Abraham himself. Their inference, however, was mistaken. We are distinctly told the rule for Jews was not binding on Gentile followers of Abraham's faith. God did not put a yoke "on the necks of Christ's disciples" which neither their fathers nor they were able to bear. The old law was abolished.

"Not at once did a severance between Jewish Christians and Gentile Christians take place. It was more manifest after the fall of Jerusalem than before. Then the custom in the synagogues of cursing apostates from the law became prevalent and established; and this would naturally rend asunder any previously existing friendly relationship."[2]

Other dark shadows fall across our path as we pursue the early history of Christendom. Paul says

---

[1] Acts xv. 1.   [2] See Westcott, *Epistle to the Hebrews*, Int.

to the Corinthians: "I fear, lest by any means, as the serpent beguiled Eve in his craftiness, your minds should be corrupted from the simplicity and the purity that is toward Christ."[1] Further, he urges Timothy to warn the brethren against "profane and old wives' fables."[2] He predicts that some would "fall away from the faith, giving heed to seducing spirits, . . . forbidding to marry, and commanding to abstain from meats."[3] Also he refers to a coming time when sound doctrine would not be endured by some having itching ears, who would turn from truth to fables.[4] Peter predicts, as near at hand, the activity of "false teachers, denying even the Master that bought them."[5] Thus were painted before the eyes of early Christians, pastures where not only the flock might feed, but where also wolves would prowl. The second Eden, like the first, would have in it a serpent "more subtle than any beast of the field which the Lord God had made."[6]

Warnings are accompanied by unmistakable allusions to *contemporary facts*. We are startled when told that there were among the Christians at Corinth those who denied the distinguishing doctrine

---

[1] 2 Cor. xi. 3.   [3] 1 Tim. iv. 1, 3.   [5] 2 Peter ii. 1.
[2] 1 Tim. iv. 7.   [4] 2 Tim. iv. 3.   [6] Gen. iii. 1.

of the Gospel. "Now," writes Paul to the Church there, "if Christ is preached that He hath been raised from the dead, how say some among you that there is no resurrection of the dead?"[1] It seems almost incredible to those who have only sunny views of primitive Christendom, that Paul should have written in his second letter to Timothy,[2] "This thou knowest, that all that are in Asia turned away from me; of whom are Phygelus and Hermogenes." How strange to read of "unruly men," "vain talkers and deceivers, teaching things they ought not, for filthy lucre's sake," and of "questionings and strifes unprofitable and vain"; and of a man heretical (or factious), who after admonition ought to be avoided;[3] and of Hymenæus and Philetus, who said the resurrection was past, and overthrew the faith of some.[4] Once more, we find the Apostle John declaring, "Even now have there arisen many antichrists; whereby we know that it is the last hour." Also, he says, "Many deceivers are gone forth into the world, even they that confess not that Jesus Christ cometh in the flesh."[5]

We have in the Epistle to the Hebrews a view

---

[1] 1 Cor. xv. 12.
[2] 2 Tim. i. 15.
[3] Titus i. 10, 11; iii. 9, 10.
[4] 2 Tim. ii. 17.
[5] 1 John ii. 18; 2 John 7.

of Christian life such as is drawn in detail nowhere else. It represents a remarkable phase in the Church's growth. Its enthusiasm, its first hope, had passed. Believers began to reckon loss and gain. Some were inclined to overrate the loss; and we learn elsewhere that dark clouds overhung the sky.

From all this we see that Christendom is historical; subject, in the lives of its professors, to common temptations. We perceive that its early difficulties were not dealt with tentatively, as if truth resulted only from free conflict of thought. "The false view was met at once by the corresponding lesson. Error called out the decisive teaching, but it had no part in creating it."[1]

In the Third Epistle of John we read of "Diotrephes, who loveth to have the pre-eminence." Was he a presbyter, a deacon, or, in modern phrase, a layman? At all events, he was an unfavourable specimen of early professors. This is not strange. But what follows is so. Diotrephes "*receiveth us not. Therefore, if I come, I will bring to remembrance his works which he doeth, prating* against us with wicked words: and not content therewith, neither doth he himself *receive* the brethren" (whom St. John

---

[1] Westcott, *Epistle to the Hebrews*, Int., xxxvii.

sent), "and them that would, he forbiddeth and casteth them out of the Church." Differences of opinion occurred even between Peter and Paul; Jewish and Gentile Churches fell into controversy; party spirit broke out in Corinth;[1] and beyond all, there was one who abused "that disciple whom Jesus loved," and would not receive those whom he sent.

Reading the New Testament for edification, we are apt to overlook these scattered notices; but they are windows through which one catches sight of existing evils around and within.

There is a curious relic of ancient date bearing the name of Barnabas, and spoken of as written by the fellow-labourer of St. Paul. Clement of Alexandria so regarded it.[2] Origen cites it as the Catholic Epistle of Barnabas,[3] and it is found in the Sinaitic manuscript of the New Testament. Westcott summarises its character thus: "It treats the Mosaic legislation as having only a symbolical meaning. It had no historical, no disciplinary value whatever. The outward embodiment of the enigmatic ordinances was a pernicious delusion. As a mere fleshly ob-

---

[1] Gal. ii. 11; Acts xv.; 1 Cor. i. 10-17.   [2] *Strom.*, vi., 84.
[3] *Contra Celsum*, i., 63.

servance circumcision was the work of an evil power."[1] The contents are inconsistent with apostolic authorship, and the production is to me a great puzzle.[2]

At the close of the first century, and early in the second, a group of letters appeared written by "Apostolic Fathers." The earliest is from the pen of Clement, Bishop of Rome, whose death is dated under the year 100 A.D. It appears possible that in the *Clementines*, to be presently noticed, there are fragments of truth respecting Clement's relatives, but they throw no light whatever upon his biography. Legends followed touching his martyrdom, and the transportation of his relics to the East, where they were said to be discovered by Greek missionaries. The first of the two epistles ascribed to Clement is genuine. There is in it nothing, properly speaking, *historical*, nor, in the exact sense, *theological*. It is simply *practical* and *religious*; it supplies no reference to any apocryphal literature.

---

[1] Westcott, *Epistle to the Hebrews*, lxxxii.

[2] There is a learned pamphlet, entitled *An Argument by Constantine Tischendorf, with a narrative of the discovery of the Sinaitic Manuscript*, translated and published by the Religious Tract Society, in which this Epistle of Barnabas is critically noticed, in a chapter on "The Testimony of Apostolic Fathers."

The next Father is Ignatius, Bishop of Antioch, martyred at Rome early in the second century—to be noticed hereafter. The use made of his writings will also be noticed in a future chapter. Exhortations to unity, faith, and the confession of Christ; a condemnation of false teachers, and an expression of a desire for speedy dismissal from a world of sin and sorrow, are characteristics of the Ignatian remains.

An epistle, by an unknown author, addressed to Diognetus is without date, but no doubt it belongs to the early part of the second century, and is a precious relic. He says: "God did not, as one might have imagined, send to men any servant, or angel, or ruler, or any who bear sway over the earth, or one to whom the government of things in the heavens has been entrusted, but the very Creator and Fashioner of all—by whom He made the heavens —by whom He enclosed the sea within its bounds —whose ordinances the stars observe—from whom the sun received the measure of his course—whom the moon obeys—whom the stars obey, following the moon in her course; by whom all things have been placed within their limits, and to whom all are subject—the heavens and the things that are therein, the earth and the things that are therein, the sea and the things therein. He gave His own

Son as a ransom for us, the holy for transgressors, the blameless for the wicked, the righteous for the unrighteous, the incorruptible for the corrupted, the immortal for those that die. What else was capable of covering our sins but His righteousness? O sweet exchange! O unsearchable operation! O benefits surpassing all expectation! that the wickedness of many should be hid in a righteous One, and that the righteousness of One should justify many transgressors." He would have Christians trust His loving-kindness, and regard Him as "Nourisher, Parent, Teacher, Counsellor, Healer, Wisdom, Light, Honour, Glory, Power, and Life."

CHAPTER II

RELIGIOUS NOVELS

WE must now notice productions different from those just described. Fiction has played a considerable part in the literature of all ages and communities. Christendom presents no exception.

Much has been written respecting one of the oldest books we have—*The Shepherd of Hermas*—belonging to the second century, and containing six visions, twelve commandments, and ten similitudes.

The Church is represented with six youths, who are bid to go and build; with stones provided, white and square, signifying apostles, bishops, and teachers, living in Gospel holiness. Other stones, representing reprobate teachers, are set aside. Then appear seven women, who are Faith and her daughters—Self-restraint, Simplicity, Guilelessness, Chastity, Intelligence, and Love. Tribulation approaches her in the form of wild beasts. Then comes a man, in shepherd's attire, from whom the book derives its title, and he delivers twelve commandments in figurative words. The ten similitudes refer to faith, fasting, repentance, and good works; and present an elaborate allegory relative to building up the Church militant and triumphant. In the ninth similitude, respecting the Church under the image of a tower, stones are represented as piled up, symbolical of righteous men during the first and second ages, and of apostles, prophets, and teachers. Those not baptised before, were after death "sealed with the seal of the Son of God." The seal is water, into which souls enter subject to death, and rise out of it appointed to life.

The *Clementines* figure in the history of early centuries. They consist of *Recognitions* and *Homilies*, with an epitome or abridgment. They all turn on the history of Clement. The Greek original of the *Recognitions* is lost, but a Latin version of it has been preserved. There is also in existence a Syriac translation of the first three books. Its circulation, with the other *Clementines*, was probably large, and its influence is to be estimated accordingly. The chief characters in this fiction are Simon Magus, the Apostle Peter, and Clement of Rome with his family.

A slight sketch of its contents will give the reader some idea of its nature and tendency.

Of Simon Magus impossible stories are told. He declares: "I have flown through the air. I have made myself a body of fire. I can make statues move, and give life to what is dead. Angels uphold me with their wings." His tricks exceed those of clever conjurers in our day. Much is said of his transformations. He appeared with other people's faces.

The title of *Recognitions* relates to Clement's family. Faustinianus is his father, Mattidia his mother; Faustus and Faustinus are twin brothers. Suddenly the mother departs from her husband, in obedience, she says, to a dream which she had feigned as an excuse for escaping the licentious solicitations of her brother-in-law. In her flight she takes the twin boys, and the father cannot learn what has become of them. At length he goes himself in search of the wanderers, leaving Clement behind, who, in his thirty-second year, travels after them. He meets with Peter at Cæsarea, and an intimate friendship springs up between the two. A beggar-woman appears, who turns out to be the lost mother. Then follows the discovery of the twins, after they had suffered shipwreck. What had become of the father? He is recognised in the person of an old workman, casually met with. A long discussion follows by the seaside respecting generation, creation, providence, the atomic theory, the human body, and other subjects, including the origin of evil. Before this talk is over, the parties enter upon heathen mythology, and describe the doings of gods and goddesses. The "novel" closes with the baptism of Mattidia in the sea, her sons being present.

The *Homilies* are not sermons, but twenty chapters going over the same ground, and giving a confused and wearisome account of Clement and Appion—the latter a grammarian of Alexandria. The chapters contain offensive descriptions, mixed up with magical absurdities. They are followed by revolting conversations and correspondence, together with amorous tales of Greek deities. Numerous pages are full of heathen mythology, with allegorical explanations. I do not, however, find any sympathy expressed with what is evil ; on the contrary, some amount of moral and religious instruction may be found amongst much of a different kind. The origin of the *Clementines* has been discussed ;[1] but the moral significance of

---

[1] It is impossible here to enter upon this question ; I can only refer to a full discussion of it in Smith's *Dictionary of Christian Biography*, article "Clementine Literature."

this early romance does not appear to me to have been sufficiently considered.

With the fictitious literature of early Christendom must be included a number of apocryphal gospels, and other writings of a similar character. Some are of later date than the third century. Indeed, their origin is uncertain ; and the earliest, probably, have been more or less interpolated and changed. *The Protevangelium of James*, translated repeatedly— fifty MSS. of it in the original are said still to exist— relates to the birth of our Lord's mother, and contains the story of Joachim, Anna, and the Christ-Child, as conveyed in early legends, and depicted by Giotto and other mediæval artists. Similar tales are found in *The Gospel of Mary's Nativity*, *The History of Joseph the Carpenter*, and *The Gospel of Thomas*. In the last of these, actions are attributed to our Saviour's boyhood derogatory to His holy character. *The Gospel of Nicodemus* describes Christ's descent into Hades. Of about twenty such works, I can notice, in addition to those now mentioned, only *The Passing of Mary* and *The Acts of Paul and Thecla*.

The Passing of Mary contains marvellous accounts of the apostles gathering about her ; together with the visit of angelic multitudes, her celestial assumption, the descent of Christ to receive her soul, the dropping of her girdle into the hands of St. Thomas, and a meeting between the Virgin and St. Paul in Paradise. *The Acts of Paul and Thecla* form an incredible story, in which the damsel is described as visiting the Apostle in prison, "enchained to him by affection."

The Virgin is the principal subject in *The Gospel of the Nativity* and *The History of Joseph the Carpenter*. *The falling asleep* and *The passing away of Mary* present a story of her birth, visits paid to her by angels, her spinning purple and scarlet for the Temple, her conception, her marriage with Joseph, her presence at his death, the gathering of the apostles at her funeral, the assumption of her body to heaven, her meeting with Paul in Paradise, and the homage paid her by angels. The picturesqueness and poetry manifest in these details are made familiar to art students by Italian painters. Such legends grew up by degrees, and vary in different recensions —Syriac, Arabic, Greek, and Latin. Tischendorf assigns their earliest date to the fourth century; but it is probable that germs of them existed at an earlier period; large additions were made afterwards.

Grote, in his *History of Greece*, justly remarks: " Neither discrepancies nor want of evidence, in reference to alleged antiquities, shocked the faith of a non-historical public. What they wanted was a picture of the past, impressive to their feelings and plausible to their imagination."[1] The remark may be applied to the credulity of many early Christians. The same author says: "Even during the third century of the Christian era, when the old forms of Paganism were waning, and when the stock of myths in existence was extremely abundant, we see this demand in great force." A spirit in the air would be likely to affect large classes distinct from each other. Christian apologists saw clearly enough the absurdities of heathen fables. How they regarded these stories, which made way among ignorant Christians, does not appear.

If some productions now noticed were heretical, most were chiefly intended to gratify curiosity and a love for the marvellous; hence their circulation is not likely to have been confined to particular sects. Orthodox and heretical people do not appear to have been gathered into distinct camps, though controversial writings may suggest that idea. People of different opinions talked together and told sensational tales; they read what was written, and the influence of fiction would be diffused over a wide circle.

---

[1] *History of Greece*, vol. i., p. 43, edit. 1869.

Perhaps some readers nowadays, after being reminded of apocryphal gospels and similar writings, may wonder why anybody should care to examine their contents. Like many things, however, which a hasty judgment would doom to destruction, these remains may be put to useful account. Examination of them serves to show, by way of contrast, the superiority of Holy Scripture, and how wisely, through Divine direction, those thoughtful men who settled the Canon set the apocryphal aside. To study these relics critically is an aid to faith ; such study has been employed in establishing the genuineness and authority of our New Testament.

More than this, they are of historical, though not of religious use, throwing light on the period to which they pertain. They are specimens of a large class circulated about the same time—a number of them known only by their titles. The works themselves have perished, a fate probably they deserved. But the fact of their existing when they did, dissipates the delusion that those who lived so near apostolic days, and honoured Christ's family and personal followers, must have been eminent Christian people, more intelligent and devout than those of aftertimes. Perhaps this mistaken idea exists still. What is more serious, no attempt appears to have been made at the time of their first circulation to expose their falsity. Wherever they were accepted their effect must have been injurious.

Before I finish notices of this kind, mention should be made of recent discoveries in an old cemetery at Panapolis, Upper Egypt. An apocalypse—a *Gospel of Peter*—has been found there. Peter, it is related, had secrets of the other world revealed to him, and the redeemed were seen "white as driven snow," while the lost were wrapt in "the blackness of darkness." The following is an extract from *The Gospel of Peter* :—

"And I saw also another place, and it was a place of chastisement ; and those that were being chastised, and the angels that were chastising, had their raiment dark according to the atmosphere of that place. And there were some there hanging by their tongues, and these were they that blaspheme the way of righteousness. And I saw the murderers and them that had conspired with them cast into a certain narrow place full of evil reptiles, and being smitten by those beasts, and wallowing there thus in that torment ; and there were set upon them worms as it were clouds of darkness. And the souls of them that had been murdered were standing and looking upon the punishment of those murderers, and saying, 'O God, righteous is Thy judgment.'"

The Gospel of Peter describes Pilate as nothing without Herod, and Nicodemus is represented as Pilate's friend. Jesus is seen sitting on Pilate's throne; and it is curious to notice that Archbishop Whately used to give, "and set *Him* [*i.e.* Jesus] on the judgment-seat" (John xix. 13), as a legitimate rendering of the original.[1] The writer describes our Lord's crucifixion as painless, and thus indicates himself as one of the Docetæ (so-called), who supposed Christ was a man *only in appearance*. People are represented as carrying lamps during the supernatural darkness at the time of the crucifixion. The writer conveys the idea that the Divine nature descended on the human Christ at His baptism, and departed whilst He hung upon the cross:—

"There was a great voice from heaven, and (the soldiers) saw the heavens opened, and two men descending thence with a great light, and approach-

---

[1] See p. 18 of the work *The Gospel according to Peter, and the Revelation of Peter*. Edited by J. Armitage Robinson, B.D., and Montague Rhodes James, M.A. In this pamphlet the writers say: "Archbishop Whately used to translate the words in John xix. 13, 'and set Him on the judgment-seat'—a legitimate rendering of the Greek." So it seems Justin Martyr read the passage (*Apol.*, i., 35).

ing the tomb. And the stone which was put at the door rolled away of itself and departed on one side; and the tomb was opened, and both the young men entered it. When therefore the soldiers saw it they awakened the centurion and the elders, for they too were hard by keeping watch; and as they declared what things they had seen, again they see coming forth from the tomb three men, and the two supporting the one, and a cross following them. And of the two the head reached unto the heavens, but the head of Him that was led overpassed the heavens. And they heard a voice from the heavens, saying 'Hast Thou preached to them that sleep?' And an answer was heard from the cross, 'Yea.'"

CHAPTER III

LANDMARKS OF EARLY ECCLESIASTICISM

IT is well to glance at this subject thus early, because here we have something visible, which must have caught the eye of the outside world at an early period. Doctrines of the Gospel might be unintelligible to outsiders, but the word *Ecclesia* placed before people what they could see and understand. The word denoted gatherings of different kinds, but it was specially employed to denote a gathering of Christian people. Its master meaning was a confederation of those who professed to obey Jesus of Nazareth. Divine authority was claimed for such societies. By Divine call, under Divine rule, they professed to meet and conduct their religious affairs.

More of a popular element appeared in some cases than in others as to the control of affairs. Christian people at Corinth were conspicuously democratic.

Bishops and deacons, as we shall see, were conspicuous in other Christian communities, but no mention of either is made in the Letters to Corinth. We have the echo of cries, "I am of Paul," "I am of Apollos," "I am of Cephas," and "I am of Christ."[1] It would seem that this Church, when assembled, contained members, some claiming to follow one teacher, and some another; others repudiated *these* party cries, whilst they adopted another, and professed in a special, if not exclusive sense, that they were followers of Jesus Christ.

It is remarkable that in the Pauline Epistles, bishops and deacons are noticed together as ecclesiastical officers only in the case of Philippi.[2] The *name*, however, of Bishop is recognised in the Apostle Paul's address to those who, in the narrative, are distinctly called Elders (Presbyters) of the Church.[3] "It is a fact now generally recognised by theologians of all shades of opinion," says Bishop Lightfoot, "that in the language of the New Testament the same office in the Church is called indifferently Bishop and Elder."[4]

---

[1] 1 Cor. i. 12.
[2] Phil. i. 1.
[3] Acts xx. 17, 28.
[4] Lightfoot on *St. Paul's Epistle to the Philippians*, p. 95.

In the Epistle to Ephesus Paul gives a picture of brotherhood and love. "And He gave some to be apostles; and some, prophets; and some, evangelists; and some, pastors and teachers; for the perfecting of the saints, unto the work of the ministry, unto the building up of the body of Christ: till we all attain unto the unity of the faith, and of the knowledge of the Son of God, unto a perfect man, unto the measure of the stature of the fulness of Christ."[1]

The Epistles to Corinth and to Ephesus convey to us two different aspects under which ecclesiastical life would appear at the time they were written. When Paul met the presbyters from Ephesus he called them Bishops.

The primitive ministry included local and itinerant agents. We read of "apostles," "prophets," "evangelists"; also of "bishops" and "angels." Seven men of good report, full of the Spirit and of wisdom, were appointed to look after poor brethren and sisters in Jerusalem. These seven disappear, and then we read of "deacons," who performed a like office. Was preaching a diaconal duty? Certainly in those days deacons did preach, but that might mean nothing more than religious conversation; for

---

[1] Eph. iv. 11-16.

Philip, in the *Eunuch's chariot*, "preached unto him Jesus." We meet, as noticed already, with *elders* at Ephesus whom Paul addressed as *bishops*.[1] Philippi, as we have seen, had bishops and deacons. Moreover, Paul uses the word "deacon" in a general as well as an official sense. Peter writes as an "elder." Timothy is named "deacon," and forbidden to rebuke an elder, but to work as "evangelist." Not one is called in the New Testament *sacerdos*, a priest.

What is meant by the mention of "angel," in the epistles to the seven Churches noticed by St. John, has been largely discussed. Origen and Jerome regard it as meaning what is generally understood by the word. Hengstenberg believes it is intended to denote an associated body of rulers—in fact, a "presbytery." Ebrard explains it as signifying some special messenger deputed to St. John, to whom he entrusted an epistle in reply. Lightfoot remarks, whether the word denotes an actual person or personification, the "angel" is made responsible for the Church : " He is punished with it, and he is rewarded with it." [2]

---

[1] The word ἐπίσκοπος, as indicative of ecclesiastical office, occurs four times in the New Testament : Acts xx. 28 ; Phil. i. 1 ; 1 Tim. iii. 2 ; Titus i. 7.

[2] *St. Paul's Epistle to the Philippians*, by Lightfoot, p. 200.

In the Epistle of Paul to Titus, we have directions given, not to a *local bishop*, but to a *missionary superintendent* appointed to ordain elders in every city of Crete where Churches were formed.[1] Evidently he had a special commission.

We catch some further glimpses of early ministerial orders in a work entitled the *Didaché*,[2] spoken of by Clement of Alexandria. There were itinerant teachers who went from place to place under what they regarded as a Divine impulse. They are called "apostles," "prophets," "teachers." We are startled by the following words in this primitive relic: "Every apostle who cometh to you, let him be received as the Lord; but he shall not remain more than one day; if, however, there be need, then the next day; but if he remain three days, he is a false prophet. But when the apostle departs, let him take nothing except bread enough to last him till he reach his resting-place for the night; but if he ask for money he is a false prophet." Were there religious tramps in those days, who made gain of godliness?

The fact that all early Churches were *not* exactly

---

[1] Titus i. 5.
[2] It has been translated and published by the Dean of Gloucester.

alike distinctly appears. Corinth, as already noticed, had no bishop, no deacons. Clement writes to them, not in his own name, but in that of his flock. Bishops distinctly appear in the letters of Ignatius to Ephesians, Magnesians, Trallians, Romans, Philadelphians, and Smyrnians. I cannot find anywhere notice of episcopal rule over a rural congregation.

Changes in an episcopal form of government have become a subject of controversy. I content myself with the result of Bishop Lightfoot's researches. The learned author admits that a bishop was still called presbyter by Irenæus; that the same estimate of office appears in Clement of Alexandria; that in the fourth and fifth centuries it was customary for a bishop to address a presbyter as a *fellow* presbyter; that there early arose a considerable exaltation of the episcopate; that the same tendency appears in notices of Ebionism; that Montanism was a reaction against this change; that the advance of episcopal power was unconnected with *sacerdotalism* in the primitive Church, though it rapidly spread at a later date; that Cyprian was champion of priestliness; and that later episcopacy was a development caused by surrounding influences.[1]

---

[1] Lightfoot on *Epistle to Philippians*, pp. 98, 226, 236, 240-245.

Little is said in the New Testament about ordination. The word denoting it means "stretching out the hand" to indicate choice. The word used in Acts xiv. 23 ("χειροτονήσαντες") would literally imply a "show of hands," and whether this was the mode of election or not, we may conclude that Paul and Barnabas called upon the believers to recommend some of their number for the office of elder; and the persons thus recommended were instructed in their duties, and had the care of the Church committed to them.[1]

The priesthood of the Gospel appears in the New Testament as pertaining to all believers. "Unto Him that loveth us, and loosed us from our sins by His blood, and He made us to be a kingdom, to *be priests* unto His God and Father," are words at the opening of the Apocalypse to the same effect.[2] "A royal priesthood" is an expression which fills us with devout astonishment; but in the Book of Revelation it embraces *the whole* redeemed Church of Christ, and is never used to signify ministers of the Gospel as *distinguished* from other people. No sacerdotal order, *in* and *over* the Church, finds place in the

---

[1] Burton's *Lectures on Ecclesiastical History—First Three Centuries*, p. 150.

[2] Rev. i. 6.

New Testament. When speaking of a priest-like ministration under the present economy, the author of the Epistle to the Hebrews extends it to the *whole multitude* of the redeemed. "Through Him [Christ, the High Priest of our profession] let *us* offer up a sacrifice of praise to God continually, that is, the fruit of lips which make confession to His name."[1] But when we turn from these passages to the literature of the second and third centuries, we discover that Christendom was in some quarters being impregnated with a notion that bishops and presbyters were mediators between God and man, like the Aaronic order.

Each of the Christian communities, with its pastor or pastors, was complete in itself; but there were bonds of union amongst them of two kinds. We find at an early period traces of commendatory letters sent by one Church to another, relative to disciples, upon their removal from place to place. Wherever a Christian traveller went, if provided with one of these certificates, he found welcome and hospitality.[2] Such documents were not given by orthodox Churches to those out of communion with

---

[1] Heb. xiii. 15. Here I follow Dean Vaughan.
[2] Tertullian, *De Præscriptionibus Hæreticorum*, c. 20.

them; hence no single practice of early Christians tended so much as this to impress a stamp of unity on collective communities recognising one another. Indeed, a person free of one Christian Church was free of others; and whilst each Church was an entire fellowship in itself, the aggregate fellowships constituted an extensive confederation. Gatherings of pastors of different local communities for counsel, and the determination of matters pertaining to the general welfare, constituted interlacing bonds. At an early period of the second century such meetings were held. They increased in Asia and in the West. Councils, however, is a term applied by Tertullian to meetings of a single Church.[1]

We proceed to notice Christian *worship*. Preaching was accompanied by praise and prayer. When we remember the musical character of Jewish service, we do not wonder that "psalms, hymns, and spiritual songs" were common with primitive believers. Pliny says, in his letter to Trajan, "Christians sang hymns to Christ as God."[2] In the primitive Church of the third, if not the second century, catechumens engaged "in a service of song and Scripture reading." This was followed by the united worship of the

---

[1] Tertullian, *De Pudicitia*.   [2] *Ep.*, I., x., 97.

"faithful," as decided and accepted Christians were called, who joined in the Holy Communion.[1] Metrical hymns, it is said, are not earlier than the days of Ambrose.

An ancient hymn, ascribed to Clement of Alexandria, is filled with adoration of the Saviour. It is figurative in character and fragmentary in form, but intensely evangelical in spirit—difficult to translate rhythmically, but clearly conveying the ideas which inspired it. As the wing to a bird, the helm to a ship, the shepherd to his flock, the husbandman to his field, and milk to an infant, such is Christ to the faithful. That is the substance of the hymn. Thoughts struggle for expression; the neck of the vessel is too narrow for the outlet of what it contains.

Bingham tells us there is evidence for set forms of worship in the third century, and adduces Hippolytus in proof. Palmer, in his *Origines*, thinks there are strong reasons for believing the so-called *Liturgy of St. James* may be traced back from the fifth to the third century. These authors, however, do not supply satisfactory proofs for their assumptions.

Perhaps the earliest indication of liturgical worship is found in a Carthaginian council of the third century.

---

[1] *Bingham's Works*, Vol. III., pp. 8-11.

Bingham[1] has shown that worship was offered, in the ante-Nicene age, to Father, Son, and Holy Spirit, but not to any saints or angels; and that it was always expressed in the language of the people. Cyprian refers to the daily celebration of the Eucharist.[2] Egyptian Christians took off their shoes on entering church, as I saw them do when I was in Alexandria.

Bishop Lightfoot remarks: "The origin of the earliest extant liturgies is a question of high importance; and with the increased interest which the subject has aroused in England of late years, it may be hoped that a solution of the problem connected with it will be seriously undertaken; but no satisfactory result will be attained unless it is approached in a thoroughly critical spirit, and without the design of supporting foregone conclusions."[3]

"There was at this time no authoritative written liturgy in use in the Church of Rome, but the prayers were modified at the discretion of the officiating minister. Under the dictation of habit and experience, however, these prayers were gradually

---

[1] *Works*, Vol. IV., chaps. ii., iii., iv.
[2] *De Orat.*
[3] *Apostolic Fathers—Clement of Rome*, i., p. 385.

assuming a fixed form ; a more or less definite order in the petitions, a greater or less constancy in the individual expressions, was already perceptible. As the chief pastor of the Romish Church would be the main instrument in thus moulding the liturgy, the prayers, without actually being written down, would assume in his mind a fixity as time went on. When, therefore, at the close of his epistle, he (Clement of Rome) asks his readers to fall on their knees, and lay down their jealousies and disputes, at the footstool of grace, his language naturally runs into those antithetical forms and measured cadences which his ministrations in the Church had rendered habitual with him when dealing with such a subject. This explanation seems to suit the facts. The prayer is not given as a quotation from an acknowledged document, but as an immediate outpouring of the heart ; yet it has all the appearance of a fixed form. This solution accords, moreover, with the notices which we find elsewhere respecting the liturgy of the early Church, which seem to point to forms of prayer more or less fluctuating, even at a later date than this."[1]

But worship was always in the common language

---

[1] Lightfoot's *Clement of Rome*, i., p. 386.

of the people. "Greeks use Greek, Romans Roman; every one in his own dialect prays to God and gives thanks. The Lord of all languages hears those who pray in different tongues. He is not as one who selects one language knowing nothing of another." This is what Origen says in his *Contra Celsum*.[1]

The first day of the week—"the Lord's day," as the Apostle John calls it—was kept sacred as far as possible. But a slave was not master of his own time, and therefore many poor people would be debarred the privilege, until after imperial authority had made it a day of rest; this was indicated by closing the law courts at that season.

It requires a great effort in our time to realise the state of society in the first three centuries, as regards the use of the first day. Now it is with us in England a holiday. Business is suspended. Certain amusements are held in abeyance. In apostolic times, and long afterwards, the first day of the week was like other days. Business and amusement went on as usual. Shops were kept open, and so were places of amusement. The Christian slave was at his master's beck and call. He was not free "to attend church," as is now

---

[1] I., viii., c. 37.

the case commonly with our domestics. The state of society must have affected Christian habits in ways difficult for us to imagine. Sunday habits, as we may call them, could not be then what they are now. A state of civilisation, in the first three centuries different from ours, must have affected many usages of Christian life. The fact is often overlooked in the use we make of early ecclesiastical precedents.

A review of New Testament teaching leaves the impression that all public worship was framed on the basis of a Jewish synagogue rather than the Jewish Temple. If worship was divinely designed to be elaborately ceremonial, as it afterwards became, it is amazing to find nothing for that purpose taught in either Gospels or Epistles. Vitringa, Bernard, and others have gone far in a theory, that primitive worshippers imitated the Jews in having desk, pulpit, alms-chest, and ark in their solemnities. What we read of Paul's exhortation at Antioch, and his joining devout women at Philippi by "the river side, where prayer was wont to be made"—seems to run on a line with Jewish customs appearing after the return from captivity. But it appears to me that, whilst in the first century a synagogue fashion obtained, there set in afterwards arrangements for relig ious service more after the Temple form, with its altar and Holy of Holies.

There are two Christian ordinances of Divine appointment—baptism and the Lord's Supper. *The Teaching of the Twelve*, Chap. VII., says: "Baptise into the name of the Father, and of the Son, and of the Holy Spirit, in running water. But, if thou hast not running water, baptise in other water; and if thou canst not in cold, then in warm. But before the baptism let the baptiser and the baptised fast." Tertullian mentions, in connection with baptism, renouncing the devil, his pomps and angels; "watching, confessing sin, dipping thrice, tasting honey and milk, and abstaining for a week afterwards from daily ablutions."[1]

What Tertullian says of baptism is remarkable. He contends that in creation God "dignified the element of water." He says: "Darkness covered the earth, and the heavens were unformed, but water, perfect, cheerful, simple, pure, supplied a vehicle worthy of God. Water was a source of life at the beginning, and is so still. It is fit to be sanctified, and to sanctify. Water, after prayer, becomes the sacrament of sanctification. Not that we obtain the Holy Spirit in water,

---

[1] *De Corona*, 3.

but, being cleansed in water, under the Angel [here Tertullian seems to allude to the Pool of Bethesda], we are prepared for the Holy Spirit." He adds: "Is it not wonderful that death should be washed away by bathing? If wonderful it ought, on that account, rather to be believed."[1] I am struck with the different tone in which baptism is spoken of by Tertullian and others, from that employed in the New Testament.

Cyprian refers to the baptismal rite as preceded by interrogation, and as being performed by aspersion or effusion, with water sanctified by a priest; unction also is referred to as administered to the baptised.[2] In all cases the name of Father, Son, and Holy Ghost was solemnly pronounced; and we notice that Easter and Pentecost were special seasons for administration.

Very strong language respecting its efficacy is also used by Justin Martyr, who calls it "the washing of salvation," "the remedy for birth sin," and "the remission of transgressions":[3] also by Clement of Alexandria, who writes: "Our transgressions are

---

[1] *De Bapt.* Tertullian dwells on baptism at length, attaching to it great efficacy.

[2] *Ep.*, lxix., 11, 12; lxx., 2, 3.

[3] All this and more may be found in his *Apol.*

remitted by one sovereign medicine, baptism, according to the Word. Being baptised we are illuminated, being illuminated we are adopted, being adopted we are perfected, being perfected we are immortal."[1] He speaks of life-giving water washing away former stains and pouring into the cleansed breast the light of heaven, of drinking in the Spirit, and being created into a new man by second birth.[2] Irenæus speaks of its regenerating power.[3] Cyprian uses strong expressions in reference to baptism : " It remits sin "; "justifies, purifies, and sanctifies"; it is the "laver of salvation"; it "makes us new men, the sons and the temples of God"; it is "a holy and heavenly washing," "a consummation of grace," "an entrance on eternal life," death to the old man, birth of the new one. These expressions are employed in his Epistles.

Cyprian declares baptismal grace is equally bestowed, but unequally retained, and that Satan, repelled by baptism, returns when faith departs. Also, invalidity of the rite is attributed to its administration by heretics and schismatics.[4]

After all I have read on the subject I find it hard

---

[1] *Pedag.*, i., 6-12.
[2] *Ad Donat.*, 3.
[3] *Adv. Har.*, iii., 19.
[4] See *Baptismo* and *De Penit.*

to define *exactly* the *kind and the degree of efficacy* the Fathers quoted attached to baptismal regeneration. It is remarkable that none of them are found disputing or criticising the strong language used by others.

As to the Lord's Supper, the frequency of its observance in the earliest age is manifest. There is a difference of opinion as to what is meant in Acts ii. 46 by "breaking bread from house to house," or, according to the marginal reading, "breaking bread at home." Some think that it refers to ordinary meals, noteworthiness of which in this connection seems unmeaning. Others, with more reason, regard it as indicating the Lord's Supper. It is plain in Acts xx. 7 that the words, "Upon the first day of the week, when the disciples came together to *break bread*, Paul preached to them"— relate to the Eucharist, and it is also plain that this ordinance was an integral part of worship. Justin Martyr's account of Sunday services accords with this view. In *The Teaching of the Twelve* we find the following injunction :—

"Thus give thanks, as regards the cup, We thank Thee, our Father, for the holy vine of David Thy servant, which Thou hast made known to us through Jesus Thy Son; to Thee be glory for ever; and as regards the broken bread, We thank Thee, our Father, for the life and the knowledge which Thou hast made known to us through Jesus Thy Son; to Thee be glory for ever. Just as this broken bread was once scattered in grains of corn over the hills, and having been gathered together became one, so let Thy Church be gathered together from the ends of the earth into Thy kingdom: for Thine is the glory and the power, through Jesus Christ for ever. But let no one eat and drink of your Eucharist except those baptised in the name of the Lord; for as regards this, the Lord hath said, 'Give not that which is holy to the dogs.'"

Ignatius calls the bread "the body of our Saviour," "the flesh of the crucified and risen Lord," and "the medicine of immortality."[1] Justin Martyr says that the food, blessed by prayer, is, we are taught, "the flesh and blood of that Jesus who was made flesh."[2] Irenæus remarks: "We offer to Him His own. The bread produced from the earth, when it receives the invocation of God, is no longer common bread, but the Eucharist, consisting of the earthly and the heavenly."[3] Such language expresses belief of a mysterious change wrought

---

[1] His Epistle.   [2] *Apol.*, 66.   [3] *Adv. Hær.*, iv., 18.

in the sacramental elements themselves, but transubstantiation of mediæval date went far beyond the primitive view of the consecrated bread and wine. The sacrifice on the altar came as imitation of Temple service.

The teaching of the Fathers touching sacraments has been so long a battle-ground, and those who have studied the subject have been so anxious to find that which favours their own views, that it is easier to pick out from them our individual opinions than to give an unbiassed view of the whole subject. For my own part, as I build my faith on the Scriptures, not on the Fathers, some of their views, so different in many respects from apostolic teaching, have no authority. That patristic teaching differed, in some respects, from apostolic is not surprising when we think of the heresies which existed in early days. If, while apostles were living, some hearers and teachers wandered into error, no wonder some readers did the same.

Festivals, in addition to the Lord's day, began to appear at an early period. Easter is conspicuous in this respect. In Asia Minor, Christians celebrated the resurrection on the fourteenth day of the first month, corresponding with our March, and were called quartadecimans. The Western Churches kept their Easter upon the Lord's day following the Jewish passover. Easterns cited as their authority the time of the Jewish passover. Other Churches, Rome amongst the rest, appealed to an apostolical tradition in support of their own view. Other festivals, including Christmas, are of later date, and can be traced to no earlier period than the fourth century.

We proceed to notice what relates to ecclesiastical discipline. Nobody was admitted to participate in the Lord's Supper who had not been baptised and were not acknowledged Christians. It was administered within closed doors. On that account, partly at least, it came to be called a mystery. Celsus attacked Christianity on the ground that "it attracted bad characters, that it issued a proclamation for an assembly of robbers." Origen replied : " It urged all men to come to Christ, that they might be healed of sin, and therefore invited all to submit to the *divinely curative* process." He says : " When those who are turned towards virtue make progress, and show that they have been led so far as to practise a better life, *then, and not before*, we invite them to participate in our mysteries, for we speak wisdom amongst them that are perfect." [1]

---

[1] *Contra Celsum*, iii., 59.

In Paul's First Epistle to the Corinthians, he refers to discipline as necessary when members transgressed Gospel law; but, in connection with this, he adds nothing about the office and action of bishop or presbyter; he entrusts the whole community with an inquiry into the case. "I verily, being absent in body but present in spirit, have already, *as though I were present*, judged him that hath so wrought this thing, in the name of our Lord Jesus, ye being gathered together, *and my spirit*, with the power of our Lord Jesus, to deliver such a one unto Satan for the destruction of the flesh, that the spirit may be saved in the day of the Lord Jesus."[1] Instead of sending an officer to perform the duty, he leaves its execution with the whole community.

With regard to discipline at a later date—the third century, for instance—I cannot discover in Cyprian's writings what errors in opinions or conduct regarding the Church, came within the range of his episcopal censure, and therefore exposed those chargeable with them, to ecclesiastical discipline. Gnosticism and Ebionitism—in other words, philosophical speculations—carried out so far as to include a denial of our Lord's divinity and atonement; also Jewish

---

[1] 1 Cor. v. 3-5.

conceptions of a law of works, opposed to salvation by grace,—these anti-Christian ideas, with their influence on character and conduct, needed to be checked. But the common tone, wherever heresy is mentioned, looks as if *all deviations* from what was *deemed orthodoxy* deserved severe treatment; and what he called schism might be only preference for one bishop before another. " Schismatics," says the good man, " have no power, no authority, cannot baptise, have no church, cannot use the creed properly, lose the savour of spiritual wisdom, have not the Holy Spirit, and are to be ranked with heathens." Cyprian compares schism to the revolt of the ten tribes, and denounces it as a denial of Christ's Church; and says those who partake in it share the guilt of its authors. " How without hope they are, and what perdition they procure."[1] Surely, in the exercise of discipline, a distinction is to be made between those errors which strike at the foundations of faith, and those which do not oppose truths of essential importance.

There lay in all this a sad forgetfulness of the wise lesson inculcated by St. Paul, in the fourteenth chapter of his Epistle to the Romans. It seems in early

---

[1] *Epistolæ*, lv., lxix.

as in later ages, that no adequate recognition of the line was drawn between what is *essential* and what is *non-essential* to Christian character. How much injustice, exclusion, and persecution might have been saved by a due regard to apostolic teaching!

CHAPTER IV

LEADERS AND SCHOOLS OF THOUGHT

CHARACTERISTICS of prominent men are discoverable under the surface of treatises and letters, indicating what they were and what they accomplished. The early diffusion of Christianity did not proceed from a spirit in the air, it did not float on the breeze of public opinion, but depended upon such as were prominent in Church history. Under God these men were the makers of Christendom. Some familiar names occur in early history, pale and shadowless, as ghosts in Dante's visions, but those we now refer to can be placed pretty distinctly before our imagination.

These leaders and their schools are of two classes—Greeks and Latins.

I. Greeks.—Justin Martyr (about A.D. 103—166) calls himself a Samaritan, meaning, probably, that he was born in Samaria, not that he was a Samaritan in race or religion. Nobody can read what he has written without seeing that he was an intelligent though not exactly an intellectual person—ready to talk with those he met, showing what was uppermost in his mind—and in the habit of travelling with his eyes and ears open. We find him pacing the colonnades of Ephesus, and walking on the seashore, where he attracted the attention of Trypho the Jew, and held conversation with him. He became converted—an important fact, showing that he was a Christian, not by descent, but by conviction. There is no notice of his holding office in any Church. He continued to wear a philosopher's cloak, and invited friends to accompany him to a philosophical school, after the Gospel had gained his heart, and he was seized with a conviction that he had a call to seek the salvation of others. Hence he wrote his famous *Apology* and his *Dialogue* with Trypho. He entered into full communion, was baptised, and appears to have spent his time as a kind of lay missionary, privately talking, wherever he went, about his Divine Saviour.

Justin Martyr in his writings dwells upon the incarnation and Divine nature of our blessed Lord— "the first-begotten of the Father, sitting above the cherubim, the King of glory, the Lord of hosts, whom

Christians worship, and not without reason." He also speaks of remission of sins, by the death of Christ, according to the teaching of Isaiah, and repeats the following truths. Christ suffered, that by dying and rising again He might overcome death. Through the crucified One, God saves those who had done what brought them into condemnation, and left them under the curse of the law. Christ took this upon Himself for the whole human race. Salvation was brought within reach of *all*, through His blood. He will come again; for there are two advents, the first without comeliness and honour, the second in beauty and glory, upon the clouds, and the angels with Him. If so great was the power of His passion, what must be His final coming! Grace is recognised in the work of salvation from first to last. It is a fountain of living water, and produces a new and regenerated race.[1]

Justin Martyr was not the founder of a distinct school; but two celebrities of that order may be found in Alexandrian history at the period before us. The Macedonian Library in that city eclipsed others in the ancient world. Aristotle's idea was there carried out "with a magnificence of execution which kings

---

[1] These passages are gathered from his writings.

alone could project, and a succession of ages secure." As the second century closed, and afterwards, Christians resided there who had their characteristic way of looking at the Gospel. Within the city were divers sects—Greek, Indian, Jewish—who had an eager desire to seek and intermeddle with all wisdom, after fashions of their own. They were not so much original thinkers, as inquisitive hearers and indomitable talkers. They made up a Neoplatonic class, employed in moulding what they acquired, into fashions of their own.

The Alexandrian school, as already suggested, had in it little of original speculation. It manifested more the product of memory than of creative thought. It was decidedly eclectic, searching into speculations of earlier days rather than discovering previously unknown veins of metaphysical wealth. Ancient schools had declined; modern sects could only fall back upon remains of early days. Heathen and Jewish speculators were hard at work, breaking in pieces anciently excavated ore and stamping upon it some impress of their own. Jules Simon, in his *Histoire de l'Ecole d'Alexandrie*, has set forth specimens of old diggings, with indications of the shape into which critics were reducing them. Plotinus and others had left much which was laid under contribution for new purposes. Christian workers, as Origen said in writing to Gregory Thaumaturgus, were like the Israelites, who, when they left Egypt, carried out of it jewels, which they employed in the tabernacle, though some of the collected treasure was turned into "a golden calf."

Irenæus appears early on the list of Greek Fathers; and though his great work is known by us chiefly from a Latin translation, it appeared originally in his native tongue. He was born in Smyrna, amongst Greek-speaking people, between A.D. 120 and 140. He removed to Lyons, in Gaul, and there devoted himself to Christian work. He became bishop in the city of his adoption, and his principal production is a *Treatise on Heresies*. To this chiefly we are indebted for what we know of errors by which early Christian Churches were bewildered. Though he writes on a subject pertaining to philosophies of the age, his volume is not composed after a philosophical method, and leaves the reader, at times, in perplexity as to the nature of systems he undertakes to criticise. At the commencement of his treatise he employs a clever illustration by noticing how a piece of glass may be mistaken for a jewel;

---

[1] *Adv. Hær.*, i., 1.

and gives that as an illustration of pretentious appearances, found, on a comparison of them with Christianity, to be as worthless as they are pretentious. His descriptions and criticisms bring before us a motley crowd of would-be philosophers, full of fantastic dreams, who attempted theories of the universe, derived from imaginary beings called Eons —supposed to come between an original First Cause and the existing constitution of the universe. These philosophers had a great deal to say about spirit and matter, and the distinction between an original power and the maker or fashioner of our visible world. The existence of matter is their great puzzle, and the result of their speculations is a theory very different indeed from the facts we find in Holy Writ. God the Creator, Jesus Christ the Saviour, and the Holy Ghost the Comforter, have no place in such dreams; and the upshot of reading this book by Irenæus is a conviction that Gnostic philosophy is a sham, and darkens counsel by words without wisdom. It is remarkable that the great subjects involved in Divine revelation—the fall of man, the moral condition of the world, the work of the Redeemer, the regeneration of souls, and the revelation of eternal life—never touched the minds and hearts of these shallow inquirers; and it would seem as if they never looked into writings by prophets and by authors of the New Testament. They lived in a fictitious realm, and lost themselves in wild wanderings.

Irenæus appeals to the Word of God, and shows how earthly things are types of the heavenly; that Abraham's faith and that of Christians are of the same nature; that patriarchs and prophets pointed to Christ; that He is the treàsure hid in Scripture, brought to light by the Cross; and that they who study, understand, and believe what is written about Him, shall shine as the firmament and the stars for ever and ever.[1] Irenæus is exceedingly valuable as a witness to the genuineness of the New Testament, from which he so largely quotes; the number of passages cited being reckoned as about four hundred; and direct quotations from St. John alone exceed eighty.

I may remark, in passing, that Irenæus touches upon one of the questions in modern theology. We find views on the subject of Freewill and Predestination, stated by this Father, at a period before controversies on the question had been evoked. He tells us, on the one hand, that men have a

[1] *Adv. Hær.*, iv., 1.

power of choice and accordant action; that the
Almighty has always treated them as responsible,
praising and blaming them according to their
conduct; that they are saved, not by compulsion,
but by persuasion. Yet, on the other hand, he
believed in a Divine predestination unto eternal life
of a number to be completed at the end of time.
Modern disputants on the mystery will not, on either
side, find in the writings of Irenæus developed views
such as have been maintained by divines in the middle
ages, and since the Reformation; but they must
admit that he certainly saw there were two sides
to the momentous question, and without penetrating
further than what appeared to be the leaning of
Scripture, he felt sure the two were reconcilable.[1]
Irenæus not only asserts great Gospel truths, such
as that Christ was very God and very man, that
He gave His soul for our souls and His flesh for
our flesh, pouring His Spirit into our nature; but
this Christian author also abounds in what we call
good common sense. With this fact I have just been
struck, in reading the twenty-eighth chapter of his
second book against heretics. His remarks on the

---

[1] *Cont. Hær.*, iv., 37 *et seq.* See *Account of Life and Writings of Irenæus*, by Beaven, Oxford.

limitation of human knowledge, and the necessity of leaving mysteries in the hands of God, are admirable.

Further, I may remark respecting Irenæus, that theories have been broached to the effect that the Pauline view of Christian doctrine was repudiated before the end of the first century, and that a Judaistic view then prevailed. But Dr. Lightfoot remarks: "Irenæus knows nothing of the religious convulsions which must have shaken its foundations, but represents the tradition as one continuous, unbroken, reaching back through the elders of the Asiatic Churches, through Papias and Polycarp, to St. John himself." Irenæus, who received his Christian education in Asia Minor, and was throughout life in communication with the Churches there, had already reached middle age when this second revolution is supposed to have occurred. "The demands on our credulity which this theory makes are enormous. And its improbability becomes only more glaring as we extend our view. For the *solidarity* of the Church is the one striking fact unmistakably revealed to us, as here and there the veil which shrouds the history of the second century is lifted. Anicetus, and Soter, and Eleutherus, and Victor at Rome, Pantænus and Clement at Alexandria,

Polycrates at Ephesus, Papias and Apollinaris at Hierapolis, Polycarp at Smyrna, Melito at Sardis, Ignatius and Serapion at Antioch, Primus and Dionysius at Corinth, Pothinus and Irenæus in Gaul, Philippus and Pinytus in Crete, Hegesippus and Narcissus in Palestine,—all are bound together by the ties of a common organisation, and the sympathy of a common creed."[1]

Clement of Alexandria (who died about A.D. 213) had for a while sympathies with heathenism; but, like Justin, he was converted to Christianity. I always think of him as a polished courtier, dignified in manners, who sought to melt down prejudices against Christianity, and met inquirers, akin in some respects to those common in our own day, so as to conciliate their minds and win them to the faith. His great mistake was to misplace knowledge in relation to religion. He divided Christians into two classes, simple believers and intellectual inquirers— *Gnostics*, as he called them (not, of course, in the heretical sense)—and to these he gave the highest place; thus cherishing a sort of philosophical ambition, at the expense, in a measure, of submission to evangelical authority. This was a leading ele-

---

[1] Lightfoot, *Epistles to Colossians and Philemon*, pp. 59, 60.

ment of error in his teaching. He flattered the intellect at the expense of a submission to that Divine teaching which is the basis of true piety. He also encouraged an ambition to seek after what is beyond human reach. And it is evident that he leaned to that side of theology which afterwards led to Pelagian errors. It is a relief, after toiling through the first book of Clement's *Pedagogue*, to take up a digest of it clearly expressed in Kaye's *Account of Clement's Writings and Opinions*.

Clement became a presbyter in the Alexandrian Church and a teacher in its catechetical school, which was an institute, not only for instructing young Christians, but for preparing agents to undertake missionary work. He was driven from Alexandria by persecution, and we can follow him afterwards to Antioch and Jerusalem.

In a book entitled *Pædagogus* (the Instructor), and another called *Stromata*, in which he describes dress, utensils, baths, spectacles, and ordinary life (he was fond of minute details), we find him giving advice to Christians, respecting conduct at home and intercourse abroad. From what I have said of Clement's calling his philosophical student of Christianity "a Gnostic," it must *not be inferred* that he sympathised with those who, in the history of ancient opinions, are known by that name; such, as we have seen, were, properly speaking, heretics or infidels altogether outside Christianity, having no sympathy with what is distinctive of it. A more serious charge against him is that he advocates a theory of accommodation, which resembles the adage of being all things to all men.[1] He seems to say a Christian, like a physician for the good of his patient, may utter what is apparently false, and refers to the case of Paul and Timotheus (Acts xvi. 1). Paul, however, only did what *seemed* inconsistent, but was not really so. This accommodation theory was perilous ground to tread. Much of the *Pædagogus* is trivial and amusing; but it serves to give a vivid idea of Alexandrian life in the second century.

With regard to Clement, let me add that in his writings sparks of imagination appear worth notice. For instance, he says: "God in His great love comes to man's help, as the mother bird flies after her young ones when they have fallen from their nest." Again, he says: "Who would prefer bondage to sonship? to sink into darkness when he might become a citizen of glory, and cultivate fields in paradise, and cleave the sky on a luminous cloud,

---

[1] *Strom.*, lib. vii., c. 9, § 53.

like Elijah?" "God invites us to salvation, saying, The land I give thee, and the sea, my child, and heaven too."[1]

Origen (about A.D. 186—254) is known all the world over for genius, learning, and industry; but it is sometimes forgotten that his life-story teems with adventure. We might suppose, if we only thought of him as a student writing books—"more," says Jerome, "than anybody can read"—that he spent all his days in quietude; whereas he passes before us amidst incessant change, and his life is romantic in circumstances from first to last. His childhood is rich in touching beautifulness. We read of his father "bending over his little bed, uncovering his breast as a shrine consecrated by the Holy Ghost, and then reverently kissing him." His mother taught him Hebrew hymns (was she a Jewess?). Together they sung praise to God, and so inspired was the boy with a martyr spirit that he "advanced close to danger, and eagerly leaped towards the conflict." It is touching to be told that he visited confessors in prison, and walked with martyrs to the place of execution, and there gave them a last kiss. When only eighteen years of age, he became virtually head

---

[1] *Exhortation to the Heathen*, x.

of a school in Alexandria. Having devoted himself to the office of a tutor, he sold his classical library that he might devote his time to Christian studies. But he long continued a layman, being absorbed in educational work. Origen was a great traveller for the age in which he lived. We meet with him at Rome, where he was not pleased with what he saw; we find him in Arabia, Palestine, and Greece. Then he returns to Alexandria to work in a large library, employing copyists and shorthand writers. He denied himself sufficient clothing, would not have more than one coat, and walked the streets without shoes. His self-denial presents a contrast to the social habits of Clement; and his self-inflicted torture is universally known.

In Palestine he entered holy orders, being there ordained presbyter—a circumstance which brought him into trouble with Demetrius of Alexandria,[1] an early friend; but they afterwards renewed former relations. Under the Emperor Philip, Origen en-

---

[1] I light upon the following passage in the Life of my old friend Dr. Hook: "It is strictly according to the courtesy of the Catholics (true Catholics, I mean) not to ordain ministers of another Church without permission from the bishop at the head of it; as Demetrius, Bishop of Alexandria, was justly offended when the bishops of Palestine ordained the celebrated Origen."

joyed Court favour. After all this he saw dark days, being tortured, condemned as a heretic, and only saved from martyrdom to die in prison, " having completed seventy years save one."

Origen was a man of higher mark than Clement. No one can question his extraordinary genius, but his writings, in many instances, lack distinctness of thought—at any rate, clearness of expression ; so that a century or two after his death Christendom was agitated by strife as to the scope of his teaching. There can be little doubt he believed in the preexistence of souls.[1] That opinion he coupled with a belief in the final restoration of sinful beings to holiness and felicity.

Origen said, in the words of Scripture, " the letter killeth, but the spirit giveth life," by which he meant that Scripture loses power when not mystically apprehended. In short, he taught there is a threefold meaning in Holy Writ—the literal, the allegorical, and the mystical. What we find in his comments on early parts of Genesis does not bring out what is commonly regarded as matter of fact. He says he will not sacrifice letter to spirit, "except after most careful examination." But as Neander and

---

[1] *De Principiis*, iii., c. 5, § 4.
[2] *Ibid.*, i., c. 6. The expression here is somewhat qualified.

others have remarked, What limits can be fixed in such a case? What becomes of creation, the fall, and the flood if this loose practice be followed?

Undoubtedly the ablest, indeed the only complete, defence of Christianity by an ante-Nicene writer is supplied by Origen in his *Contra Celsum*. He goes exhaustively over the whole ground occupied by antagonists. He examines every hole and corner of the enemy's fortifications, and leaves nothing standing. He is more patient in his inquiries, more explicit in his replies, than any other early defender of the faith. He goes on through chapters xlvi. to lxii., lxv. to lxxi., cxxix. to cxxxii., and in every instance silences his opponents. We find it wearisome to read his arguments all through. What must have been his patience to write them! He declares that early believers understood Christian doctrines in different ways, and refers to views of the resurrection, and to discussions touching ceremonial observances.[1]

Within extensive limits, Origen allowed scope for free thought. There is remarkable haziness in some of his writings upon points of importance. St. Paul's doctrine of justification by faith, regeneration through

---

[1] See *De Principiis*, iv., 1; *Ibid.*, iii., 1; iv., 44; *Contra Celsum*, iii., 11.

the work of the Holy Spirit, and other vital truths, do not appear, I think, to have fixed his attention. Yet he speaks of Christ's death as "*a ransom to redeem sinners from Satan*, to whom they had sold themselves"; also he refers to the Divine Saviour as a "propitiation for sin."[1] Some heretical opinions he treated leniently.

Origen was philosophical in his habits, after a fashion of his own, and it is interesting to notice what he says of Greek sages. He speaks of Socrates as eulogised by Euripides and Sophocles, and then adds: "It is poor praise to be extolled on the stage, and to be called the wisest of men, on account of the victims he offered to demons."[2] "Plato," he remarks, "puts in Socrates' mouth words more appropriate than are recorded of him by others." Aristotle he curtly notices as fleeing from Athens, afraid of persecution.[3] Origen applies to heathen philosophers the language of Paul to the Romans, as "vain in their imaginations," and carried away; their "foolish hearts" being "darkened."[4]

The debt we owe to his memory as a Biblicist is immense. We find it equalled when we turn to his apologetic treatise in reply to Celsus. Celsus attacked

---

[1] Com. Rom. ii. 13.
[2] *Contra Cels.*, vii., 6.
[3] *Ibid.*, i., 65.
[4] *Ibid.*, vii., 47.

the credibility of the Gospels, and Origen met him on historical grounds in a manner and to an extent never attempted before. It is often forgotten that the same man, who imperilled the historical integrity of Holy Writ by his method of interpretation, did more than any one else to establish the credit and authority of the four Evangelists. In this line he was in advance of Justin and Tertullian. With a force of reasoning superior to theirs, he, with a minuteness of detail and a patience wearisome to modern readers, tracks Celsus through all the windings of his sophistical objections. Nor should it be forgotten that the Christian school of Alexandria was a catechetical institute, preparing the young for discipleship and communion; and also a missionary society for the propagation of the Gospel. Origen was an eloquent advocate for proclaiming to the heathen the unsearchable riches of Christ.

Justice, commonly, has not been done to Origen. His allegorising habit offends some who give common sense a proper place in Biblical study; but obligations to him, under which competent students of Scripture are laid, surely ought not to be forgotten. In connection with his name, we should recall especially the memorable passage which occurs in his writings and which is the germ of Butler's *Analogy*: " He who believes the Scriptures to have proceeded from Him who is the author of nature, may well expect to find the same sort of difficulties in it as are found in the constitution of nature."[1] This is the inscription on the monument of Butler in Bristol Cathedral. The inscription was written by Dr. Southey.

To the intellectual and moral character of Origen must be assigned a chief place amongst celebrities in the early Church. Milner[2] betrays a prejudice against him in a comparison he draws between Origen and Cyprian. They were by natural endowment, educational training, and lifelong circumstances, striking contrasts. Their temptations and failings were not of the same kind. If philosophy was a drawback in the character of the Alexandrian teacher, priestly assumption, on the part of the Carthaginian bishop, may also be deemed a drawback, only of another kind. Origen remained a simple presbyter to the day of his death, never aspiring, it would appear, to any higher office; and of his eminence in this respect we have a monument in his Homilies taken down from his lips when employed as lecturer in his catechetical school. He maintained, it appears, that to the consecration of

---

[1] *Philocal*, 28.   [2] *Church Hist.*, Vol. I., chap. xv.

bishops, the presence and consent of the people were essential, and that bishops were called, not to command, but to serve the Church, and that they ought to discharge their duties with modesty and humility.[1]

Neale, in his *Holy Eastern Church*—" Alexandria," gives a comprehensive digest of Origen's opinions, and though evidently no admirer of the philosophical Alexandrian, yet acquits him of the charge of heresy, as to the doctrine of a Trinity, Father, Son, and Holy Ghost, and of the Incarnation. Neale regards Origen as having been a mystic rather than a heretic.

I have made free remarks on the Alexandrian school in general, and on Clement and Origen in particular; it is but just to insist on the bright side —sometimes very bright—afforded by an impartial study of the entire character of their instructions. Much of what these Fathers say indicative of a Divine element in ancient philosophy, is but an amplification of what Scripture means by "the spirit of man being a candle of the Lord." We must admit that whatever thoughts, true and good, are found in works by illustrious Greeks, were lighted up by Him who made man in His own image,

---

[1] Fleury's *Eccl. Hist.*, by Herbert, i., 359. He refers to *In Jud.*, Hom. 4.

however fallen and dark afterward mankind might be. The Alexandrian recognised, that wisdom of old—outside and far short of Jewish inspiration—came as precursor of instructions conveyed in the New Testament. Paul did not scruple, when preaching at Athens, to quote from one of the poets of the people, " For we are also His offspring. . . . And certain men clave to Paul, and believed : among whom also was Dionysius the Areopagite, and a woman named Damaris, and others with them."[1]

There is another notability connected with Alexandria, who claims more attention than he generally receives. He comes soon after Clement and Origen. I allude to Dionysius, the Great, as he is sometimes called, who held the commanding Egyptian patriarchate for some years. He had not, I apprehend, the social qualities which marked Clement of Alexandria, and made him such a favourite with his fellow-citizens as he seems to have been ; nor had Dionysius the varied brilliant erudition of Origen ; but the natural gifts and the acquired endowments of this Patriarch of Alexandria place him amongst the first Churchmen of his age. No one of that period occupies such a leading place in the

---

[1] Acts xvii. 28.

History by Eusebius, and appears there under so many aspects, as Dionysius. His life was full of incident, and his ecclesiastical ability and influence surpassed that of most contemporaries. His epistles were very numerous, and they seem to have fallen into the hands of Eusebius. They are autobiographical, and the copious extracts given by the historian are, some of them, very entertaining. He relates much respecting himself, and many of his adventures were of an interesting order. We learn how he was going to a festival, and was seized by soldiers, who stripped him of all but a linen garment, and carried him away upon an unsaddled ass. He said it was a duty to suffer anything rather than to afflict the Church of God, and that it was better to suffer martyrdom than to offer sacrifice in honour of idols. Page after page in the History by Eusebius is filled with letters written by Dionysius, and we learn more respecting him than we do of any other individual. The story which interests me more than any other is one relating to Nepos and his schism. The schism sprang from certain millenarian views which agitated the Church at that day. "When I was at Arsinöe," Dionysius says, "this doctrine was afloat, so that apostacies and schisms followed. I called the presbyters and brethren together, and exhorted them carefully to state the views they had adopted. They produced a book, which they regarded as a kind of armour, and an impregnable fortress; and I sat with them for three days from morning to night endeavouring to refute the opinions it contained. I was pleased with the sincerity and intelligence of the brethren. Moderately and methodically we proposed questions, expressed doubts, and made concessions; carefully avoiding all that was offensive. We did not evade objections; and, as far as possible, we kept to the subject before us, not ashamed where reason prevailed, to change opinion and acknowledge truth. We received, with single hearts before God, whatever was established by the Holy Scriptures. At length the founder and leader of the doctrine under consideration, in the hearing of all present, avowed that he would no longer adhere to the opinions he had adopted, being fully convinced by opposite arguments. The brethren present rejoiced at the result of the conference, and at the conciliatory spirit manifested by all who were present."

If this account be trustworthy, as I hope it is,

---

[1] Eusebius, *Eccl. Hist.*, vii., c. 24.

such a model discussion is worthy of praise and imitation. The principal opponent was convinced, "through the opening made into his heart."

This good Bishop Dionysius has been accused of inconsistency and a want of independence—common charges against amiable people and successful peacemakers—and he is chiefly complimented for courtly concessions and churchly tact. But, as far as I can see, after much reading on the subject, there is no ground whatever for regarding Dionysius as a time-server.

II. Latin Fathers.—Clement, Bishop of Rome, wrote to the Church there in Greek, but he belongs to the Western section of Christendom. It is interesting to compare his Epistle to the Corinthians with that of St. Paul to the Romans. Both letters contain quotations from the Septuagint. The schismatical character of the people addressed shows that they were the same at the end of the century as in the middle. And one cannot but notice the harmony of Paul's doctrine of justification with Clement's rebuke of its antinomian perversion. The latter is eminently devout in spirit. "Open our eyes, O Lord, that we may know Thee, and feel Thy presence." "Help those who need help." "Lord and Creator, pity and forgive." "Through Christ we pour out our hearts to Thee." There is no strictly dogmatic teaching in the letter.

On the list of Latin Fathers comes Tertullian (about 160—240), an African, born in Carthage. The dates of his birth and his death are uncertain, but we gather that his parents were heathen, and that Christianity was the choice of his riper years. He studied Greek, and was acquainted with Homer. He preferred history and poetry to philosophical studies: for the latter he had no taste; and, judging from what we know of him, no aptitude. Gospel facts, however, laid hold on his understanding and touched his heart. From facts he passed to doctrines. Thus he gained foothold on what he made his own for life and death. He studied Roman law, and legal habits appear in his works. Often, in reading him, we detect the special pleader, intent, after a one-sided fashion, upon making out a case; but without any consciousness of unworthy motives, for they never swayed him.

Tertullian was not a philosopher, in the common acceptation of the term, though he had a way of his own in that direction; and, in his ecclesiastical views, account must be taken of influence exerted over him by Montanus. Montanus has been hardly dealt with; sometimes he is represented as claiming to be an incarnation of the Paraclete—a charge never substantiated.[1] There might be attributed to him extraordinary Divine gifts; perhaps he claimed such himself, in an age when supernatural endowments were not supposed to have been wholly withdrawn. What is probably the case, as he professed to be a Reformer, he was excited by corruptions he saw increasing at the time; dwelt extravagantly upon the necessity of some spiritual revival to check the tide; and referred to the Holy Ghost in ways disapproved by sober-minded Christians. Those who deplore existing evils, and look on an age in which they live as backsliding from God, generally take pessimist views of all around; they are apt to seclude themselves from those on whom they might exercise an influence by intercourse, and to say, "Stand by, for I am holier than thou." Montanus, no doubt, was an unamiable man, likely to have what good was in him evil spoken of. Such people may draw towards themselves those who are like-minded, but they are sure to repel non-sympathisers. Charges of immorality were brought against the Montanists by Cyril of Jerusalem; but Dr. Newman candidly

---

[1] Burton's *Eccl. Hist.*, ii., 158; Mossman's *Hist. of the Catholic Church*, chaps. xv., xvii., xviii.; Smith's *Dict. of Christian Biog.*, art. "Montanus."

remarks, " These charges are not borne out by other writers." [1]

Tertullian is considered by Bishop Kaye to have been orthodox on the whole, and might have passed muster in an examination upon the XXXIX. Articles; but certainly he diverged from Catholic teaching in his view of the soul, to which he attributed a sort of corporeity, citing, in support of his notion, the parable of Dives and Lazarus. Tertullian was out of sympathy with philosophers. "What," he asked, "has Athens to do with Jerusalem, the Academy with the Church? Our school is of Solomon's Porch. Away with those who have brought forward a stoic, and a platonic, and dialectic Christianity! To us there is no need of curious questioning, now that we have Christ; nor of inquiry, now that we have the Gospel. In that we believe, we desire to know nothing besides."[2] He contended for an unphilosophised Christianity; but, like some other people, he had, after all, a philosophy of his own, for which, with characteristic spirit, he was prepared to do battle. He blamed Gnostic allegories; yet he allegorised in his own way. He speaks of the twelve wells of Elim as types of the twelve Apostles, and of the ark

---

[1] See Oxford translation of *St. Cyril of Jerusalem*, p. 206.
[2] *De Præs. Hær.*, 7, 8.

as a type of the Church. "It mattereth not," he says, "whether, according to that figure, the raven, the kite, the wolf, the dog, and the serpent shall be in the Church; the idolater is assuredly not contained within the figure of the ark. No animal was made an emblem of the idolater. That which was not in the ark may not be in the Church."[1]

Tertullian's controversy with Marcion figures largely in ante-Nicene history, but is too wide and intricate to be disposed of in a few sentences. I have only room to say that Marcion identified matter with moral evil, or rather that he believed the former was a source of the latter; that the creator of our material world is really the author of evil and God of the Old Testament; but that the God of the New Testament is the Saviour of men, and the source of all that is really true and good. This theory Tertullian exposed with amazing force and eloquence, establishing the unity and authority of the two Biblical records. His work is a wonderful production.[2]

Tertullian's repellent style was not likely to win over to his views persons he addressed. Of his

---

[1] *De Idol.*, 24.
[2] I have been much struck by a perusal of *Cont. Marcionem*.

intellectual gifts there can be but one opinion; but I must confess there is no other apologist I find so difficult to follow. He presents, in his defence of Christianity, a labyrinth of thoughts, the consecutiveness of which—the way in and the way out—it is difficult to trace. But there are expressions of his never to be forgotten. " The blood of the martyrs is the seed of the Church " has become an aphorism which can never die. A grim humour now and then flashes up, as when he talks of persecutors making martyrs and idols, after the same fashion, "with crosses and stakes, axes and saws, knives and nails." "We are," he says, "thrown into a fire to be melted down like iron, lead, and other metals." His Punic dialect requires at times a special lexicon to make it intelligible; and, unfortunately, his Latin has done much to make many divines since rather hard to read, as he is himself.

Let me add, Tertullian had a keen perception of other people's imperfections, and was by no means charitable in construction of their motives. He unsparingly condemned what he did not like, and hence he made numerous personal enemies. This fact explains his unpopularity. Apt to censure others, they retaliated by censuring him. He was no heretic, nor indeed, voluntarily, a schismatic;

but I regard him as just the person to create an idea of his being both.

Though married, Tertullian had no family, and his asceticism unfitted him for domestic and social enjoyments; yet there comes out something genial in his notice of the Agape. "We eat as worshipping God by night; talk as knowing that He listens. Having washed our hands and lighted the lamps, each sings according to ability. Prayer concludes the feast."

Cyprian, whom we have noticed already, called Tertullian his master. We think of the master as rude and unpolished, and his disciple as refined and polite. The latter, it is said, had a retentive memory and active habits, with command of others, proving him to have possessed business power. Pontinus, his deacon, says: "His countenance was grave, yet cheerful, neither too severe nor too placid; his dress was in harmony with this, neither pretentious nor mean, neither extravagant nor penurious." From the same authority we learn that Cyprian's house was free to all comers. No widow went away with an empty lap from his hospitable door. When pestilence raged, he said it was a test whether the healthy would nurse the sick. He worked hard to keep the Church unspotted from the world.

Cyprian was more of an ecclesiastic than a theologian; devoted to the experimental and practical side of religion rather than the doctrinal. But, in his epistles, he dwells with devout interest upon Christ as our Lord and God, truly Divine whilst truly human; as our King and Judge; as the Sacrifice for our sin, and the High Priest of our profession; as loving us with infinite pity, and redeeming us by His cross and passion; as Protector, Guardian, Shepherd, Captain; crowned Himself, and giving crowns to His true soldiers. Christians, in Cyprian's esteem, must live *in* Christ, *by* Christ, *with* Christ, awaiting sufferings for His sake. Christ gives to us as much as we believe, not according to our merit, but His mercy.[1]

Cyprian wrote a treatise on *Unity*. Reading it, I find it is a plea for episcopal *uniformity*. "This unity," he says, "we hold, especially we bishops, that we may approve the episcopate to be one and undivided." From beginning to end he is thinking of the episcopal form as a bond of brother-

---

[1] Shepherd, in his *History of the Church of Rome*, attacks the writings of Cyprian, disputing their genuineness. The critic was answered in the *Quarterly Review*, June, 1853. I remember the controversy, and on reading Shepherd's *History* saw the ground he took was untenable.

hood, oblivious of the fact that episcopacy was being professed, at that very moment, where strife between bishop and bishop, between Church and Church (all of episcopal order), prevailed to the disgrace of Christendom. The shadow of unity in an outward form was left, but the substance of union was gone. Parties were professed Episcopalians, yet quarrelling together as to whether certain men were included in the order. Cyprian did not see, though it was plain enough, that uniformity might remain in Church government, and yet the unity of the Spirit not be kept in bonds of peace. Certainly, Episcopalianism is no more a bond of union than other forms of ecclesiastical government, seeing that bishops, like other people, then quarrelled one with another. The controversy, which grieved sorely the heart of the good Carthaginian prelate, demonstrated the fallacy of his favourite argument. We see in modern times episcopal communities holding fast their fundamental principle, and yet full of intestine strife. On the other hand, denominations adopting diversified methods of government may and do live in concord and charity one with another. Brotherly love, not ecclesiastical agreement, is the secret of real unity. Cyprian denounced " heretics and schismatics as not gathered in Christ's name," but as people "like Korah and Uzziah."

Citing the words of our Lord, "Thou art Peter, and upon this rock I will build My Church, and the gates of hell shall not prevail against it," Cyprian remarks: "In order to manifest unity, Christ has by His own authority so placed the source of the same unity to begin from one. Certainly the other Apostles also had what Peter was endowed with, an equal fellowship both of honour and power; but a commencement is made from unity, that the Church may be set before us as one." This utterance is ambiguous. Hence a dispute arises between Roman and Anglo Catholics, into which it would on these pages be foreign to enter.

Of the benevolence, and, under some circumstances, the tenderness of Cyprian, there can be no doubt, but he was a strict disciplinarian. "Discipline," he says, "is a protection against Satan's wiles. He cannot bite feet shod with this defence. To relax discipline is injurious to the safety and welfare of the Church. Laxity is hurtful, and severity is benevolent; but it is to be tempered with mercy, like the dealings of God." In this way Cyprian writes letter after letter. Immorality the good man would not tolerate; but when I read what he has written, I must say that schism, heresy, and the conduct of the lapsed, beyond other offences aroused his indignation. For all this he was reviled; "but discipline," he says, "must not be abandoned."[1] After all he was a man of deep spirituality and devotion. An eminent Nonconformist friend of mine used to speak of his piety in the strongest terms of admiration.

We know little respecting the details of Cyprian's private life, but we have a full account of his death. The incidents are carefully preserved. The main source of his joy was the life to come. The walls of the earthly house, he said, tottered, and the roof shook. The ship was tossed, and the mariner hastened to the harbour. Thus he wrote, as he longed for home and rest. "Paradise," he said, in his touching treatise on *Mortality*, "we reckon as our native land. Patriarchs are our parents, and we long to salute our ancestry. Earth is shut, but Heaven opens. Death comes, and Immortality follows. Faith, made ready for martyrdom, will not be without reward."

In concluding what I have to say of Cyprian, let me remark that, while I differ from his ecclesiastical

---

[1] *Ep.*, lix., 4.

views, there is no one of the Fathers who impresses me so much by his beautiful devoutness of heart and life. His realisation of God, Christ, and Eternity is wonderful. He endured as seeing Him who is invisible. I regard him as spiritually akin to George Herbert and Thomas Ken.

The ascetic influence of Cyprian, following as he did Tertullian in this respect, has been often noticed. Very much of early hermit life, and, through that, of mediæval monachism, which, after all, was an improvement upon some previous ascetic examples, may, I think, be traced to the writings of the Carthaginian bishop, whose piety and good intentions no one can fairly doubt.

Asceticism, in its decided shape, made its appearance in the third century. Two typical examples, earliest and most pronounced, occurred within that period—Paul and Antony. We are told that Paul died in A.D. 343, a hundred and thirty years old; Antony in 356, at the age of a hundred and five. More than half their lives, therefore, pertain to the age under present review. No contemporary account of them remains, but we have a full-length portrait of Antony by Athanasius. It is, no doubt, based upon traditions, looked at in the light of an age when asceticism was attracting admiration and reverence from illustrious Churchmen. How far the famous biography of Antony is to be trusted, is a puzzle to unprejudiced critics; at any rate, it indicates that before the reign of Constantine the hermit habit had begun to be developed. Paul and Antony appear together. Paul dwelt in a cave, close to a palm tree and a water spring, leaves and dates supplying him with clothing and food, for forty-three years. Afterwards bread was brought every day by a faithful raven. Antony visited him, not long before his death, and on the way met with a centaur, who fled at the sight of the cross, after helping the old man to find out where Paul was. The raven came as usual to Paul that day, but with a double portion for him and his guest. Antony saw the soul of Paul carried up to heaven, attended by angels, prophets, and apostles, a grave being dug for his body by a couple of lions. Other incredible marvels are related; how Antony was tempted in a desert far away from all human abodes, by devils who came to him in the guise of beautiful women. From youth to age he never changed his clothing, and, dying in the odour of sanctity, left behind him traditions piously collected and preserved by his admirers. Contradictory stories are told about Antony's knowledge of Scripture;

some saying that he could read, others that he could not, and that he learned all he knew from what he heard. At all events this noted saint was no student of the Bible; and much of what is related by Athanasius about him throws a dark shadow across the period in which he lived.[1]

As the distinguished Fathers described pass in review before us, we are in the presence of a fact quite new in the history of mankind. Here are men of different countries, languages, habits, and idiosyncrasies, brought together by a bond of belief, sympathy, and affection. Africans and Europeans, Greeks and Latins, the philosophical and those unaccustomed to abstract speculation, are found embracing the Gospel which reveals God the Father, Christ the Son, and the Holy Ghost, sanctifier and comforter of souls. Thus men became *one* in a sense never understood before. Their faith rested on a Divine Prophet, Lord, and King, and was such as never entered into human minds to conceive before

---

[1] I have seen doubts cast on Athanasius' authorship of Antony's Life. I do not know on what grounds. Cardinal Newman remarks, "I conceive no question can be raised as to its integrity." That such a man as Athanasius could write such a book as the Life of Antony, shows how much superstition existed in his days. Plenty of what Protestants count superstitions may be found in writers of the fourth and fifth centuries.

Christ's time. They were "new creatures," weaned from earthly ambition and self-indulgence, ready to die for Him who died for them. It perplexes reason to account for this : the Divine origin of Christianity is the only solution.

To say that the primitive Church believed Jesus of Nazareth to be *only* a man is to contradict the consensus of patristic teaching. " Who knows not the works of Irenæus, and Melito, and the rest, in all of which Christ is described as both *God and man* ? " are the words of Eusebius ; and he adds : " There was a certain Natalius, who lived, not in remote times, but in our own. He was seduced by Asclepediorus, and Theodotus, a money-changer."[1] Such is the origin assigned by the historian Eusebius to a belief in Christ's sole humanity.

Agreement as to the Divine personality of Jesus Christ was a bond of unity strong enough to bear the strain of subordinate controversies, both as to doctrinal opinion and ecclesiastical observance. Polycarp adhered to the tradition that Easter should be kept on the fourteenth day of the month, whatever might be the day of the week ; but Anicetus maintained that the feast of the resurrection should be

---

[1] Eusebius, *Eccl. Hist.*, v., 28.

confined to the first day. Polycarp visited Rome in the middle of the second century, with the hope he might convince his brother that the Oriental season of observance was the proper one. Failing in that respect, he united, notwithstanding, in the holy commemoration, inviting the Bishop of Smyrna to officiate in the service.

Nor was this union confined to one point : Christian doctrine with regard to Christ was a whole ; what He was, stood in relation to what He did, according to the perception of primitive teachers. Redemption, in its doctrinal view, was not fully developed until a later period, and some peculiar ideas held for a time respecting it have long since dropped out of controversy ; but a comprehensive belief obtained that Christ, by His obedience and sacrifice, by " His agony and bloody sweat, His cross and passion," made an atonement for the sins of the world.[1]

---

[1] I may here take the opportunity of noticing the division which Kurtz makes in his *Church History* (Period I., Div. ii.) respecting the second and third centuries,—the former of these periods, which he calls *Post Apostolic*, lasting down to A.D. 170 ; the latter, denominated *Old Catholic*, reaching to the time of Constantine. Kurtz rests this distinction on theological grounds, A.D. 170 being the time of Irenæus, the early great champion against heretics, and also the time when the Trinitarian con-

Tertullian has a remarkable passage touching the doctrine of our Lord's person. "The mystery of the dispensation is guarded, which distributes the Unity into a Trinity, Father, Son, and Holy Spirit—Three, not in condition, but degree, not in substance, but in form, not in power, but in aspect; of one substance, of one power as He is one God, in name, Father, Son, and Holy Ghost. He is the one only God, yet must be believed according to His own economy. The Unity, which derives the Trinity out of itself, is so far from being destroyed, that it is administered by it." Tertullian, in his own crabbed style, thus maintains the Unity of the Triune Godhead to be a doctrine of the primitive Church at large, and not a particular opinion of his own.[1] He adduces a number of considerations supporting the Trinity and Unity of the Divine existence, giving it not merely as an individual opinion, but as a prime article of the Catholic faith. Here we have a so-called schismatic contending for doctrinal orthodoxy. Praxeas held a

---

troversy may be said to have commenced. The first period includes the Apostolic Fathers and Justin Martyr; the second, Irenæus, Hippolytus, Clement of Alexandria, Origen, and Dionysius among the Greeks; Tertullian, Cyprian, Arnobius, and Lactantius among the Latins.

[1] *Adversus Praxean*, 2, 3.

new doctrine, involving denial of the Trinity; its popularity arose from its novelty. It was new, and, on that account, had a special charm for minds of a certain order. I may add, " Artemas, like his predecessor Theodotus, believed Jesus Christ to be a mere man, and denied His pre-existence, though he allowed His miraculous conception."[1]

---

[1] Burton's *Eccl. Hist.*, ii., pp. 223, 387.

CHAPTER V

DIFFUSION OF CHRISTIANITY

THIS may be said to have been provided for from the beginning. The prophecy of bruising the serpent's head, the call of Abraham, the mission of Moses, and the whole Jewish dispensation prepared for the Gospel. The Greek language was ready to receive the Old Testament in the Septuagint. Plato and other philosophers had prepared for early patristic literature. The last century of ancient heathendom, by means of politics and war, prepared for the Christian era. Struggles in Rome, battles in Spain and Africa—all helped to clear the way for Messiah's empire over the wide world.

From A.D. 31 the world was open to the Divine mission of the Church. Providence had prepared a way for ministers of the Word, so that for a while it had free course.

Christ's commission was to preach the Gospel to

every creature, and that commission rested on the fact that God had "made of one blood every nation of men to dwell on the face of the earth."

It is interesting to notice how the Mediterranean was open in the first century, so as to admit the passage of Apostles from one place to another. "It may be observed," says Dr. Arnold, "that two out of the three ships in which the Apostle Paul performed his voyage from Palestine to Rome were ships of Alexandria; which seems to indicate that vessels from that place sailing direct to Italy were more easily to be found than from any other port in the Eastern provinces."[1]

The same author adds afterwards: "The evils of war were no longer felt or dreaded. Four legions only were stationed in the whole of Asia Minor and Syria. The piracy once so great an evil on the coasts of Cilicia and Pamphylia, was now so reduced as to offer no obstacles to the trade or general intercourse which was carried on by sea." Arnold is here speaking of the Augustan era, and he includes in his notices "an established conveyance for letters." He calls the first eighty years of the second century "the prime of manhood in the Roman empire."

---

[1] *Later Roman Empire*, ii., p. 377.

From A.D. 31 to A.D. 58 the empire, so far as the government was concerned, lay open to Christian missions. So far God had levelled a road where His servants could walk and work. The valley was exalted, the mountain was made low; crooked things became straight, and rough places plain. Facilities for travelling and for correspondence, to an unprecedented extent, existed when Paul and others were passing to and fro from province to province on Divine errands. Had wars then raged round the Mediterranean shores, or Cilician pirates swept its waters, as they did a century earlier, how would Apostles have accomplished what they did?

The Fathers bear witness to the spread of the Gospel. "There is not one nation of men," says Justin Martyr, " whether barbarians or Greeks, or by whatever name distinguished, whether nomads, who live in waggons, or those who are without houses, or pastoral people dwelling in tents, among whom prayers and thanksgivings are not offered to the Father and Creator of all things, through the name of the crucified Jesus."[1] Tertullian paints a still bolder and more highly coloured picture, which, after being toned down, leaves a decisive testimony to the

---

[1] *Dial. Tryph.*, 117.

wide extent of Christian influence. "If we wished," says he, "to act the avowed enemy, not the secret avenger only, would strength of numbers and forces be wanting to us? We are a people of yesterday, and yet we have filled every place belonging to you— Cities, Islands, Castles, Towns, Assemblies, your very camp, your tribes, companies, palace, senate, forums. We leave you your temples only. We can count your armies; our number in a single province will be greater. If so large a body of men as we were to break away from you into some remote corner of the globe, surely the loss of so many citizens, of whatever sort they might be, would cover your kingdom with shame, and would punish by the very desertion of you."[1] To this witness, borne to the number of Christians within the pale of Roman civilisation, may be added another relative to tribes outside—Moors, Spaniards, Gauls, Britons, Sarmatians, Dacians, Germans, and Scythians. Irenæus, in a more sober strain, speaks of the truths of the Gospel being written in the hearts of barbarian people by the Holy Spirit.[2] Origen declares that Christianity had won myriads of converts from among all nations,[3] and Arnobius mentions distant

---

[1] *Apol.*, 37. [2] *Adv. Hær.*, iii., 4, 2.
[3] *Contra Celsum*, i., 27.

realms where believers might be found.[1] The defenders of the Christian faith would not have dared to write in this way, if its wide-spread influence had not been an unquestionable fact.

Antioch, the first missionary station of Christendom, maintained a prominent position among the Churches during the period under review. In the time of Ignatius its moral power must have been great, and in a city of 200,000 inhabitants the disciples, who were there first called Christians, found, under such a pastor, a wide sphere for their activity. The number of professors at Antioch in the fourth century indicates the progress which had been previously going on. Pliny, in his letter to Trajan, throws light on the advance of Christianity in Asia Minor; for he tells his imperial friend that the temples of the gods were almost forsaken, and animals for sacrifices found few purchasers.

The history of particular Churches becomes obscure after the apostolic age, but the names of bishops presiding over some of them have been preserved. Only scanty notices can be found of Macedonia and Corinth, Greece and Athens, but there were traditions in after times of bishops and catechetical schools

---

[1] *Ad Gentes*, i., 16.

there between the first and fourth centuries. The Church at Rome was the most important of the West, and in the middle of the second century had forty-six presbyters, besides the Bishop-in-chief.

Africa received the Gospel in apostolic times. The Evangelist Mark is reported to have laid the foundation of the Church in Alexandria, which witnessed, in the year 235, a council, whither had come twenty bishops from different places in the neighbourhood. Carthage had a flourishing Church in the second century. Cyprian there assembled a council of eighty-seven bishops, and half a century later the Donatist pastors met in the same place to the number of 270. No doubt some dioceses were small. In Western Europe, Spain could reckon at the Synod of Elibeus nineteen bishops; and, at the Council of Arles, as we shall see, three British bishops were present. The Churches of Lyons and Vienne, in Gaul, seem to have been spiritually prosperous at the time of the persecution in the last half of the second century, their close connection with Asia Minor at that period being a very important fact.

"The Gospel was propagated chiefly by preaching and by personal intercourse; to a considerable extent also through Sacred Scriptures, which were early translated into different tongues. Communication in different parts of the empire, from Damascus to Britain, was comparatively easy and safe. Highways made for commerce and Roman legions served also the messengers of peace and the conquests of the Cross. Besides the regular ministry, slaves, and women particularly, appear to have performed missionary service, and to have introduced the Christian life into all circles of society."

Thus then, by turning over page after page, written seventeen or eighteen hundred years since, we, as it were, hold in our hands telegrams forwarded by witnesses of Christian victories won so long ago.

One thing is often overlooked in the early diffusion of Christianity. Our Lord said, "The kingdom of heaven is like leaven, which a woman took and hid in three measures of meal till the whole was leavened." So, unremarked by the world, did the Word of God work effectually. No account is or could be preserved of hidden influences amongst humble people. Dean Milman says: "Christianity sunk deeply into depths of the human heart, unmoved by tumults which so fiercely agitated the surface of the Christian world. Far below, less observed, less visible in its mode of operation, though manifest in its effects, was that profound conviction of the truth of the Gospel, that infelt sense of its blessings, which enabled it to pursue its course of conversion throughout the world, to bring the Roman mind more completely under subjection, and one by one to subdue the barbarian tribes which began to overspread and mingle with the Greek and Latin population of the empire."

The beneficence of Christians promoted the spread of the Gospel. We find depicted scenes of horror in Armenia under the Emperor Maximinus, during a time of famine, and deadly disease which followed in the wake of want. People ate noxious herbs and wisps of hay; some, wasted to skeletons, stumbled in the highway, and fell, gasping the words, "Hunger! hunger!" Then "the evidences of Christian piety and zeal became manifest, for Christians were the only persons who manifested humanity in their conduct. They buried the dead, and, collecting together the famished, distributed bread; so that their conduct was noticed and praised by all, and men glorified the Christians' God."[1]

Eusebius writes, "Throughout every city and village, like a replenished barn floor, Churches were rapidly found abounding, and filled with members from every people." There is perhaps a touch of rhetoric here, but the learned author, whilst many

---

[1] *Latin Christianity*, i., p. 255.

still opposed Christianity, would hardly have ventured on such a report if there had not been patent facts to bear it out. Other broad statements occur in other writers. Pliny, in his letter to Trajan (A.D. 107), after describing what he had done with the new sect, remarks: "The matter appears to me to require that I should ask your counsel, especially on account of the number who are in danger of suffering, of both sexes, of every order." Temples were almost deserted—victims rarely found a purchaser. Tertullian used strong language touching the spread of the Gospel, but facts, if not fully justifying every word, confirm the substance of his assertion. If we examine a map of the Empire in the fourth century, we find it includes Palestine, Syria, Asia Minor, Cyprus, Egypt, Greece, Illyricum, Italy, Gaul, Spain, and Britain—Christianity penetrated them all.

Facts illustrating the propagation of the Gospel are beyond dispute; details of success have been filled in partially by the researches of scholars. The pith of numerous particulars has been published by Wiltsch, in his German *Handbook of Church Geography and Statistics*, translated into English by Leitch. This branch of study has been cultivated by Romanists and neglected by Protestants. No doubt, in collections by Baronius and Mansi (who supply material for such digests) there is a great deal which few critics outside their communion can accept; but that does not justify our rushing to the extreme of regarding all particulars they supply as mere inventions. Some of them appear to me quite trustworthy, and I have found it interesting to turn over Wiltsch's pages when I have been studying particular branches of Church history. For instance, after reading Arnold's glowing description of Rhodes (a place which I well remember passing on my way from Beyrout to Smyrna), I opened Wiltsch to see if he had anything to say about the early history of Christianity in that island, and I found that he notices a Bishop of Rhodes at the Council of Nice in A.D. 325. This bishop's name stands third in succession, carrying back the episcopate at Rhodes into the third century, and the introduction of it there, most likely, to a still earlier date. Arnold speaks of heathen Rhodes as distinguished by "justice and mutual kindness," and a "spirit of general benevolence, and of forbearance even towards enemies."[1] If so, were not the Rhodians a people prepared of the Lord for receiving His truth?

The diffusion of the Gospel before the age of

---

[1] Arnold's *Hist. of Rome*, ii., p. 415.

Constantine must altogether have been very extensive, for imperial and other conversions certainly proceeded more or less from an impression that paganism was a losing cause. Roman idolatry and popular superstition in town and country had to be overcome; and the labour needed for this purpose must have been immense. Effective propagation could not but be gradual. "Many persons," says a modern missionary, "think that the conversion of a few hundreds to Christianity should reform a whole province. It is not so. It never was so since the first dawn of the kingdom of God. The progress of ideas has always been slow, and only by comparing one age with another can progress and improvement be marked."[1]

It is very remarkable to learn that at the death of Gregory Thaumaturgus of Neo-Cæsarea, in the third century, the number of heathens remaining in his diocese amounted only to seventeen, exactly corresponding with the number of Christians when he was ordained to episcopal office. Gregory's namesake of Nyssa, in a romantic eulogium on the "wonder-worker," tells a curious story, how, at a festival of some local deity, the place was too small

---

[1] *Light in Africa*, by James Macdonald, p. 135.

to hold the crowds, and the people cried, "Zeus, make room for us!" After this Gregory exclaimed, "There shall be granted you larger room than you pray for, or ever have known." A fearful pestilence followed, which was regarded as a fulfilment of the speaker's prophecy. The disease was accompanied by other calamities. They yielded to the bishop's intercession, and this led to numerous conversions. I give the story as I find it.[1]

The number of believers in Rome is a subject of much interest. "In the capital," says Bishop Lightfoot, "there is every reason to think the Christians were as influential and bore as large a proportion to the heathen population as in any part of the Empire, except possibly some districts of Africa, and some exceptional cities elsewhere, such as Antioch. Now, in an extant letter of Cornelius, who was Bishop of Rome from 250 to 252, it is stated that the number of widows and others receiving the alms of the Church was over 1,500. Unfortunately the whole number of the Christians is not recorded; but in the Church of Antioch, somewhat later, we find that the proportion

---

[1] Smith's *Christian Biography*; articles, "Gregory Thaum." and "Gregory of Nyssa."

of these recipients of alms was three for every hundred. Assuming this same proportion to hold for Rome (and there is at all events no reason for supposing it less), we should get 50,000 as the whole number of Roman Christians. Now at the very lowest estimate the population of Rome amounted to one million (some make it a million and a half), so that the Christians at this time would form somewhat less than one-twentieth of the whole." [1]

Other means besides preaching promoted the cause. For instance, a Christian woman was taken captive by Iberians—a Spanish colony at the foot of the Caucasus, their settlement being separated by Colchis from the Euxine Sea. She was known for her piety, and her fame reached the queen of the country, who had a sick child, and thought the woman's prayers might save his life. She accordingly sent and requested her intercessions, which were earnestly offered, and proved successful. Upon his restoration, the mother herself becoming ill, she requested prayers on her own account; she also recovered, and when the stranger was thanked for what she had done, she replied, "This work is not

---

[1] "Comparative Progress of Ancient and Modern Missions." A paper read at the Annual Meeting of the S.P.G., 1873.

mine, but Christ's the Son of God, who made the world." The conversion of the queen followed, and led further to that of the king, who also betook himself to the exercise of prayer, to faith in Christ, and to the building of an oratory for Divine worship. A change in the weather, and a miracle in placing a pillar of this oratory on its base, are related, after the manner of the age, as the result of these royal conversions. The authority of an Iberian prince is cited by Socrates the historian for the story, part of which must be numbered amongst other beliefs of that credulous age. The same narrative—which, in reference to the captive's prayers and the royal conversions, I accept—is repeated in other words by Theodoret and Sozomen, historians living at the same period, contemporary with Socrates, about a century and a half after the Iberian conversions; and I give it as the most interesting I can find connected with the Christianisation of Gothic tribes in the North-East.[1]

Christianity reached Britain at an early period, but how we do not know. Much has been written about Plautus, Pudens, and Claudia (names mentioned by the Apostle Paul, and by the poet Martial), in

---

[1] Theodoret, i., 24; Sozomen, ii., 7; Socrates, i., 20.

order to show that the persons so named came to our island in the first century; but the attempt, to my mind, is inconclusive. A slight glimmer of facts may perhaps be found in Mello, a Gallic bishop of the third century, said to have been a native of our country.

In looking back upon the progress of Christianity, as imperfectly indicated in this chapter, we see, in what relates to Greece and Italy, how the Gospel in its practical effects proved itself to be derived from Him who "went about doing good." Epicureans and Stoics competed with Apostles and their followers in what they offered to mankind, as consolations amidst darkly chequered life-scenes. The doctrine that pleasure, not duty, gratification, not self-restraint, is the pole-star of fallen humanity—welcome enough under emperors who sought popularity by providing amusements, when voluptuousness ran riot to an enormous extent: that doctrine left people in sickness and sorrow without help or hope. The Stoic principle had a noble side; but how humiliating it was to its pride, that it had no power to rise above calamity, and could only defy the foe it could not conquer! How the assumptions of these sects were put to shame by a gospel which offered contentment in time, and happiness in eternity, and inspired lowly, quiet strength amidst unavoidable suffering! Stoicism crushed affection ; Christianity exalted it. When we turn from controversies and ceremonies to the cardiphonia—the heart utterances of saints —we discover proof after proof of heroism such as Stoics never reached, united to pleasures such as it entered not into the hearts of Epicureans to conceive.

We must now come farther West, and notice the introduction of evangelical truth to our own country.

King Lucius figures in stories related by Geoffrey of Monmouth as a British ruler and Church founder in the second century. And it is a curious fact that at the time of the Reformation this fictitious tradition was cited in proof that an ancient British monarch exercised authority in Ireland over the Church there in the second century.[1] Thus, by irony of fate, an argument originating in mediæval times was turned to Protestant account under Henry VIII., when it was urged that Popes, so early, acknowledged sovereigns to be supreme in their dominions over Church as well as State.

Putting aside traditions as to causes of diffused Christianity in Britain at an early period, proof of

[1] Olden's *Church of Ireland*, p. 297.

the fact may, I think, be found in intercourse between Roman Christian soldiers and inhabitants of our island—perhaps through marriage between the foreigners and natives. We shall soon see that at a council in the fourth century three British bishops took part.

With regard to population in different countries touched by Christianity, it is interesting to discover lower and upper grades. The poor had the Gospel preached to them, and multitudes destitute of life's comforts found consolation in Christian promises; also, it may be noticed that in the reign of Decius believers at Rome included people of wealth, "that vessels of gold and silver were used in religious worship, and that many proselytes sold their lands and houses to increase the public riches of the sect." So writes the historian Gibbon, adding as censure, unsupported by evidence, that liberality to the Church was bestowed at the expense of poor relatives.[1]

If we take a modern map of the globe, and include in our idea of the world all the continents and islands of the two hemispheres, the enumeration of countries touched by the Gospel in the first three centuries

---

[1] *Decline and Fall* (Milman's edition), i., p. 503.

may seem a scanty result; but when compared with the limited knowledge of the earth's surface at that period, the impression we receive is very different. Take Claudius Ptolemy's map of the world in the second century. It is limited to the eastern half. There is no America at all; and little is seen of Africa beyond strips on the Mediterranean shores. The Indian Ocean is a waste of unknown waters; and India itself is little more than a *terra incognita*, to which writers in the fourth and fifth centuries refer in a blundering way. No distinct indication of China appears. The northern part of Europe is quite obscure; in fact, the Roman and Greek empires make up the known world. When we compare all this with the spread of Christian preaching within the first three centuries, we cannot but exclaim, "What hath God wrought!"

CHAPTER VI

PERSECUTION AND HEROISM

AS to charges against primitive Christians, light is thrown by accusations levelled at Socrates. He was accused of weaning children from parents, inspiring people with a conceit of their superior wisdom, and thus undermining sentiments of filial duty and loyal submission. He was further charged with political as well as religious innovation, with discrediting the constitution of their country, and dishonouring the gods of Greece. Also unfair citations were made from his oral teaching, construed as being adverse to the State. Moreover, when brought before his judges, he made no defence, and did not desire to be acquitted. To crown all, his enemies were exasperated by his claiming to fulfil a Divine mission.[1]

---

[1] All these particulars are abundantly illustrated in Grote's *History of Greece*, vol. viii., new edit., pp. 273, 281.

Somewhat parallel to these charges were those brought against primitive Christians. They were accused of abandoning ancestral customs, of dishonouring domestic piety, and of rebelling against laws of the land. Doctrines inculcated by them were construed as disloyal and antisocial—words being torn from their original connection. When arraigned before their judges, those accused were silent or only made a confession of faith, not desiring acquittal. This limited parallel, which I have ventured to suggest, relates to persecutors rather than victims. In most cases, the *animus* which moved the former was hatred of goodness seen in the latter. Intellectually, no comparison is possible between the marvellously gifted Athenian and the mentally commonplace character of most primitive believers; but how far above the philosophy of the Greek sage rose the truths which strengthened and comforted Christian sufferers!

What I have now stated by no means fully explains the cause of persecution. Roman authority came into collision with Christianity partly on political grounds. Christ said, " I am a King," " My kingdom is not of this world." This was a claim which, when known, was likely to rouse Roman jealousy and antagonism. At first, in Trajan's time, it does not seem to have done so; but afterwards it did, especially when Diocletian occupied the throne. Prevalent superstition also for some time kindled a flame to consume the Church. Priests, and poets in service to heathenism, could not but regard those who denounced their gods, and said, "An idol is nothing in the world," as coming into destructive collision with their cause. Nor did Pagan philosophy prove, in many ways, otherwise than inimical. First it looked on the Gospel with disdain; afterwards it endeavoured to dig up its foundations.

It is impossible to study, on the one hand, Christianity as it really is according to Scripture, and as it came actually to be through its converting power, and, on the other hand, imperial pretensions, claiming mastery over mankind, without foresight that the two forces would come into collision. Neither could be consistent with itself, without being antagonistic to the other. The Empire embodied an idea of nationality, and was responsible for maintaining unity of interest, purpose, and endeavour. Sympathy in the worship of Pagan gods, who for ages had been adored in Rome, appeared essential to the realisation of imperial ideas. How could it be endured to see the worship of Jesus taking the place of what had been paid to Jupiter, "father of gods and men"? One can understand how Roman rulers would regard such a change. People of other nations could be tolerated in the honours paid to their ancient deities, but it was quite another thing to allow enthusiasts to propagate sentiments of a kind calculated to revolutionise Roman society. Had Christians formed a nationality, and only asked for such freedom as was conceded to other races, the case would have been different.

Rome subordinated religion to imperialism; Christianity regarded religion as above what is political. While Roman citizens remained Pagan, their government would inevitably clash with the Church. Christians did not rebel against imperial authority in civil affairs, but they could not sacrifice their consciences to political rule. There existed between the two parties incompatibility, which could cease only under a policy of toleration.

Pliny was ruler of Bithynia Pontus, and his famous letter referring to provincial persecution is a contemporary evidence of State warfare against the Gospel. This letter is assigned to different dates; the latest is A.D. 111.

Nero was an enemy to Christians, and after the great fire in Rome, while he was emperor, his Majesty is said to have accused them of kindling it, and caused Christians, covered with pitch, to be set on fire, that their blazing bodies might illuminate his palace gardens. Without attempting to explain the incident, I quote the statement by Clement of Rome, that the Apostles Peter and Paul were, at that time, martyrs for Christ, and "gathered around them a multitude of the elect, who set a glorious example." "Whether they were martyred at the same time with the great bulk of the sufferers in the year of the fire (A.D. 64), or whether they were isolated victims of the spent wave of persecution (A.D. 67 or 68), we need not stop to inquire."[1]

All the succeeding emperors did not follow Nero's example. Hadrian (A.D. 113—137) is described as "tolerant, eclectic, inquiring"; Antoninus Pius (A.D. 138—161) as "loving righteousness and mercy." Marcus Aurelius (A.D. 161—180) is spoken of as acquitting those against whom there was no charge but that of Christianity.

Early in the second century a perpetual edict appeared, that in all places people should follow Roman customs—a law which might be construed to mean they must conform to religious as well as civil institutes. Also, it is to be remembered, that

[1] Lightfoot's *Clement of Rome*, i., p. 351.

Justin Martyr, in his second *Apology*, speaks of *recent* severe persecution; and before the close of the second century there were martyrdoms in Gaul. Under Decius (A.D. 249—251) an outburst of persecuting fury occurred, and torments were inflicted on professors of the Gospel.

Gallienus, when left sole emperor in A.D. 261, extinguished a persecution which Valerian, his predecessor, had commenced. Aurelian, who reigned from A.D. 270 to 275, has been represented as planning a destructive attack on the Christian Church,[1] but there is no convincing proof of particulars. That he was cruel and disliked Christianity is probable. Eusebius says, in the progress of Aurelian's reign, " he began to cherish different sentiments with regard to us, from those he had done." [2]

In the reign of Decius, people were required to testify that they adhered to the national worship by offering sacrifices, and partaking of banquets in honour of the gods. Commissioners were appointed to carry out the edict, and some people, from fear, forsook the faith. They obtained certificates of apostacy, and one of these documents has been

---

[1] See *Rome and the Early Christians*, by the Rev. W. Ware Published in America.
[2] Eusebius, *Eccl. Hist.*, vii., 30.

lately published.¹ It attests that "a man of seventy-two, with a scar on his right eyebrow, had sacrificed and poured out libations." People who had yielded to persecution thus sheltered themselves. After persecution ceased some of this class sought restoration to Church privileges by submitting to prescribed penance. Penitential rules were laid down for the purpose. Those who suffered and survived persecution won the admiration of their brethren, and sometimes, by supplication on behalf of the fallen, secured their restoration to fellowship, or mitigated severities of discipline. This influence was sometimes abused on the part of those who employed and those who were relieved by such intercession.

An edict of Diocletian (A.D. 303) threatened the total destruction of Christianity. Churches were to be pulled down and Scriptures burnt. Eusebius tells us: "We saw with our own eyes houses of prayer destroyed; also Holy Scriptures cast into the flames. The shepherds of the people were captured, and made the sport of enemies. We shall not mention those who were shaken by persecution and sunk into

---

¹ This is stated on the authority of an article by Professor Harnack in the *Theologische Literaturzeitung*, 1894, No. 2. See Lactantius, *De Mozt*, cc. 15, 16, 34; and Eusebius, *H. E.*, viii., 6, 8.

the depths of watery gulfs. Here was one scourged with rods, another tormented on the rack. People were dragged a long distance by the feet." The historian speaks of "illustrious martyrs who filled every place with the celebrity of their names, and obtained crowns of martyrdom." Sufferers in Egypt, Phenicia, Thebes, Alexandria, and Phrygia are mentioned in harrowing detail.[1]

To the last heathen emperors believed in the efficacy of persecution, and an inscription is copied by Gruter in his *Corpus Inscriptorium* to that effect.

Of the noble army of martyrs I begin with Ignatius. This saintly man is supposed to be noticed by Lucian, in one of his satires, as a prisoner in Syria, to whom Christians of Asia Minor sent money, and who wrote letters to important cities, forwarding them by persons whom Lucian mockingly calls "messengers of the dead." The epistles of Ignatius, written after his being condemned to death, contain, with numerous spiritual exhortations, expressions of his own experience—as glorying in the Cross, as not worthy to be called a Bishop, as full of love for those to whom he wrote, and as fired with passionate zeal for his Saviour.

Paul said : "I am already being offered, and the

[1] *Eccl. Hist.*, viii.

time of my departure is come. I have fought the good fight, I have finished the course, I have kept the faith; henceforth there is laid up for me the crown of righteousness, which the Lord, the righteous Judge, shall give me at that day; and not only to me, but also to all them that have loved His appearing." Ignatius goes beyond this, and, in a different tone, *craves* after martyrdom, longing to be devoured by lions. This feeling seems to have been not uncommon with primitive believers. We are anxious to do them justice, but it must be admitted that some things which we cannot approve mingled with others worthy of renown. A soldier in battle, often in almost suicidal ways, rushes on hostile bayonets, yet we do not, on that account, withhold the meed of honour. We praise patriotism and pardon rashness. Shall we, then, coldly criticise these early heroes, and fail to appreciate their wonderful endurance? They have produced effects on after times; and we may well send up a prayer-song to the Captain of Salvation, who "was made perfect through suffering,"—

> "Great Chief of faithful souls, arise!
> None else can lead the martyr-band,
> Who teach the brave how peril flies,
> When faith, unarmed, lifts up the hand."

The Martyrdom of Ignatius, professedly written by those who accompanied him on his voyage to Rome, is considered by some not trustworthy; but there is no reason at all for doubting that the bishop was thrown to wild beasts in the newly built Coliseum at Rome. He died in the reign of the Emperor Trajan, who ascended the throne in A.D. 98.[1]

Next in celebrity comes the martyrdom of Polycarp under the Emperor Decius. A note, of no authority, attached to a letter, purporting to be written by the Church of which he was bishop, states that he was executed "on the second of the month Xanthicus, the seventh before the Calends of March (or May), on a great Sabbath, at the eighth hour." It is suspicious that dates in early Church history become more precise as time rolls on. Polycarp was Bishop of Smyrna, a city more populous in our time than it was in his. Now it sweeps along the Mediterranean beach, in a line of French-looking shops and warehouses, full of European commerce, opening into an Oriental town of mosques and Turkish dwellings, backed by thick groups of cypress trees. Then it

---

[1] Much has been said of numerous *Christians* devoured by wild beasts in the Coliseum. Legends refer to them, but I have sought in vain for plain historical evidence of any other instance than that of Ignatius.

must have been very different from what it is now; though heavy calamities—which have often occurred in our time—were, eighteen hundred years ago, its melancholy lot; for a contemporary of Polycarp speaks of it as visited by plague, fire, and earthquake, " its stately houses overturned, its temples ruined."

An account of Polycarp's last days, which some regard as a writing of later date founded on tradition, has in it some miraculous occurrences—a feature which appears in most martyrologies of the primitive age written years afterwards. Eusebius, in his *Ecclesiastical History*, who has much to say about Polycarp, gives the substance of it.

He tells us how the venerable martyr, when the persecution broke out, remained unmoved, but was persuaded by his friends to retire to a farmhouse outside the city; how his pursuers caught a couple of boys and made them show the way to that retreat; how he received these men in an upper room, saying, " The will of the Lord be done," and then offered them refreshment; and how, when taken to the Stadium or amphitheatre, and urged to forswear the Saviour, he exclaimed, " Eighty and six years have I served Him, and He never did me wrong, and how can I now blaspheme my King? I am a Christian." He was first threatened to be torn by wild beasts, and next to be burnt alive—a fate which followed. When the crowd seized wood and straw from shops and baths to feed the flames, he loosed his girdle, laid by his clothes, and prepared to take off his shoes, but he refused to be fastened to the stake. Clasping his hands, he offered this prayer: "Father of Thy well-beloved and blessed Son, Jesus Christ, through whom we have received the knowledge of Thee, the God of angels and powers, of all creation, and the family of the righteous, that live before Thee, I bless Thee, that Thou hast thought me worthy to share in the number of the martyrs, and in the cup of Christ, unto the resurrection of eternal life. On this account and for all things I praise Thee, I bless Thee, I glorify Thee, through the eternal Priest, Jesus Christ, Thy well-beloved Son, through whom glory be to Thee, with Him, in the Holy Ghost, both now and for ever. Amen."[1]

The spot where he suffered is outside the city, in the hollow of hills, commanding a view of the azure

---

[1] Abridged from Eusebius, iv., c. 15. Dr. Lightfoot, referring to the record of incidents in the document, which he considers a contemporary one, remarks: "The simplicity with which the narrator records omens and occurrences easily explicable in themselves, but invested by their surcharged feelings with a miraculous character, is highly natural" (*Essays on Supernatural*

Mediterranean, skirted by mountains, and enlivened by ships.

Eusebius—after showing how Justin Martyr suffered, and after mentioning martyrs who died before him —proceeds to give the trials of those who suffered for their faith in Gaul. That Christianity reached this province from the East, at a very early period, traditions and monuments sufficiently prove. Roman civilisation had preceded and given proofs of imperial power ; yet other mementoes betokening a connection with Churches of Eastern Christendom show that, not from Italy, but from Asia Minor, the Gospel was first carried to Greek colonies west of the Mediterranean. Inhabitants of Lyons and the neighbourhood were amongst the earliest converts in that part of the world ; and traditionary annals of Churches there are filled with accounts of martyrs. These supply materials for one of the most interesting chapters of Eusebius—the first of the Fifth Book. "Two chief cities," he says, "surpassing all the rest, were Lyons

---

Religion, p. 103). That the record is not a forgery, Dr. Lightfoot proves most satisfactorily. The story that a dove flew out of the wounded body is wanting in Eusebius, and in some MSS. of the original *Martyrdom*. Such a marvel would be *unnatural* indeed ! Imagination, under the circumstances, would add something to real facts.

and Vienne." Lyons, with its commercial enterprise, its crowded population, and its public buildings, is known by almost everybody nowadays; yet how many travellers pass by the neighbouring town of Vienne, with its glass houses and metal foundries, its coal pits and smoke, without feeling any interest in the place! But Vienne took precedence of Lyons in the second century, and there it was that a flourishing Church existed. The amphitheatre—scene of the martyrdom described by Eusebius—is found, from excavations, to have been a building of great magnitude. It is interesting to recollect, that when the heroism described by the historian aroused the hatred of heathens, and inspired the admiration of Christians, the hilly banks of the Rhone were fair and beautiful, clothed with verdure and rich in fruitfulness. One heroine, in the sufferings she endured and the fame she won, surpasses the rest, and of her Eusebius gives an affecting description.

Blandina,[1] a maiden slave, whilst all were trembling, and her mistress was a martyr, feared that, through weakness, she would fail in her confession, but she was filled with such power that her tormentors acknowledged themselves overcome. "On the last day of

---

[1] Eusebius, *Eccl. Hist.*, v., c. 1.

the shows, Blandina was brought out with a youth, Ponticus, about fifteen years old." After scourging and exposure to the wild beasts, she was confined in a net and tossed by a bull. It is confessed that no woman amongst the persecuted had ever endured such sufferings. Extracts from original documents dwell upon the savage conduct of the persecutors with agonising minuteness, and outbursts of indignation occur, which we do not wonder at. We are nevertheless told that the persecuted prayed for those who were bitter in their hostility. The passage occurs in a chapter entitled "Those that had fallen away kindly restored by the pious martyrs," from which I gather that what follows must refer to some who shrank back at first and then recovered fortitude. The narrative becomes rather confused: towards the close, however, it is said of the valiant ones, "They did not arrogate any superiority over backsliders, but the things wherein they excelled supplied what was deficient in others."[1]

Another female martyr is well known. Her name was Perpetua, and she is considered, by modern authorities, to have suffered under Septimius Severus; but the date cannot be determined. A framework of

[1] *Eccl. Hist.*, v., c. 2.

legend rather than history, including visions of some poetical beauty, has grown up around her name. No doubt can be felt respecting the reality of her martyrdom ; and, taking "The Acts" recording her sufferings and death as so far trustworthy, she was a youthful wife who had just given birth to a child, and who, on that account, as well as others, was entreated to save her life by renouncing her faith. But she remained firm, and died under the executioner's hand. She was a native of Carthage, and in the neighbourhood of that city sealed the truth with her life. Symphorinus was another Gallican martyr, who suffered at Autun under Marcus Aurelius, according to Gregory of Tours.[1] His story is amplified by Ruinart and others.

Of the martyrdom of Cyprian we have few details. His life prepared him for death; his death glorified his life. When persecution came, in A.D. 257, Cyprian prudently retired from publicity, till he felt the cause he loved recalled him to the front. His execution was the result. Soldiers surrounded his garden. The report spread that he was seized. It is sufficient to say, that when the magistrate pronounced sentence, "Our pleasure is that Thascius Cyprianus be executed

---

[1] *Hist.*, ii., 15.

by the sword," the victim answered, " Thanks be to God."[1]

The patience of the martyrs, and their behaviour towards those who inflicted upon them horrible cruelties, are beyond all praise. Few attempted to escape: indeed, in some instances, as already suggested, martyrdom was eagerly sought; Christians neither resisted persecution nor resented injustice, but prayed for their murderers. Arnobius, in his Seven Books "adversus Gentes," writes : " Since we have learned from Christ's teaching, that evil ought not to be requited with evil, that it is better to suffer wrong than to inflict it, that we should rather shed our own, than stain our consciences with another's blood, an unthankful world is now enjoying a benefit from Christ, inasmuch as, through Him, ferocity has been softened and has withheld its hand from a fellow-creature." Arnobius wrote this in the early part of the fourth century, probably A.D. 303. Lactantius, a pupil of Arnobius, has left a tract on " The Death of Persecutors," in which he points out the untimely end of those emperors who had manifested a hatred of Christianity, painting their characters, however truly, after a spirit and manner not in keeping with that of Arnobius. I

---

[1] Short Life by his Deacon, Pontius.

may add, that the tone of feeling manifested in the genuine Catacomb inscriptions, is in harmony with the sentiment expressed by Arnobius.

The heroism of which I have spoken often reached a pitch of endurance which makes one's blood run chill. It defied fire and steel, faggot and sword, and, what seem worse, pincers tearing the flesh, and the deadly gaze of a lion's eyes, as he paused to leap on his helpless prey. There was a calm steady faith which saw Him who is invisible, an intensity of feeling which benumbed physical agony—a subjugation of body, demonstrating a mastery of soul. It is plain, from what we read in details given by Eusebius, that martyrs in their final conflict were in a state above that of common mortals. Miracles they did not wonder at—such things seemed to them matters of course; if they really did not exist, that made no difference in their apprehension. I think this explains a good deal that we meet with in old martyrologies.

The number of martyrs in the ante-Nicene period is a contested point, magnified, no doubt, in Church Martyrology, and minimised unjustly by Dodwell and Gibbon; what makes calculation unsatisfactory is, that Eusebius, whilst he mentions certain sufferers individually, indicates there were more, without suggesting how many. The inscriptions and remains in the Catacombs lead to no reliable conclusions.[1]

---

[1] I do not know any book in which there is a more dispassionate inquiry into the extent of early persecutions than Maitland's *Church of the Catacombs*. He judiciously takes up the question as to the restoration of the lapsed at Carthage (see pp. 93-117); as to Catacomb inscriptions (see pp. 127-34), and the poetry of Prudentius on the martyrs (146-50). He justly remarks respecting tales afterwards told that "in them every principle of probability is violated: between them and the authentic records of martyrdom there exists not the slightest analogy" (p. 154).

PART II

CHAPTER 1

CHURCH AND STATE UNDER CONSTANTINE

IN the year A.D. 312—as Eusebius, twenty years afterwards, learned from his Majesty—one day, about noon, a luminous cross appeared in the sky to Constantine, with the inscription "*By this conquer*"; and afterwards he had a dream, in which Christ appeared with the same sign, and commanded him to use it as the emblem on his standard. There is no reason to regard this story as a fable, or as something miraculous. Perhaps at the time he did see something which he thus interpreted, and had a dream, in accordance with it; but it is remarkable this story remained a secret, and was not related till long afterwards. Eusebius, who communicates it, adds, the sight *struck the army with amazement*, implying that his soldiers, like himself, witnessed the marvel. It is not improbable that other influences predisposed him to adopt Christianity; for it appears that, through his own reflections, he saw polytheism was foolish and false. Probably conversation with the clergy deepened this conviction. However, Constantine's life after he professed Christianity was not such as to interpret his conversion, according to the strict meaning of that term. He built churches, and did what he could to promote religious uniformity, but his memory is laden with charges of crime.

Early in his reign, an ecclesiastical council was held at Arles, where three episcopal representatives from Britain were present; and the chief point discussed was the proper time for keeping Easter, Western Churches then differing from the Oriental in that respect. The British now agreed to adopt the Roman practice.

In 312 Constantine issued an edict of toleration which protected Christians from being persecuted; and places of worship previously closed were allowed to be used. At the same time ecclesiastical property was applied to its original purpose. Christians who had been banished returned to their homes; martyrs' goods were restored to their families; churches and cemeteries were returned to their proper owners, and subjects of the empire were exhorted to worship the true God. About the same time Constantine published *An Oration on Idolatry*, in which he granted what would be called religious liberty. "Let every one do what his soul desires," was the imperial exhortation. Amongst particular laws enacted by Constantine, special notice has been taken of one forbidding that shops and courts of law should be opened on the first day of the week—a fact to which religious motives have been attached. It would be gratefully welcomed by Christian people, and showed that the Emperor had respect for their religion; but we must not be too hasty in determining the motives which influenced this legislative policy. At all events, a new holiday would be popular with most people.

We meet at that crisis with a troublesome, unruly sect, which increased in numbers as time rolled on, known as *Donatists* from their leader Donatus. Notices of them are abundant in the Church histories of the period, but what we learn concerning them is chiefly from those who were their opponents. Their taking up arms in self-defence, on professedly religious grounds, is a fact the full treatment of which involves questions leading to discussions beyond the limits of this work.[1]

---

[1] I think that Archdeacon Farrar is just when he says: "The Donatists began as rigid Evangelicals, they ended as ruthless brigands; the Catholics began as tolerant Churchmen, and ended as bitter Catholics."—*Lives of the Fathers*, ii., p. 52.

Constantine spent a large part of his reign in the East; there, it is said, tragical events in his family occurred; and there he divided his dominions between his sons. In 337 he completed and dedicated the Church of the Holy Apostles in his Eastern capital. About the same time he ordered the sign of the cross to be engraved on his military shields, and prohibited profane mysteries and gladiatorial combats. Best of all, he caused a multiplication of books containing sacred Scriptures.

One of his last acts was to submit to baptism. Eusebius informs us his death was mourned at Rome, but does not mention any royal visit there during his latter years. The baptistery at the Lateran is falsely ascribed to him, unless it means a bequest of money for the purpose, as the edifice was not built till about a century after his decease. In truth, Church traditions, unsupported by historical facts, have largely influenced Roman beliefs on the subject. Much which is reported, as to what he did for the Vatican and for St. Peter's, is without sufficient foundation.

I may here add, the exact attitude of his mind towards theological doctrine it is difficult to discover; at first he treated the Arian controversy as of little consequence, and his subsequent conduct indicated waverings of opinion. His sister Constantia leaned to the heterodox side, and she persuaded him to recall Arius from exile. When Athanasius refused to acknowledge the heretic at Alexandria, his Majesty banished that orthodox bishop to Gaul.

The main ecclesiastical incident in his reign is the Council of Nicea, and to this we must now direct attention.

Here we reach an unprecedented era. There had been controversy between heretics and champions of truth prepared to man the walls against foreign foes. Now we touch a period when strife comes to the front, and the Arian controversy creates an excitement such as it had never done before. At the same time other theological questions are seen coming up; and after the union between Church and State had taken place, questions arose requiring study on the subject. How far they were apprehended is by no means plain.

Different tendencies of thought obtained in ante-Nicene times touching the nature of our Lord. Some impaired the brightness of His glory by distinctions made between Him and the Father. Others blended the two, so as to convey an idea of absolute identity. The former class were led by Paul of Samosata, who said the man Jesus was "inhabited by the Word—an impersonal power, distinct from wisdom, inherent in God as an attribute," which descended from heaven upon the Nazarene at His baptism. The latter class followed Sabellius, who confounded the Father and Son, denying the orthodox distinction, and regarding Father and Son only as different *aspects* of the same Being.

In the third century Sabellianism was less prominent than the opinion of Paul of Samosata, and amongst heterodox thinkers, the idea of difference between the Divine Father and Son obtained ascendency.

After Constantine professed Christianity the difference now indicated came under his notice. Imperfectly acquainted with theological speculations, he felt neither aptitude nor inclination for such an inquiry. Looking at it through a political haze, chiefly if not only anxious to extinguish strife amongst his subjects and to promote imperial interests, he addressed a letter to the different parties, saying: "Listen to me, your friend and servant. I ask nor answer questions, which are not upon any injunction of your law, but arise from the altercation of barren leisure; at least, keep them to yourselves, and do not publish them. Your contention is not about any capital commandment; neither of you is introducing any novel scheme of worship; you are of one and the same way of thinking, so that it is in your power to unite in one communion."[1]

Constantine ere long discovered his theological ignorance, and his political mistake, in supposing a question of such importance as that could be settled by compromise or neglect. From one end of his dominions to the other there were thoughtful men deeply interested in the subject, who justly attached to it supreme importance. Hence some conference seemed needful for an authoritative decision on the subject.

Constantine resolved that a council should be held at Nicea, in the Eastern division of the empire, where his Majesty resided at the time. Nicea was capital of Bithynia, situated on a lake furnishing means of access from the Propontis, and not far from the imperial palace. "Bishops of Italy and from other parts will be present," wrote his Majesty, "and I shall be at hand as spectator and as participator in what is done." He commanded public provision should be made for conveying members to the place of assembly; and the historian Ammianus Marcellinus tells us high-

---

[1] Eusebius, *Vita Constantini*, i. 63-70.

ways were crowded by bishops galloping to the synod, so that public posts for travelling were nearly ruined. I may add that not long after the famous gathering, part of the place occupied by it was destroyed by earthquake: restored, however, in the year 368. It is now a miserable spot, but the neighbourhood is richly wooded.

It was not till a fortnight or so after the bishops had assembled, that Constantine made his appearance. The day of opening (A.D. 323) is uncertain, as dates vary from May 20th to 29th, and from June 14th to June 19th.[1]

The exact number of persons cannot be ascertained, but probably there were above three hundred bishops and presbyters included. The assembly met in a church at first; afterwards we find them in a hall of assembly, prepared for the occasion. On each side sat dignitaries, and when all was ready, the doors opened, up rose the clergy, and in came his Majesty, "clothed in purple, sparkling with gems." Invited by the bishops, he sat down in a gilded chair, and the clergy resumed their seats.

The three most remarkable men in that gathering were Arius, Alexander, and Athanasius. Arius

---

[1] In what follows I avail myself of Stanley's *Eastern Church*.

was advanced in life, tall, like Saul of old, and popular amongst friends for courteous manners, though pronounced by others proud, austere, and quarrelsome, "wriggling like a snake." In 313 he had charge of a church in Alexandria, and at one time, so it is said, had his eye fixed on the patriarchate of that magnificent city. He was more a debater than a philosopher, more clever in argument than profound in conception. There is in existence a fragment of his entitled *Thalia*, denoting a *banquet*, and made up of verses, "written for the sea, the mill, and the road," whatever that may mean.[1] Alexander, Bishop of Alexandria, was another person of importance; but he was eclipsed by Athanasius, his deacon and secretary, only twenty-seven years of age, not tall, but "with a face beautiful as an angel." Julian called him "a dwarf, not a man."

Eastern Churches were largely represented in this conclave, but Hosius, a Spaniard, was the only Western prelate.

There were three principal groups in the council. One followed Arius; a second was devoted to Athanasius; the third, by far most numerous, at

---

[1] Socrates, *Ecclesiastical History*, i., 9, refers to the book as "loose and dissolute."

first only wished to hand down the old orthodoxy. They at last ranged themselves under the youthful Alexandrian. Some of the clergy probably were illiterate. Spyridion, "the shepherd" or sheep-farmer, was one. His remains are preserved in Corfu Cathedral, and are there yearly carried about the streets in procession.[1]

Aetius headed a party distinguished by extreme views and the violence with which they enforced them. He spoke of the Son as *unlike* the Father. His followers were denounced by opponents as utterly godless. Certainly he seems to have surpassed Arius in heretical beliefs. Another thing which made him obnoxious to episcopalians was his denial of any distinction between bishops and presbyters, and also of any obligation to keep Easter. His followers did not fast or pray for departed souls—points held firmly by some on the orthodox side.

---

[1] *Itinéraire de L'Orient*, p. 246. An absurd story is told of Spyridion's replacing the heads of some decapitated horses; but doing it in haste, black heads were fixed on white shoulders and white on black ones. Sozomen (*Hist.*, i., c. 11) tells us some one entrusted a treasure to the care of Spyridion's daughter, who for safety buried it in her father's garden. She died, and the father went to the girl's grave, and was there told where the treasure was hidden !!

Eusebius says of the assembly: "Officers and soldiers drawn up in order with naked swords kept the vestibule of the palace, and through their midst the men of God passed without fear and entered into the inner hall. There some sat near the Emperor, and others occupied couches on either side. Any one might have thought it a picture of the kingdom of Christ, and a dream rather than a reality."[1]

Constantine, in connection with the council, it would seem, invited the members to a banquet. That must have been to them a memorable day, when they were first seated at a royal table, as memories of past trials crossed their minds. Several of their number had been persecuted for righteousness' sake, and endured a great fight of affliction. They had taken joyfully the spoiling of their goods, and been made a gazing-stock by reproaches and afflictions; but now "the Lord had turned away their captivity, and they were like them that dream. Their mouth was filled with laughter, and their tongue with singing. They said, The Lord hath done great things for us, whereof we are glad." What had happened must have seemed miraculous.

---

[1] *De Vita Constant.*, iii., 15.

Diocletian's persecution, which lasted for ten years, when churches were burnt down, and martyrs slain, and Scriptures consumed, had ended only with Constantine's edicts of toleration in A.D. 311 and 313. This last date was ten years before the Nicean assembly. The guests at the imperial banquet had but to look a few years back to the period when their fathers died deaths of martyrdom.

Knowing what human nature is, and the effect produced by royal notice, we cannot but infer that the visit of bishops and other ecclesiastics to the Nicean palace, and the attention shown them, would elevate the guests in social rank. This would be a small matter compared with the elevation, in point of official influence, to which the union of Church and State raised the guests. They were now not merely religious officers, but possessors of secular influence as well. That was a fact which the history of the Church demonstrated before the world. The power which bishops and clergy possessed in social affairs and in legal authority is illustrated in numerous details.[1]

The outcome of controversy between orthodox

---

[1] See a long article on "Bishops" in Smith's *Dictionary of Christian Antiquities*.

and Arians appears in the Nicene Creed; and it is interesting to compare this with that bearing the name of "the Apostles' Creed." That is chiefly historical; the Nicene is essentially dogmatic. It develops through Scripture study, philosophical meditation, and logical inference, doctrines involved in earlier formularies and writings. The earlier creed referred simply to evangelical facts; the Nicene is a decidedly theological formula. No contradiction exists between the two. The latter only expands the former. There is growth in the Church's confession, after three centuries of thoughtfulness. Some expressions in our English translation of the Greek formula grate harshly on our ears; but the original did not produce the same effect on those who first listened to it.

It has been remarked that the Greek word denoting *similarity* adopted by semi-Arians resembles the orthodox symbol so closely, that *difference of a mere diphthong* in this case produced violent controversy between *Homoiousians* and *Homoousians*. Only criticism of a shallow sort can estimate a difference of fact by counting letters denoting that difference. "Essentially the same" and "similar to each other" point in distinct directions. Besides, in the present case it is a mistake to confine the main dispute to semi-Arians and orthodox, for the contention chiefly lay between decided Arians and those decidedly orthodox. The anti-Athanasians consisted of those who said the Son was of *like* substance, *not the same*; as well as others who believed He was a different Being created *out of nothing*.

The Arians, it is said, early presented a draft of their creed, which created an uproar, and the document was torn in pieces. Afterwards Eusebius, Bishop of Cæsarea, proposed a formula, omitting the word *consubstantial*, an omission zealously opposed by the orthodox party.

The Greek term Ὁμοούσιος, meaning what the Latin *consubstantial* and the English *same substance* express, became a party cry of the orthodox, under the leadership of Athanasius. It was intended to express the true and proper Divinity of our Lord, indicating that He possessed the same perfections as God the Father and God the Holy Ghost. There were divines at that period who believed in the Holy Trinity, but objected to the Athanasian watchword, and would not use it. Others disliked the use of that term, and preferred to speak of Christ as "the inscrutable," "the unoriginate," "the eternal Son, by incomprehensible generation." They said, "He is the Son of God, not by adoption, but nature."

In the whole of the Nicean controversy, and for a long time afterwards, when other questions arose respecting the mystery of Divine existence, there seems to have been an absence of regard for the expostulation: "Canst thou by searching find out God? canst thou find out the Almighty unto perfection? It is as high as heaven; what canst thou do? deeper than hades; what canst thou know? The measure thereof is longer than the earth, and broader than the sea."[1] Disputants, more or less, seemed to forget the infinite and unsearchable nature of the Divine Being, to whom reasonings founded upon created modes of existence are inapplicable. Metaphysical thoughts, when applied to the self-existent One, lay open to the rebuke: "Thou thoughtest that I was altogether such an one as thyself; but I will reprove thee, and set them in order before thine eyes."[2] It is, in some instances, painful to read descriptions touching the Divine nature as if it were no more incomprehensible than our own.

In the fourth century amenities were not cultivated in controversy. Orthodox champions called the Arians "profligates," "idolaters," "Jews, worse than heathen," "animals," "satanic partisans, and guilty

---

[1] Job xi. 7-9.   [2] Psalm l. 21.

of the unpardonable sin"; Athanasius was not free from blame in this respect, but he relaxed in severity of language the older he grew. At the same time the Arians were not behindhand in violence; and an incident in their warfare stands unparalleled. Arians accused Athanasius of murder. An Arian bishop named Arsenius was persuaded to hide himself. Afterwards, so runs the story, the orthodox champion was charged with taking away the man's life. A withered hand was shown as belonging to the victim, and as employed by the orthodox leader for magical purposes. It turned out that Arsenius was still alive, with two hands like other folks.

After the Nicene formulary had been adopted, Constantine commended it to his subjects, and urged its acceptance as tending to their "temporal welfare." "Some," he says, "were won by hoping for temporal support, or by the prospect of gaining influence, or by courtesy of manner, or by substantial presents." "Most unworthy motives," Dr. Kaye [1] mildly remarks.

Speaking of Arianism after the death of Constantine, Socrates tells us it was diffused throughout the Court and amongst the imperial household and guards. The mischief extended, but it was chiefly confined to the East.[2]

Council of Nicea, p. 50. [2] Socrates, Eccl Hist i., c. 6.

The personal history of Constantine, so far as it is noticeable on these pages, closed in A.D. 337. Then he died at Hiæropolis; and just before his departure from this life he submitted to the rite of Christian baptism. He expired at noon on the feast of Pentecost. It is said that he granted to the Roman pontiff and clergy, a number of dignities and privileges, all of them showing a desire to make the imperial a model for pontifical dignity. The pontiff was to occupy the Lateran palaces, to wear the diadem, collar, and purple cloak, and to carry the sceptre.[1]

"The legislation of Constantine," says Dr. Stubbs, "gave a coercive and material force to rules which had been hitherto matters of conscience and consensus. The Church was empowered to enforce her doctrinal decisions, her rules of discipline, and her frame of administration; and that so completely, that from this date, the ecclesiastical administration in Christian countries, under the empire, became so wedded to the secular administration as to be at times almost indistinguishable from it, except on close investigation."[2]

---

[1] See *Divi Gratiam Universe Juris Canonici*, etc. (Lugduni, MDLIII.). The forgery was probably based on a tradition.

[2] *Lectures on Mediæval and Modern History*, by Bishop Stubbs, p. 338.

On the effect of union between Church and State on the Church in Rome, Dean Milman remarks: " On the one hand, the bishop and the clergy are already aspiring to a sacerdotal power and preeminence, hardly attained, hardly aimed at, in any other part of Christendom. The pontiff cannot rest below a magnificence which would contrast as strongly with the life of the primitive bishop, as that of Lucullus with that of Fabricius. The prodigality of the offerings to the Church and to the clergy, those more especially by bequest, is so immoderate that a law is necessary to restrain the profuseness on the one hand, the avidity on the other—a law which the statesman Ambrose, and the monk Jerome approve, as demanded by the abuses of the times. ' Priests of idols, mimes, charioteers, harlots may receive bequests; it is interdicted, and wisely interdicted, only to ecclesiastics and monks.' The Church may already seem to have taken the place of the Emperor as universal legatee. As men before bought by this posthumous adulation the favour of Cæsar, so would they now that of God. Heredipety, or legacy-hunting, is inveighed against, in the clergy especially, as by the older satirists. Jerome, in his *Epistles*, is the Juvenal of his time—without his grossness indeed, for Christianity no doubt had greatly raised the standard of morals. The heathen, as represented by such men as Prætextatus[1] (they now seem to have retired into a separate community, and stood in relation to the general society, as the Christians had stood to the heathen under Vespasian or the Antonines), had partaken in the moral advancement. But with this great exception, this repulsive licence, Jerome, both in the vehemence of his denunciation and in his description of the vices, manners, habits of Rome, might seem to be writing of pre-Christian times."[2]

The union between Church and State, as it is termed, began under Constantine, but on what exact terms does not distinctly appear. How far the author had formed a distinct theory on the subject, if he did frame any theory at all, it is impossible to say. The practical development we shall see as we proceed.

---

[1] There was a Bishop of this name, over the diocese of Rouen, accused of aiding King Chilperic's son in plots against his father. He was attacked and slain; some counted him a martyr. (See Smith's *Dict. Biog.*)

[2] *Latin Christianity*, vol. i., p. 70. It would appear that the wealth of ecclesiastics was to be attributed largely to testamentary bequests. "The law of Constantine, which empowered the clergy to receive testamentary bequests and to hold land, was a gift which could scarcely have been exceeded if he had granted them two provinces of the empire" (Milman's *History of Christianity*, iii., p. 380).

CHAPTER II

SUBSEQUENT EMPERORS

CONSTANTINE II., Constantius, and Constans followed their father on the throne—all three under the age of twenty-one. They divided the empire between them: Constantine II. holding Gaul and Britain; Constans ruling Italy, together with Africa; and Constantius having for his share Thrace and the East. Constantine II. was killed in a skirmish on the Alps in A.D. 340; and Constans in an insurrection, ten years afterwards. Constantius then became sole emperor, and died as he was preparing to defend his rule against Julian, who succeeded him.

During the reigns of Constantine's sons, between the years A.D. 337—361, we meet with a succession of controversies between orthodox and Arian parties, which distress a right-minded reader. Amidst a succession of conflicting events and opinions, one reads of two restorations of Athanasius from exile; intrigues of Arians against this renowned champion of orthodoxy; his fresh expulsion from Alexandria; the intrusion into the Church there of the noted George, a Cappadocian advocate of Arian heresy; the division of its abettors into three groups of semi-Arians, Anomeans, and Acacians; a series of Councils at Ancyra, Rimini, and Seleucia, full of earnest disputation and a multitude of creeds :— these facts altogether make a painful impression on minds imbued with brotherly love and evangelical orthodoxy.[1] I must say that these reminiscences throw a dark shadow over that ecclesiastical era. I find abundant dogmatic zeal absorbing different parties, associated with little of that charity which hopeth all things and endureth all things.

Moral and spiritual lights which shone during the first three centuries were sadly bedimmed in distinguished quarters during the fourth. At the same time, even where Christian piety was deepest, it must be confessed asceticism appeared in the ascendant. Monasteries, as we shall see, began to flourish in post-Nicean times.

The reign of Julian (361—363) brings before us

---

[1] See Robertson's *History of the Christian Church*, vol. i., pp. 327-330.

a startling crisis. He aimed at the restoration of Paganism, and withdrew from bishops the privileges they had enjoyed. He totally rejected the religion of "the Galilæan," as he scornfully styled our Saviour. Socrates has a chapter in his *Ecclesiastical History* entitled "Martyrs at Merus in Phrygia, under the reign of Julian."[1] The restoration of a pagan temple exasperated the Christian inhabitants, some of whom rushed into the edifice, and smashed in pieces an image which had been erected there. They were required to "expiate their crime"; how does not appear. On their refusal they were laid on a gridiron, and burnt to death, exclaiming, so it is said, "If you wish to eat broiled flesh, turn us on the other side also, lest we should appear up half cooked."[2] The doubtful story thus related by a Church historian, while it testifies to heathen cruelty, does no honour to Christian religion. Incidents of Julian's reign are recorded, but no light is thrown on his fundamental policy. He possessed some good qualities; he supported hospitals, was moral in his conduct, a man with mental gifts and some amiable dispositions; but Socrates tells us he extorted immense sums of money from the Christians

---

[1] Socrates, *Ecclesiastical History*, iii., c. 15.
[2] *Ibid.*, iii., c. 15.

and ridiculed them in pamphlets which he wrote. It is said he tortured a young man named Theodore, whom heathens brought before him, and who excited admiration by his fortitude.[1]

Jovian, in A.D. 363, succeeded Julian, but did not accept office till the army declared in favour of the Church. He departed from Julian's policy, and restored Christian privileges denied by his predecessor. He wrote to the governors of provinces, directing that his subjects should assemble for worship, serve God with reverence, and receive the faith accepted by Constantine. He revived on behalf of Churches and clergy, also of widows and virgins, those privileges which Julian had withdrawn, and, whilst renewing them, Jovian made no laws against those who did not embrace the Gospel.[2] After the Emperor Jovian came Valentine I. and Valens (A.D. 364), then Gratian and Valentinian II. (A.D. 375—395). Valentine I. was tolerant, but Valentinian II. was a minor, and his mother, Justina —a staunch Arian—ruled in the name of her son, doing what she could to promote her own views in Milan, the seat of government.

Theodosius I. (A.D. 527—562) commenced his wide

---

[1] Socrates, iii., c. 19.
[2] *Ibid.*, iii., c. 22, 24-26.

imperial sway with this majestic declaration : " I will not permit, throughout my dominions, any other religion than that which obliges us to worship the Son of God in unity of essence with the Father and the Holy Ghost in the adorable Trinity." The story runs that he put the question to the Senate, according to Republican form, whether Jupiter or Christ should be God of the empire. As the result Jupiter was deposed, and old temples were destroyed or turned into churches. Soon afterwards the Sibylline Books were burnt. Paganism was dead, and with it died its literature, of which Claudian was the last poet.

An instance of persecution occurred during the reign of Theodosius.

In the north of Spain, under the shadow of the Pyrenees, towards the end of the fourth century, there sprang up a movement under Priscillian, a man of learning, wealth, and influence, who was led astray by Manichæan principles. A bishop or two countenanced his course. A synod at Saragossa condemned the teacher and his party, but this did not prevent his election to a bishopric. The orthodox applied to the Emperor Gratian, who ascended the throne in A.D. 375. He was urged to suppress the sect, but such a measure was prevented by bribery. Priscillian's wealth—"the silver spear," as it was called—being skilfully employed, Priscillianists for a while prospered; but afterwards, when Maximus, on the murder of Gratian, usurped the throne, Priscillian's fortunes underwent a change, which led to his deposition. He attempted a counter movement, but failed.

He believed in two primeval principles, light and darkness, in eternal conflict, and he had heterodox views of the Trinity. The general outline of Priscillianism included fantastic allegories, daring cosmogonies, and astrological fancies, combined with the severest asceticism. Priscillianists have been accused of immorality, but, as Gibbon says, "if the Priscillianists violated the laws of nature, it was, not by the licentiousness, but by the austerity of their lives."[1]

Priscillianists were summoned before a synod at Bordeaux in A.D. 384, when their leader maintained that the assembly was incompetent to try the case, and appealed to the Emperor. Martin of Tours and Ambrose of Milan interposed to stay proceedings, not from sympathy, or from a policy of toleration, but from opposition to secular interference. Other

---

[1] Gibbon's *Decline and Fall of the Roman Empire*, ii., p. 527.

bishops were for destroying schism by force, and sought imperial condemnation of the movement. Priscillian, and a lady who was his disciple, were condemned to die. It was probably for political ends that this deed was done. Christians in general felt no longer oppressed by State control, as was the case before; still a sect, small and feeble, might come under the lash of intolerance.

Certainly what is now meant by religious liberty was then unknown.

I have, in this chapter, passed over the last few Western emperors, as of no ecclesiastical importance. But after the separation of East and West, Justinian, who reigned in the East from A.D. 527 to 565, appears prominent in ecclesiastical matters, and requires distinct notice.

He walked in the steps of Constantine, so far as to bring the Church under State rule as much as possible. He directed his attention to theological questions, but, whilst ascetic in some of his habits, was not exemplary in his moral conduct. He married Theodora, a woman of fascinating manners, who had led a wild and reckless life before her marriage, not afterwards. She possessed great abilities, and exerted great influence over government, both in politics and religion. Her husband, a man of intellectual ability, managed affairs much according to his own will, except when his imperial consort obtained mastery. His Pandects, consisting of an extensive body of laws, won for him great renown, and became precedents for after rulers. In three respects he claims notice—as a Church ruler, as under his wife's influence, and as builder of a church the most wonderful in the world. As a religious ruler, his code of laws dealt with theological doctrine, hierarchal order, and the treatment of heresy. One great object of his, was to unite Constantinople and Rome, so as to form a theocracy for government of the world. As to his wife, she shared in some of his plans, but, in one rather amusing instance, thwarted a scheme he had devised for a missionary enterprise in Africa. He had planned sending out a priest holding views like his own, but the Empress, discovering his design, resolved to thwart it; and accordingly stole a march upon his Majesty. She found a priest according to her own mind, not her husband's, and managed to send him out to take possession of the field *before* any other missionary could arrive. The manœuvre was amusing and successful. She sent orders which defeated her husband's plan, and secured the arrival first of her own agent, who took possession of the mission, and succeeded in his work. In some matters the Emperor and Empress were of one mind, as in the case of the "three chapters," a matter which figures largely in the ecclesiastical disputes of that period. The last of Justinian's achievements was the erection of the magnificent cathedral at Constantinople, long since transformed into a mosque. The church in which Chrysostom preached had been burnt down, and the Emperor replaced it by another, which included spoils gathered from Rome, Athens, Baalbec, and Ephesus. They are still to be seen in the Great Mosque of Constantinople, which when completed drew from the founder the exclamation, "I have outdone thee, Solomon!" It is a wonderful building.

The massive construction which forms the church attached to the Monastery of St. Catherine, at Mount Sinai, is traditionally connected with the name of Justinian, as having had to do with its early history; it has received many additions since. The church retains a grand picture of the Transfiguration, together with portraits of Justinian and Theodora, in mosaic, with silver lamps shedding light upon them. How far traditions in the East respecting these royal personages, and others, such as Constantine and his mother Helena, in connection with building and decorating ecclesiastical edifices, are to be trusted by travellers, I am not prepared to say.

The recognised law of Christian life was at this period sought, not only in the Holy Scriptures, but in patristic writings, the canons of councils, and the Theodosian and Justinian codes. As if this collection of human decisions did not suffice, a *New Canon*, as it is called, was provided in a Greek original and Latin version. The first part contained laws generally accepted in the Greek Church, with the Latin canons of Sardica, and a code adopted at Carthage for African believers. The second part presents decretals on cases submitted by various parties, and also Spanish and Gallican decisions. The New Canon included particular *penitentials*, so-named, in which daily prayers are supplied and alms deeds are prescribed.

Constantine had granted privileges to those who adopted what was called a religious life. An enactment, with a view to the increase of population, had deprived unmarried women of all bequests, except from their own relatives. This told disadvantageously on persons who took vows of celibacy, and it was now repealed; and special privileges were secured to unmarried women. Virgins were allowed to make wills before they came of age. Also a law of wider scope was passed in favour of men who preferred, in cases of dispute, episcopal decisions, to such as came from secular authority. Owing to legal restrictions, difficulties had arisen in securing privileges for certain people; but such difficulties were now swept away in the case of those who obtained priestly certificates in their favour. To all this may be added the building of churches out of State funds. Help was also afforded to the clergy by their being placed on the civil list.[1]

I may add that, after the union of Church and State, the clergy were invested with juridical powers. They could authoritatively settle disputes where both parties were in clerical orders, and also in cases where disputants were prepared to abide by priestly decisions. Succeeding Emperors published edicts to check encroachments of ecclesiastical upon civil power, and bishops were left no right, in certain cases, to judge clerks where the latter were opposed to it. Episcopal courts had no coercive jurisdiction over laymen. Some changes were made by Justinian, who entirely exempted bishops from lay control, and prevented priests from being degraded without episcopal assent.[2] After Justinian, further changes were

[1] Sozomen, *Eccl. Hist.*, i., 9.
[2] *Church History* by Waddington, p. 221.

not made in the Eastern Church; but in the West, during darkness and disorder, some additional immunities were bestowed on the priesthood.

At the close of Justinian's reign, we find that monasteries were more numerous than they had been. Whatever might be the effect of social seclusion on the part of monks and hermits in earlier days, their withdrawment now from common walks of life, in its influence on society, must have inflicted injury in proportion to the personal piety which these recluses might possess. If they really were lights in the world, what a pity they should put themselves under extinguishers in cells and out-of-the-way hermitages. Increasing luxury, noticed by Gregory Nazianzen and Jerome, must have had a bad effect on families, drawing them away from the simplicity of Gospel life, and, in many cases, extinguishing them as lights in the world.

The number of professed believers, no doubt, vastly increased during imperial reigns under consideration; imposing city churches, East and West, were multiplied, and attracted spectators, if not always spiritual worshippers. Christianity became a stronger social and political power than it had ever been; but as *a really spiritual force*, there is reason to believe it was not what it had been in days of suffering under Diocletian.

As we shall see in the following chapter, the temper and conduct of some Church leaders, resembling worldly men—in short, the history of post-Nicene councils, under vouchsafement of imperial patronage —added much, in spite of professed orthodoxy, to the increasing shadows of early Christendom.

When the Church had been united to the State, organisations of dioceses and grouping of them in order were arranged according to imperial models. Rome, Constantinople, Alexandria, and Antioch stood first amongst ecclesiastical sees, and were distinguished as *patriarchates*. Rome, in this respect, became foremost and supreme amongst Italians, including Sicily, Sardinia, and Corsica. There was no other Church in the Western world to compete with Rome. In the East, Patriarchs of Antioch and Alexandria corresponded in extent of influence with the prefects of the empire ruling those great cities. When Constantinople had become the throne of Constantine, the bishop of that city took precedence in Christendom next to the Bishop of Rome. Constantinople, in the East, stood in relation to other Oriental sees as did the Roman one to those of the West. Christendom thus became an ecclesiastical reflection of the political empire.

I may add, Antioch did not meekly submit to

priority claimed on the part of Rome. Sozomen, under date A.D. 341, remarks that bishops assembled at Antioch sent a letter to their brother at Rome, "replete in rhetorical elegance, but couched in a tone of irony and defiance." These Easterns said, they were willing to remain in communion with Rome, if Rome confirmed their deposition of certain bishops, and their choice of those who were to succeed.[1]

It is but appropriate to add that, at the period now reviewed, there existed a disposition to maintain as large an amount of visible uniformity as possible, both in government and worship. The first of these instances, *on the whole*, is apparent when we remember the institute of patriarchates, professed or implied, East and West, though disturbed here and there by Donatists and Novatian sects. The second broad instance, with minor variations, is found touching Easter celebrations, observance of baptism and the Eucharist, also Mariolatry and fasting.[2] There were diversities of usage with substantial unity.

---

[1] Sozomen, *Eccl. Hist.*, iii., c. 8.
[2] Socrates, v., c. 22.

CHAPTER III

POST-NICENE COUNCILS

THEODOSIUS the Great included within his rule the entire old imperial dominions. Eminently orthodox, he zealously supported the doctrine settled at Nicea. Even on that occasion, however, the assembly was, while ecumenical in name, not so in fact.

No doubt there was a charm in Church conclaves; generally churchmen were proud of them, but Gregory Nazianzen, probably in reference to provincial councils, said: "To tell the truth, I shun these meetings, for I have seen none of them come to a good end. It is easier to set up oneself as judge of others, than to succeed in putting away one's own wrong-doing. I withdraw myself, and in solitude find rest for my soul."[1] Probably Gregory was, in this respect, no true type of the episcopal class to

---

[1] *Epist. ad Procop.*

which he belonged. Gregory's friend, Basil the Great, remarked, possibly in reference to General Councils: "The substance of God is beyond human understanding. For my part, I believe that the conception passes the reach of rational creatures. No one knoweth the Son but the Father."[1] Neither Gregory nor Basil were of that bustling order which loves to speak at public meetings; though, independently of that, Gregory had a decided opinion on the mysterious question then agitating Christendom.

Pursuing the recorded history of General Councils, we notice that what is said of the second, held at Constantinople, A.D. 381, appears in a hazy condition. There were present at the opening thirty-six semi-Arians, who soon retired, and left only one hundred and fifty members. No Latin bishops were present. Acts of the council we find preserved contain the creed and seven canons. The creed declared that the Spirit proceeded from the Father. The filioque clause was added in a Spanish assembly to be noticed hereafter.

The next General Council assembled at Ephesus

---

[1] *Ad Eun.*, iii., 6. See *Basil the Great* (S.P.C.K.), chap. vi., also p. 87.

in A.D. 431 ; and that its discussions may be understood, reference must be made to a controversy which then agitated the East.

Reverence for the Virgin had been increasing for some time. Images of her were set up in churches, enthroned, with the infant Jesus in her arms. Now appeared language respecting Mary of an unprecedented kind. Even Gregory Nazianzen said, "If any one considers that Mary was not Mother of God, Christ is severed from the Godhead." Zeal for our Lord's Divinity was perverted into strange forms of expression ; for instance, the distinguished Father I have just named affirmed, " If any one says our Saviour ran through the Virgin, as through a canal, and was not formed in her, in a Divine as well as in a human fashion—Divine, as being without a human father, human, as being by the law of fœtal growth—and further, if one says the man was first formed, and that then God assumed the man, he is to be condemned."[1]

This strange idea of passing through the Virgin " as a canal " appears in allusion to a Valentinian

---

[1] " Letter of Gregory to Cledonius," col. 178. See Swainson's *Nicene and Apostles' Creeds*, p. 83.

theory; for Epiphanius says, "The Valentinians affirmed that Christ brought down His body from above, and that, as water flows through a conduit, so He passed through the Virgin, taking nothing from her."[1] Scarcely any speculations exhibit more strikingly the shady side of patristic theology than do those in reference to the mysterious subject of the Incarnation.

In the state of thought existing at that period, Nestorius, Patriarch of Constantinople, contended against the practice of calling the Virgin "Mother of God," and insisted upon distinguishing between what was Divine and what was human in the person of our Lord. Nestorius firmly maintained the position that "it is impossible God should be born of a woman."

A report of that utterance was circulated far and wide, and it was indignantly branded as heresy. The idea of Nestorius produced an immense sensation in Alexandria, where an opposite tendency of thought obtained under the teaching of Cyril. He was

---

[1] Reading Chrysostom's *Homily IV.*, on the Gospel of Matthew chap.) i., p. 17), I am struck with the absence of such speculations on the "conception" of our Lord as were so common at that period. He says, "Above all nature is her conception," and then leaves it. The sermon is eminently practical.

particularly zealous in advocating Mary's Divine motherhood, and was intensely angry with his Constantinopolitan brother, who denied it. Cyril, not Nestorius, carried with him public opinion at that time ; and what are we to think of the animus of Evagrius the historian, who, after relating sufferings of Nestorius, endured at the hands of fellow-Christians, remarks, " I learn from one who wrote an account of his demise that, when his tongue had been eaten through with worms, he departed to *the greater and everlasting judgment* which awaited him " ? [1]

When we find the Virgin Mary called " Mother of God," we cannot be surprised at the mariolatry which followed. Before the period under review an apocryphal Gospel had been in existence, containing an account of her nativity, and, besides this, a story of her ascent to heaven. Also, Ambrose had spoken of her birth as somewhat miraculous, and Augustine did not reckon her as born in sin, like others ; but as was natural, the doctrine of her being Mother of God gave an impetus to mariolatry, then in its earliest stage, but developing afterwards until it covered Christendom. With the Virgin, Anna, her

---

[1] Evagrius, *Eccl. Hist.*, i., c. 7.

mother, became an object of devout veneration, and Justinian dedicated to her a church in Constantinople.[1] A foundation was thus gradually laid for that wonderfully extended worship of Mary which obtained in Europe before the Reformation, and still exists in Roman Catholic countries.

We now turn attention to the General Council held at Ephesus in A.D. 431.

In what I have to say of it I shall chiefly follow Neale, who gives an account of it in his *History of the Patriarchate of Alexandria*, and I say this lest I should be suspected of partisanship on the other side. According to Neale, Cyril and his followers would not wait for the arrival of John of Antioch, who supported Nestorius, but held a meeting, at once, of those opposed to the latter divine. Seven sessions were held by the bishops present in the city. They condemned Nestorius, and when John of Antioch arrived afterwards, the case had really been settled. Cyril was master of the proceedings. Documents were read, also the creed of Nicea, and a letter from Cyril to Nestorius. " You have heard that letter," said Cyril. " I believe it not to be at variance with the faith of Nicea. If your

---
[1] In this account of mariolatry I follow Kurtz's *Church Hist.*, v § 57.

opinions are different, say so." A hundred and twenty bishops expressed adherence to the doctrine of Cyril, and the rest manifested concurrence by acclamation. Another letter by Nestorius was read, and pronounced to be at variance with the Nicene decision. Then came shouts, "Anathema to the heretic Nestorius!" "Anathema to them who will not anathematise him!" Two professed friends of the accused said, however dear to them Nestorius was, Christ was dearer. Extracts were read from the Fathers, and sentence of excommunication was pronounced on the heretic. Other sessions followed, and the deliberations ended. Troubles, however, were yet to come. A message arrived from the Emperor, and the bishops had to appear before an imperial commissioner. So also had John of Antioch after he arrived. The message from the Emperor was read, to the effect that he approved of the deposition of Nestorius, and *that of Cyril also!*

As a specimen of feeling which existed between opposite parties, Cyril called Nestorius "a sleepless beast plotting against Jesus Christ"; and Neale says in a note, "These words have been by most historians taken to apply to Nestorius, and perhaps they might not untruly be said of him "; [1] but the vehemence of his expressions against Nestorius, who was, at all events, as yet uncondemned by the Church, can neither be justified nor excused. Popular feeling was on the side of the Council, and the Fathers were conducted by torchlight to their several lodgings. Women went before with perfumes, and the city was generally illuminated.

The Emperor was not present in the Council, but he received a deputation of eight members at Chalcedon, where he spent five days in listening to arguments on both sides. Upon his return to

---

[1] Neale, *History of the Holy Eastern Church : The Patriarchate of Alexandria*, i., p. 256. L'Abbé and Mansi are great authorities for Councils of the Church, and a handy *Manual of Councils* has been edited by Landon. On the Council of Ephesus and the Nestorian controversy read Swainson's *Nicene and Apostles' Creeds*, chaps. viii. and ix. I find the following incidents connected with the Council noticed by the Roman Catholic historian M. L'Abbé Fleury. They are gathered from documents of the period. "A company of servants came out and stopped some of us, took away our horses from us, wounded some, and pursued us with clubs and stones a great way." "Soldiers drew their swords and took up stones, at the same time threatening us." One of the parties said, " They have twice put bills on our houses, as a mark that they intended to assault us." " A great tumult arose because those who were with St. Cyril [that is, the Catholics] could not bear the sight of Nestorius " (see vol. iii., pp. 358, 364, 368, 377).

Constantinople his Majesty commanded some on the orthodox side to attend him there, and to consecrate a bishop in the place of Nestorius, whom he ordered to leave Ephesus and reside in his monastery near Antioch. That seems to have been a main result of the proceedings.

The absence of a devout spirit of inquiry, and the presence of personal strife, on both sides, each aiming at victory over the other, are obvious enough.

It is easier to condemn Nestorius on the one hand, and Cyril on the other, for language they employed in this controversy, than to form an adequate theory respecting the union of Divinity and humanity in Christ. Hooker remarks: "It is not in man's ability either to express perfectly, or to conceive the manner, how this [the union] was brought about. But the strength of our faith is tried by those things wherein our wits and capacities are not strong. Howbeit, because this Divine mystery is more true than plain, divers having framed the same to their own conceits and fancies are found in their own expositions more plain than true."[1]

The grand old city where the Council of Ephesus

---

[1] Hooker's *Works*, Keble's edition, vol. ii., p. 284.

was held has now disappeared, except in ruins left, which it takes about four hours to traverse, as I found when there. Two isolated mountains rise on the plain; to the north-east Ayaslouk is built, and Mont Prion occupies the centre of the town. Ayaslouk has a beautiful mosque, built at the end of the fifteenth century; and near to this are the remains of an aqueduct resting on piles of white marble, covered with inscriptions.

Another Council was held at Ephesus in A.D. 449, which has been branded by the name of the "Robber Synod." But it is difficult to discover in what respect, either in the legality of its convocation, or the number and dignity of the assembled prelates, consists its inferiority to some more honoured Councils. Two Imperial Commissioners attended to maintain order amongst the bishops, and peace in the city. Dioscorus, Patriarch of Alexandria, by the imperial command assumed the presidency. No less than three hundred and sixty ecclesiastics were present. Though adopting accustomed formalities, it "degenerated into turbulence and personal conflict. Its acts were marked with the same indecent precipitations: questions were carried by factious acclamations within, and the Council was overawed by riotous mobs without." Some of the cries recorded are: "Away with Eusebius! Banish Eusebius! Let him be burned alive! As he cuts asunder the two natures in Christ, so let him be cut asunder!" When the president put the question, "Is the doctrine that there are two natures after the Incarnation to be tolerated?" the answer was, "Anathema to him who so says." Hands were held up in attestation of the cry. There was entire unanimity, a result of interference on the part of soldiery—Dioscorus, the Patriarch of Alexandria, being the animating spirit, as he was the presiding genius, of the meeting. One Flavianus, attacked by those present, died under blows instigated by an Eutychian monk, named Barsumus.[1]

The assembly known as the Fourth General Council met in A.D. 451, at Chalcedon—opposite Constantinople,[2] occupying about the same local position as Scutari does—where stood the well-known hospital in the Crimean War. The orthodox doctrine of our Lord's nature was in opposition to the heresies of Nestorius and Eutyches, the former

---

[1] Barsumus brought with him a thousand monks to the Robber Council. He ventured to appear at Chalcedon in 451, when he was hooted at as a murderer.

[2] Chalcedon had a suburb, from which the Synod of "the Oak," assembled to defame the character of Chrysostom, derived its name.

separating and the latter confounding the Divine and human natures of the Saviour. "There is little," says Dr. Swainson, who made the subject his special study, "to command our respect, apart from the conduct of the laymen who interfered from time to time, although even they occasionally acted as partisans. From the heathenish cry of the orthodox 'Barsumus to the arena' (meaning, as Fleury, a Roman Catholic historian, quietly suggests, 'cast him to the lions of the amphitheatre') down to the abject terror of the Egyptian bishops, who rolled themselves upon the pavement, asking fruitlessly for compassion on their grey hairs, we see that there was no room for debate."[1]

This Council of Chalcedon appears, according to different authorities, to have been a disgraceful affair. L'Abbé, in his standard work on councils, says respecting it, that when Theodoret, Bishop of Cyrus, and friend of Nestorius, made his appearance, the Eastern prelates shouted, "The faith is destroyed; cast out the teacher of Nestorius." Egyptians shouted, "Long live the orthodox Empress; she has cast out Nestorius." When Theodoret had finished a speech, the opposite party shouted, "Don't call

---

[1] Swainson's *Nicene and Apostles' Creeds*, p. 123.

him a bishop. Cast out the fighter against God, cast out the Jew!"[1]

This is what took place within the Council. Theodoret, in one of his letters (169), relates what occurred outside. After saying what enormous crowds came to hear him preach "from a platform near the roof," he adds, "All the clergy, with the excellent monks, were utterly opposed to me, so that when we came back, after the visit of the pious Emperor, stone-throwing began, and many of my companions were wounded by the people and false monks." That which chiefly injured Theodoret's reputation was not that he had taught heresy, but that he was a friend of Nestorius, and consequently suspected of sympathy in his views.[2]

The only bright spot we can discover in connection with the assembly at Chalcedon is the letter written by Leo, Bishop of Rome, and read to the Fathers present. Instead of striving to penetrate the mystery of the Incarnation, he wisely confined

---

[1] L'Abbé's *Councils*, iv., pp. 102, 103.

[2] Gregory the Great wrote a synodical letter in 591, in which he declares that he received and reverenced the Four General Councils in the same manner as the Four Gospels, adding, " I bear the same respect to the fifth."—Fleury, *History*, Book xxxv.,

13

himself to what is revealed in Scripture, where the fact is set forth for devout contemplation by spiritually minded readers. " From the mother of the Lord our nature was assumed, but not our fault. Because the nativity was miraculous, we must not view the (human) nature as different from ours. He that is true God is true man. Each form ($\mu o\rho\phi\acute{\eta}$) does what is proper to itself, in communion with the other; the Word doing that which belongs to the Word, the flesh that which belongs to the flesh. To hunger, to thirst, to be weary, and to sleep are evidently human; to feed five thousand with five loaves, to bestow on the Samaritan woman the living water, the draught of which would grant to her that she should thirst no more, to walk over the sea with footsteps that sank not in it, and to calm down the rising waves in the storm, are undoubtedly Divine. As, therefore, it is not of the same nature to weep in tender affection over the friend that was dead, and to call that friend again to life when he had been dead four days; to hang upon the cross, and, turning light into darkness, to make all the elements tremble; to be pierced with nails, and to open the gates of paradise to the faith of the robber: so it is not of the same nature to say, ' I and the Father are one,' and to say, ' The

Father is greater than I.' From us, His is a humanity less than the Father; from the Father, His is a Divinity equal with the Father."[1]

One more *General Council*, so-called, numbered as the fifth, was held at Constantinople in A.D. 553. Only one hundred and sixty-four bishops were present, and they represented the Eastern Church. The meeting is often styled the Second Council of Constantinople. Vigilius, Bishop of Rome, protested against it, and did not attend, though he repeatedly received invitations. When his successor, Pelagius I., acknowledged this Council, the Churches of Northern Italy, Africa, and Illyria separated from Rome, and continued in what was deemed a state of schism, until the time of Gregory I.[2]

In looking back upon the Councils under review, it is worth particular notice, that none of them *actually* represented Christendom at large, the vastly

---

[1] The letter is given in Leo's *Works*, Migne, liv., Ep. 38, p. 757.

[2] "Those who appeal to the decisions of General Councils ought to show that the decisions are concordant, but it is well remarked, 'Practically the decrees of the fourth and fifth councils are mutually inconsistent, and it is impossible to accept both. Theodorus was reinstated at Chalcedon, in spite of what he had written; and what he had written was anathematised at Constantinople, in spite of his reinstatement."—*Select Library of Nicene and Post-Nicene Fathers*, vol. iii., p. 13.

predominant character being Oriental, their appointment originating with the temporal, not the ecclesiastical power—for they were summoned at the imperial bidding. That at Nicea was theological in spirit and form, but disciplinary also in result, excluding Arians from the Church; the Council of Ephesus was decidedly doctrinal, but it took practically a disciplinary form by pronouncing Nestorius a heretic and casting him out of the Church. The next meeting at Chalcedon decided the orthodox doctrine of our Lord's person, in opposition to Nestorian and Eutychian heresies, and was signalised by the reading of Leo's admirable letter. This last Council which comes within our notice was greatly under the control of the Emperor Justinian, who wished to establish supremacy over dogmatic conclusions—in fact a superiority in this respect of Constantinople to Rome.

Anathema is a term which bristles up ever and anon in proceedings of Councils. What exactly it meant, what were the penalties included in it, are questions discussed by learned churchmen. The malediction certainly included a total separation of heretics from the Church; not only from local Churches where they worshipped, but from the Catholic Church at large. Separation involved serious social punishments, together with those which were ecclesiastical. No orthodox person was permitted to have intercourse with the heterodox. None of the latter could give evidence in an ecclesiastical court against one of the other class ; nor were they entitled to succeed in a family inheritance.[1] The civil law gave force to the decree that heretics should be stripped of the power of making their wills. After the sixth century, penalties for the anathematised became more severe. A question has arisen whether anathemas included a *curse*, along with excommunication. Prebendary Thorndike thought the Fathers and Councils did not *imprecate* heretics, praying for their destruction, and quotes from Vincentius : " Let him be anathema, that is, let him be severed, set aside, shut out, lest the direful contagion of one sheep, with any mixture of venom, stain the innocent."[2] At best this only includes what it did *not mean*, while a meaning most unchristian remains sufficiently obvious.

---

[1] Bingham's *Works*, vol. vi., pp. 250, 261, 264.

[2] Thorndike's *Works*, II., part i., p. 340. But Swainson remarks in his book on *Nicene and Apostolic Creeds*, p. 105 : " The anathematising of a layman was, at the Council of Ephesus, considered to be a punishment of the same class as the deposition of a bishop or clerk. It can scarcely be

What I have just been describing relates to General, or so-called *Ecumenical*, Councils, though they really did not reach the nominal extent. Other minor councils were held, at which I glance before closing this chapter.

Dupin gives an account of councils which were local and limited, held in the fifth century at different places within the limits of France—such as Orange, Arles, Anjou, Tours, etc. In these conclaves decisions were reached, as to the ordination of priests, local Church matters requiring settlement, in relation to morals and manners. Canonical questions of various kinds came before such gatherings, and no doubt excited local interest; cases occur manifesting pastoral attention and minuteness of oversight, as to the conduct of priests and parishioners, beyond what we might expect.[1]

We find when Gaul was divided between Franks,

---

conceived that at this time (A.D. 431) the penalty was considered to involve eternal consequences. On the contrary, the rules were very precise—a heretic might be admitted to communion on his death-bed." But the question arises, on what terms?

[1] Dupin's *Hist. of Eccl. Writers*, vol. iii. Much curious information as to minor ecclesiastical matters may be gleaned from Fleury's *Eccl. Hist.*, vol. iv.

Burgundians, and Goths, the kings of one nation were not willing to let their bishops attend councils held by another division. Ancient forms of episcopal election were recommended; and in this matter it would appear that Church and State were not in perfect harmony. We find minute regulations recorded with regard to Sabbath observance and Church customs. People were not permitted to travel on Sunday with horses, cattle, and carriages. "Our will," says one canon of a council in Gaul, "is that people refrain from tilling ground, pruning vines, mowing grass, and making hedges, that they may have more time to attend church." People present at Divine service were not to wear swords, except in time of war or when on journeys; and laymen were not to leave worship till the Lord's Prayer was said and the benediction given.[1]

Sometimes, in Wales for instance, councils became courts of justice, and it is on record that at Llandaff, sentence of excommunication was pronounced on a king of Glamorgan for having slain another king, and two others for killing certain relatives. Settlement of disputes between individuals was accomplished in connection with these meetings, also censures

---

[1] Fleury, *Eccl. Hist.*, vol. iv., p. 142.

were pronounced, pardons bestowed, and justifications of conduct declared. Councils were frequent: fifteen were held at Constantinople before the end of the sixth century; and I find altogether more than three hundred occurred before the close of that period.

Churches or halls of assembly such as might exist in those days, we may make visible to our imagination, but the character of debaters and listeners we cannot penetrate. Some historical persons taking part in debate, we are somewhat acquainted with; but as to people listening and reaching conclusions, we are utterly at a loss.

CHAPTER IV

EASTERN SEES, BISHOPS, AND FAMILIES

I. WHEN Christendom was established Constantine founded at *Jerusalem* the Church of the Holy Sepulchre. He desired the building should surpass all churches in the world by the beauty of its walls, columns, and marbles. It answered, we are told, to prophecies in Scripture of the New Jerusalem, and was built, as supposed, over the tomb of our Lord. Eusebius describes it as overlaid with gold, the crowning part being the altar, which rose to the summit of the roof. Porticoes were on each side of the court.

Constantine's mother, Helena, visited the Holy City, and there discovered the house of Caiaphas; but the "invention of the Cross," as she regarded it, was the crowning result of her researches. Cyril was Bishop of Jerusalem at that time. He has left his catechetical lectures as records of his theological teaching—orthodox on the whole, but very rudimentary. He has much to say in his thirteenth lecture respecting the burial of Christ; but he is so absorbed in the spiritual side of his subject that he settles no question as to the archæology of the sepulchre. My inquiries when I was in the church which bears that name led me to no decision of the question which has so long puzzled antiquarians.[1]

II. The disciples were called Christians first at *Antioch* is a landmark in ecclesiastical history, and we are told of a church there at an early period, which stood in the centre of a large court, and was octangular in shape. The floor was paved with polished marbles; walls and columns were adorned with images and precious stones.

Comparatively recent explorations have revealed much which enables us to imagine what existed on

---

[1] The impression made by trustworthy accounts of the moral and religious state of the Jerusalem inhabitants and pilgrims in the fourth century is very sad. A letter written at that time by Gregory of Nyssa is sufficient proof of this.

Villemain, in his *Tableau de l'Eloquence Chrétienne au IV. Siècle*, p. 111, has a notice of Gregory Nyssa. It is curious to find that this Gregory, who was one of the pillars of the Church in the Constantinopolitan Council, is regarded by some critics as a universalist. See Farrar's *Lives of the Fathers*, "Gregory of Nyssa."

mountains between Antioch, Aleppo, and Apamea at the time. We are told of more than a hundred and fifty cities within a space of thirty or forty leagues, with houses, galleries, and subterranean kitchens ; also of churches flanked with towers and surrounded by tombs, crosses, and sculptures testifying Gospel triumphs in early ages. The ancient Emesa—metropolis of the province—on the right bank of the Orontes, had under the Emperor Constantinus a church built there renowned for beauty. A few years ago a noble basilica could be identified as having stood on the spot, with five bays, divided by double columns. What remained of it lately was used for Divine worship by Dionysius the Bishop. Other buildings, with Greek inscriptions, are still found in that Mohammedan country, testifying to an early existence there of the Christian religion. Lingering upon ancient ruins there are still to be found words such as "Christ is with us," "The Lord preserve thy coming in and thy going out from this time and for evermore." Such inscriptions demonstrate the existence of Christianity in that country before Mohammedan times.

We now turn to memorials of men with whom we are more familiar than with these architectural remains.

In the middle of the fourth century, there lived at Antioch a widow lady named Arethusa, left with a little boy, who in his manhood became a master of Greek eloquence, and stayed its "sun from going down a whole day." The city professed Christianity; but as to a large part of the population, this was little more than nominal. In the great Eastern cities of the empire, especially Antioch and Constantinople, the mass of a so-called Christian population was largely infected by dominant vices—inordinate luxury, sensuality, avarice, and display. Christianity was in part paganised before it had made appreciable progress towards the destruction of ancient Paganism. But the sincere and ardent piety of many amongst the women in the city kept alive a flame of faith which would otherwise have been smothered.[1] When Chrysostom was a child the fire burnt brightly on the hearth-stone where he played.

At a very early age Chrysostom was ordained a Scripture-reader. Theodosius the Great was associated with Gratian in the empire in 379, and we are told that about that period Antioch contained 100,000 inhabitants, 3,000 of whom were supported

---

[1] Neale's *Patriarchate of Antioch*, edited by Williams, xxi., *et seq.*

out of the public oblations.[1] We may judge from this circumstance the position of Antioch in Chrysostom's day.

He soon made a deep impression on the citizens, especially by the delivery of his famous " Homilies on the Statues." A riot had occurred in the city, and the mob broke into pieces statues of the Emperor Theodosius and his wife.

The incident deeply affected Chrysostom, and he delivered a course of sermons on the occasion. They could not fail to produce an impression. He touched on the sins of citizens ; the fortitude and patience of loyal people ; the duty of obeying magistrates ; thanksgivings due for deliverance from calamity, and the return of their bishop after a satisfactory interview with the Emperor. It is remarkable that in almost all these sermons are rebukes for profane swearing.

The state of Antioch at the time was far from satisfactory, and a vast amount of superstition seems to have been a besetting sin of people there ; a century afterwards and more, the historian Evagrius tells a story which shows how Antioch and the

---

[1] Gibbon's *Decline and Fall of the Roman Empire* (Milman's Edition), i., p. 514.

neighbourhood had been steeped in beliefs and practices most absurd.

Evagrius had a decided taste for the marvellous, and describes a visit he paid to the famous pillar saint, Simeon, and saw the rustics dancing round, whilst "a star shot along the balustrade"—an incident occurring "only on the commemorations of the saint."[1] In a page close to the notice of this marvel, the historian records the translation of "the Divine Ignatius," or the "more solid bones of the martyr," from Rome to Antioch, where a temple was raised to his honour. Hence followed a public festival which was periodically maintained down to the days when Evagrius lived, and was sanctioned by even the prelate Gregory.[2] The historian also relates a display at Apameia of the life-giving wood of the cross, which Evagrius was permitted to adore and kiss, after which a blaze burst out of "unconsuming fire," not once or twice, but as often as "the priest made a circuit of the place." The same authority states that miracles were wrought there by "Zozimus and John."[3] The narrator speaks of the sacred head which had belonged to a pillar saint—a relic regarded as a protection of the Eastern army—" Not

---

[1] *Eccl. Hist.*, i., 13.   [2] *Ibid.*, i., 16.   [3] *Ibid.*, iv., 7.

a hair had perished," we are told, "but was in the same state as when the saint was alive."[1] Such were beliefs in the neighbourhood when Evagrius was young, whose birth has been fixed about A.D. 536.

This date is much later than Chrysostom's time, but it shows the superstition which existed after he left the city and neighbourhood. Perhaps, with all his powerful appeals in many ways, he did little to check the tide in that direction. Indeed, with all his intellectual power and eloquence, like others of ecclesiastical influence, Chrysostom failed to detect and expose superstition, which increased after he was gone, and deluged dark ages with a flood of mischief.

III. Constantinople.—Gregory Nazianzen in A.D. 379 was invited to Constantinople. In a poem he left behind him he says of the Church at that time: "It had passed through the death of infidelity, and there was left but the last breath of life." He said he had come to the city to defend the faith; and what the people needed was solid teaching, to deliver them from the spider webs of subtlety in which they had been caught. Constantinople was in a miserably

---

[1] *Eccl. Hist.*, i., 13.

divided state. The fact was Arianism and other errors had taken possession of the place; and the prospect before Gregory, when he entered upon his new charge, was by no means inviting. He occupied a house where he lodged and preached, and this he called the *New Shiloh*. "There," he said, "the ark was fixed after its forty years' wandering in the desert."[1]

The Emperor Theodosius turned Arians out of churches, and bestowed the episcopate on Gregory, who, as a man of retired habits and contemplative tastes, was not at all fitted for that position. It is said he neighed like a stabled horse for green pastures. Ullman, in his *Life of Gregory*, quotes one of his dreams as an index to his character. "Sweet sleep embraced me, and in it a dream presented to my mind my church Anastasia, the object of my daily longing. I was seated, as it appeared to me, on a high-raised chair. Somewhat lower on either side of me sat the presbyters—leaders of the flock. Next stood, in robes of dazzling whiteness, the deacons, a picture of angelic adornment. The people arranged themselves in ranks, clustering like bees around the pulpit, pressing for nearer access. Others flocked in from the market towns and highways to

---

[1] *Orat.*, xlii., 26; *Opera*, i., 766.

hear my discourse; while from the upper range of seats holy virgins and noble ladies bent forward with attentive ears."

Gregory Nazianzen is far too interesting a person to be lost sight of on leaving Constantinople. He was not likely to please the people of that city. "They wanted 'a king like the nations,' a man who had a presence, who would figure and parade and rustle in silk; some Lord Mayor's preacher or West End divine, who could hold forth and lay down the law, and be what is thought dignified and grand; whereas they had no one but poor, dear, good Gregory, a monk of Nazianzus, a personage who, in spite of his acknowledged learning and eloquence, was but a child, had no knowledge of the world, no manners, no conversation, and no address."[1] He returned to his native city, and found things in confusion there, whereupon he strove to reduce them to order, and then retired to Arianzus, with its shady wood and a fountain—his favourite walk. There he died in 389 or 390.

Untoward incidents occurred. The second general council was held at Constantinople, which we have noticed already,[2] and must hasten on to the episcopate

---

[1] Newman's *Hist. Sketches*, ii., p. 84. [2] See p. 163.

of Chrysostom, who entered on his ministry at Constantinople, where he was elected as Archbishop and afterwards enthroned, A.D. 398.

Let us imagine the church where he preached. Not a vestige remains of the original St. Sophia built by Constantine; that was burnt during a riot in Chrysostom's time. As we approach the edifice where he ministered, we find beggars lying by the roadside, and can picture the preacher ascending his pulpit. The great and noble are present to hear him, and among them are ladies in costly attire who have come in gilded chariots drawn by white horses. There they sit in their pomp and glory, careful lest their dresses be rumpled and spoiled. Gentlemen, too, are there with their slaves, making themselves conspicuous and important by their manner of wearing the toga. The preacher begins, and his eloquence soon evokes a demonstration of delight; clapping is heard throughout the building. You might fancy yourself in a theatre. Looking round sternly, the orator exclaims, " Many testify their delight at our discourse by their applause, and then hasten to the circus to speed on the games with louder cheers." " I desire not your clamour," he said, " but that you hear me with calmness and attend to my admonitions."

Reproof, however, only elicits fresh acclamations, to be put down by stronger rebukes. Men come to light the lamps, and the attention of the congregation is at once diverted. "While I explain the Scriptures, you turn away your eyes to the lamps and the lighters. How great an indifference! I kindle for you the light of Scripture; on my tongue burns the fire of instruction."[1]

The sermon over, the people hurry away before the prayers. "Your hurrying away," he says, "the moment my sermon is ended shows that none of my words have been received and treasured up in your souls, or they would have detained you and led you to receive the holy mysteries with reverence. Some who tarry listen mechanically to the prayers. Then pressing one against another, many leave the church; and even those who remain to the communion include some who are irreverent."

Pickpockets avail themselves of a crowded congregation to ply their trade. Confusion at church equalled hubbub at baths. Chat, joke, and repartee

---

[1] For examples of the kind selected, see Homilies on 1 Corinthians, Nos. xxxvi., xxxix., xl.; Ephesians, vi., xv., xx.; Matthew, xxx., xlix. Villemain, *Tableau de l'Éloquence Chrétienne au IV. Siècle*. It is remarkable that the well-known prayer of Chrysostom, at the close of Morning and Evening Service in the Church of England, begins with "*Almighty God,*"

mingled with laughter during prayer. Woe to any unpopular preacher who took the bishop's place; he was pretty sure to be hooted. Such was the character of those who came to the Easter communion, and amongst them were some addicted to gross vice.

As regards Chrysostom's doctrine, whilst orthodox according to the Nicene Creed, it did not include those views of Divine grace which Augustine held. Chrysostom believed in free-will, and was touched by Pelagian ideas, though he believed in the mediation and atonement of Christ. He did not distinguish between justification and holiness, but took a broad view of both. So far there was no difference between him and the Bishop of Hippo; though certainly these two on other important subjects moved along different lines.

Passages might be cited which lean in a Pelagian direction, yet Chrysostom could say in relation to the riches of Divine grace, "It is as though one should take a miserable leper, and transform him into a

---

and then includes the words, "and dost promise that when two or three are gathered together in *Thy name Thou* wilt grant their requests." These are words of Jesus Christ. The true and proper Divinity of our Lord is distinctly recognised—an important fact in the historical theology of the fourth century.

youth of surpassing beauty, with lustrous cheeks
and eyes like sunbeams, and then, in the flower of
his age, to clothe him with purple, and crown him
with the diadem of royalty." " Far more than we
sinners owe, Christ hath paid, as much more as an
ocean exceeds a drop."

What strikes me as wonderful in Chrysostom's
preaching is the thorough reality of what he says.
He does not give a poet's dream or a philosopher's
speculation, but *realities—objects seen and felt*, not
like a starlight night, but as a noonday sun.

Further, as to the substance of Chrysostom's
preaching, we find that he believed in the intercession
of departed saints, and urged his hearers to seek
their help. " Let us constantly visit them," he says,
" touch their shrines, and with faith embrace their
relics, that we may derive blessings from them."
" Let us, not only on their festivals, but at other
times, invoke them to become our protectors ; for they
can use much boldness of speech when dead ; more,
indeed, than when they were alive (for now they bear
in their bodies the marks of the Lord Jesus Christ).
Let us, therefore, procure for ourselves, through them,
favours from God." [1] Moreover he believed departed

---

[1] *Hom. in Invent. et Maxim.*—Stephens' *Life of Chrysostom*,
p. 187.

souls were benefited by prayers on the part of survivors. "Let us assist them," he exclaimed, "according to our power." "When the people stand with uplifted hands, a priestly assembly, and the awful sacrifice lies displayed, how shall we not prevail with God on their behalf."[1]

Chrysostom describes the monastic life of his day: "The cock crows, all reverently rise, and, lifting up hands, sing a hymn, suitable and full of the love of God. When day is coming on they have a season of rest, and then proceed to the reading of Scripture. At the third, sixth, and ninth hours they perform their devotions. Instead of hastening to the baths when relieved from their labours, they betake themselves, not to highly seasoned dishes, but to bread and salt, herbs and pulse. After a short time they go to rest, on a bed made for repose, not luxury. They fear no robbers, and when they die are carried to the grave with hymns. There is thanksgiving, joy, and great glory."[2] I have condensed the preacher's description.

The discourses of Chrysostom are described as being simple, inartificial, popular, and sometimes conversational.

---

[1] *Hom. IV.*, on Epistle to Philippians.
[2] *Hom. XIV.*, on 1 Timothy.

Chrysostom has bequeathed a number of letters belonging to the period of his banishment. They are addressed to his deaconesses, for whom profound respect is blended with pure affection. Others are written to bishops, presbyters, deacons, monks, missionaries, and friends, besides acquaintances attached in the course of his journey.

We meet with passages in the course of this correspondence which show how widely remote Chrysostom was from the mind and taste of our own times in some points, although in others he seems so congenial. "He lived when the minds of Christians had for generations been inured to scenes of persecution," and "fierce opposition of party against party"; and people, however amiable and gentle by nature, become infected by the prevailing mode of thought. He "would look at things, more or less, from the same point of view as the generality of men amongst whom he lived."[1]

He asks for funds to support charities he had established; now returning thanks for letters, next complaining of silence; here stimulating hope, and there requesting prayer. His correspondence is an

---

[1] *St. Chrysostom, his Life and Times*, by Rev. W. R. W. Stephens, pp. 388, 389

index to his inner life, such as we possess for few historical names. We are able to trace him from stage to stage on a perilous journey to his place of exile, sometimes conveyed in a palanquin, a mule before, and a mule behind. For some distance he travels through a beautiful country, watered and clothed with fertility; but in the latter part of his journey different scenery produces a corresponding effect on the exile's sensitive nature.

He writes to Christian ladies—Olympias and Theodora. We find, in one of these letters, a tone of defiance towards the Empress, like what had burst out in his sermons; but his general mode of expression is that of patient endurance. The arrival of Sabiniana, a deaconess, who cheered him when he reached his destination at Cucusus, is noticed with joy in an epistle he sends to his friend Olympias : " My lady arrived here the day I did knocked up, thoroughly wearied, being of advanced age, when travel is toilsome, yet in earnestness like a girl." It is very touching to find, after reading one of his letters where he complains of a man's silence, that this poor fellow was at the time scourged and racked.

Chrysostom's adventures on his journey to Cappadocia were alarming. Freebooters infested the pass of Mount Taurus. They were an Isaurian race, wild and barbarous, and we do not wonder that he met with such people, but we are startled to learn he was actually assailed by a band of *monks* at Cæsarea. He says: "Nothing availed to stop their violence; they even frightened the soldiers of the prefecture.... The Mayor of the city heard what was going on and hastened to assist," but these "wild beasts," so Chrysostom calls them, "would not listen to the magistrate." The absence in Chrysostom's correspondence of severe reflections on his persecutors is very remarkable, and bears witness to his Christian spirit. After disappointed hopes of returning to his flock, he died on the borders of the Euxine Sea.[1]

The last days of this great preacher were filled with trouble. His boldness displeased her Majesty. The royal enmity he resented, and spoke of eating at Jezebel's table so as to leave no doubt who Jezebel was.

Once he mounted his ambo, exclaiming, " Herodias is dancing and calls for the head of John in a charger." " Herodias " was believed to mean her Majesty; still it is possible the preacher only meant to refer to the Scripture narrative. Certainly he had enemies, at home and abroad, who warped his words into the worst meaning; and, by their combination,

---

[1] *Epistles*, 9, 10, 12, 14, 120—137, and many others.

a meeting known as the "Synod of the Oak" formally degraded and deposed the preacher. Many citizens were prevented from interposing on his behalf by a private surrender of himself into the hands of his enemies.

IV. From Constantinople we now travel to Cæsarea, a city of Cappadocia, an important place during the later empire, said to contain a population of nearly half a million; but such a report must be received with allowance, at a period when taking a census was mainly guesswork. The historian Eusebius, to whom we are so much indebted for what we know of the Christian Church, was Bishop of Cæsarea from about 313 to the end of 339, but his episcopal labours do not appear to have been remarkable. He was succeeded by Basil, who figures conspicuously in the annals of his age. He was a remarkable member of a remarkable family. Grandson of a saintly woman named Macrina, he used to tell how much he owed to her early love and teaching, who, to use his own words, "formed and fashioned him by her pious doctrine." He had a sister, also named Macrina, in saintliness a copy of her grandmother, and whose sympathy he shared in one illness after another; so that "a child could see his body was like a shell, and he must soon die, unless God spared him for further repentance."

He describes himself as timid and reserved, wanting spirit, and of sluggish temperament, "the common defect of Cappadocians." "I am ashamed to tell you,' he once wrote, "how I pass night and day in this lonely nook, resembling one angry with his ship, as too much tossed, and who leaves it for a boat, in which he finds himself sick and miserable." Full of trouble, he was always seeking rest, and finding none. His life, according to his own complaints, abounded in sorrow, " disease making him tender as a plant and chaining him down to a single spot," yet he was full of playfulness with friends and relations. Withal he appears to have been self-contained and sensitive, though courageous; full of complaints, yet cheerful, and thanking God for everything; from first to last unworldly and devout; in weakness submissive, in health at work for the Church's help and God's glory. There was a touch of humour in his complaints. When an angry official threatened to tear out his liver, if he did not yield in a certain dispute, " I should be much obliged if you would do so," was his reply, "for my liver gives me a great deal of trouble."[1]

---

[1] His epistles are very numerous, and interesting specimens are given by Cardinal Newman in his *Historical Sketches*, vol. ii. In Smith's *Biographical Dict.* is an exhaustive article extending more than thirteen double column pages closely printed.

Basil and Gregory Nazianzen had been early friends and fellow-students at Athens, contemporary with Julian, afterwards the apostate. The two former resembled each other in some respects, being highly gifted, sincerely pious, and of ascetic habits, but after different types. It is interesting to notice the intense admiration of the beautiful in nature which the two friends cultivated and expressed. Basil looked on earth and sky not only with poetic feeling, but with scientific knowledge such as the age supplied. He classified birds according to their wings, and included them with beetles and bats in the same order. Bees seem to have been a favourite study, and he speaks of the monarch among them as not elected by votes; for democracies, Basil remarks, "raise unworthy favourites to power, whereas, through nature, the largest and most beautiful creatures attain supremacy."[1]

V. Nazianus was a town in the south-west of Cappadocia, a place of no importance in itself, but the name has become familiar to students of Church history in connection with celebrities, who have redeemed the place from obscurity. Cappadocia was of wide extent, with many districts, containing a mountain range, where different languages were

---

[1] *Ep.*, 188.

spoken. Interest gathers round the name of Gregory Nazianzen[1] from its being borne by the celebrity already noticed at Constantinople; but Nazianus is worthy of attention because his name presents an example of unique *family life* when hermits, monks, and other cenobites were held in renown. It is a fact worthy of special notice that there were still bishops in those days who, with wives married to them before their consecration, had boys and girls as olive trees round their tables.

Basil the Great, after having been presbyter in the Church of Cæsarea, became archbishop of the diocese. He possessed a nature capable of ruling others, and this made duty the daily pleasure of his life. At Cæsarea a new town arose, including an hospital and an asylum for strangers, with other provisions for daily wants—all paid for with money raised by Basil, whilst he reserved for himself the care of lepers.

Basil and Gregory Nazianzen were great letter-writers, and relics we possess of their communications afford illustrations of contemporary habits. We

---

[1] I have only touched those points, in the history of Gregory and Basil, where they were connected with Constantinople and Cæsarea. Their friendship was interesting and affecting both from its lights and shadows. A cloud came over it: Basil died first.

gather that orthodox people under the heretical Emperor Valens suffered distressing persecution, and old men, women, and children might be seen worshipping, like Scotch Covenanters, on hills and in deserts, under winter frost and scorching heat of summer's sun. Strange irregularities obtained, and one meets with a story how a deacon gathered together a company of young people, and led them about dancing, "to the sorrow of the godly and the merriment of the profane." We are told of a lady who had for chaplain a bishop who was her slave. We learn that people behaved irreverently at church, and that simony obtained amongst clergymen. A whole district was covered with incompetent priests, none of them being fit for office, and discipline being resisted by the people. Basil himself excommunicated a whole district, because the inhabitants harboured an excommunicated delinquent.

The name of Gregory Nazianzen's mother was Nonna, a lady of rank, child of Christian parents, described in glowing terms by her son "as holy in her life"; to her example he attributed his father's conversion, and to her intercessions the sanctity of their home. The bishop, her husband, had by birth belonged to the Hypsistarian sect, which blended into one system Christianity and heathenism.

Nonna's life was retired and uneventful, but "overshadowed," as her eloquent son remarks in one of his orations, by "such domestic sorrows as fall to the lot of a mother." Her health was commonly good, but in the year A.D. 371 she suffered from a severe illness, which brought home Gregory, who, on his arrival, found that danger was passed; her recovery being attributed to "cakes of bread, marked by a cross and blessed by her son." Three years afterwards her husband died, and the widow survived the loss only a short time. It is touching to learn that she died as she was kneeling to receive the Lord's Supper.

Basil the Great and Gregory of Nyssa are both well known among the celebrities of the fourth century, and their family history is further connected through their two sisters. Macrina, namesake of her grandmother, was intellectual, as well as pious. To Basil she was a counsellor, being his elder by two years. Educated by her mother Emmelia, she became an accomplished woman, familiar with patristic literature, and with classical authors also. She committed to memory the Psalter and the Canticles, and is described by her brother as surpassing all the young people of her age. She attracted the affection of a young advocate, who died soon afterwards, when she devoted herself to a virgin life. A widowed mother and an infant brother were now her care, increased by the management of a large estate. She condescended to humble employments, and often made and baked the household bread with her own hands.

The establishment of a religious sisterhood resulted from her ascetic piety. She had sorrow on sorrow, through losing a brother and a sister, bereavements which affected her health and contributed to shorten her days. Her sufferings were extreme, and her death story is affecting. Gregory beginning to talk of his sufferings under the Emperor Valens, she checked him, saying he owed all he had done to parental education and prayer. Dusk came on; lights were brought in, when she signed herself with the cross and finished life together with her prayers. At an earlier period the grandmother Macrina, with her husband, were forced to flee during a season of persecution, and had to dwell as outcasts.

VI. Cyrus, a city and diocese of Syria, lying on the river Ænoparus, became somewhat noted in the fifth century, from a bishop who was consecrated to the see in A.D. 423, and who figured prominently amongst episcopal controversialists. His name was Theodoret. He was a Scripture commentator, Church historian, and a popular preacher. His epistolary remains are numerous, and they furnish the chief authority for details of his busy life. The letter, in his works numbered CLXXX., relative to Cyril, is very shocking, but I cannot accept it as genuine without some proof. Baronius (vi., 23) contests its genuineness. It looks to me like a fictitious production to illustrate what some people thought of Cyril. Passing through strange adventures and deeply involved in controversies, Theodoret showed power and self-command, though, on the whole, he appears a man of irritable temper. His see was situated between the river Euphrates and the spurs of a mountain range, and was forty miles in length, embracing monasteries containing two hundred and fifty inmates; also a large number of hermitages. Its distinct parishes are set down as no less than eight hundred. The bishop speaks of miracles wrought, heretics converted, and persecution endured. According to his own account he was at one time stoned and nearly killed, but he lived down opposition, and was victorious over foes. The city of Cyrus was small, the buildings mean; but, at Theodoret's own expense, the place was improved, and he constructed aqueducts for watering fields and gardens. He mentions the absence of lawsuits amongst his parishioners. On the whole he does not seem to have been contented with his bishopric, and speaks with great delight of Antioch, a city he often visited. There, he informs us, he was very popular. People folded him in their arms, kissed his head and breast, some even his knees, declaring he preached "like one of the apostles." John the Patriarch, as he heard him, would rise from his seat and applaud the preacher with both hands. Such is Theodoret's own account; and his whole autobiography shows he was on excellent terms with himself.

He plunged into controversy, and was much mixed up with disputes about Nestorius and Eutyches, the former being an old companion and favourite. Theodoret was a remarkably active and clever man, but I do not accept all his stories, or endorse all his opinions as I understand them.

Of all which I have read of Theodoret's writings, the work entitled *Dialogues* appears to me most interesting and valuable. The title conveys no idea of the subject, but it is really a long critical dissertation on the union of Christ's Divine and human nature. One of the interlocutors is named Orthodox, and he is master of the argument. The book contains as much as would cover three hundred pages of moderate octavo, and is full of patristic learning and acute reasoning in support of our Lord's Divinity

The *Dialogues* give a deeper impression of the author's ability than any other of his writings. It is pronounced by Precentor Venables[1] to be the most valuable of Theodoret's controversial works; I think justly so. Independently of its argumentative force, it contains a catena of passages from the early Fathers on the union of two natures, Divine and human, in the person of our Lord and Saviour.[2]

In closing this chapter relative to the East, there is one celebrity who, though not a bishop, and unconnected with episcopal families, may be introduced here, from his connection with the north-east. I refer to Ephrem the Syrian, as he is called, who lived in the fourth century, and who has come to be known amongst English readers through his *Rhythms*, translated in the Oxford series of Anglo-Catholic works.

"When I was a child, lying in my mother's lap, I saw in a dream what became a reality. From my tongue sprang a vine twig which reached toward heaven, and brought forth leaves and fruit

---

[1] Smith's *Christian Biog.*, iv., pp. 304 *et seq.*

[2] Theodoret's work is translated in the quarto *Select Library of Fathers*, vol. iii (Oxford).

abundantly. As more were plucked, the clusters multiplied."[1]

The *Rhythms* are full of Christ, and Ephrem must be regarded as an evangelical writer; but his forms of thought and expression are so foreign to our habits that few will get to the end of the volume.

Commenting on the first chapter of Ezekiel, Ephrem remarks: "The faces of the lion, who is the king of beasts, represent to us the kings and princes of the world, who have come under and been subdued to the yoke of the Church, which is represented by the chariot; or to the Gospel, which selfsame Gospel the chariot represents. The faces of the eagle again are that we may know—that is, from above—that He which shall come, is to be. But by the faces of the birds and the beasts he represents the nations, differing in their habits, who have received the Gospel, and wrought at its spiritual toils. The hand that was beneath the wings of the cherubs represents to us that it was the might of Him, who is the Son of Man, which supporteth the chariot in which He rides."

Strange stories are told of Ephrem. He was wandering in the outskirts of Cæsarea, when he was

---

[1] *Rhythms of St. Ephrem the Syrian*, p. 164.

taken to a church, where he saw St. Basil arrayed in shining robes and seated in a pulpit, with a jewelled mitre on his head, and surrounded by a number of priests, magnificently enrobed. This drew forth from him an exclamation: "I fear our labour is in vain. For if we, who have given up the world, have advanced so little in holiness, what spiritual gifts can we expect to find in one surrounded by so much pomp and glory?" This looks like an imagination on the part of a man who was shocked at the pomp of religious services, and lamented the decay of Christian simplicity. And then the story goes on to say that Basil rose, with the Holy Ghost in the form of a dove on his shoulder, and sent his archdeacon to invite Ephrem into the pulpit. They embraced one another. The same miracle is said to have occurred elsewhere.

CHAPTER V

AFRICAN CHURCHES

1. LET us cross the Mediterranean to "Alexandria the beautiful"—"Crown of Cities," "Mart of the World"—in its meridian splendour during the fourth century.

We meet there with a blind man (born A.D. 309, died 395) named Didymus. He was taught to write on tablets, was renowned as a mathematician, and, by listening to Holy Scripture, learned much of it by heart. It is said that, though blind, "he had an angel's eye," and also that he was famed for his asceticism. He was head of a catechetical school in the city.

Athanasius became Bishop of Alexandria in A.D. 326. A faction disturbed his peace, and his ecclesiastical throne was usurped by George of Cappadocia. Athanasius suffered exile over and over again, and his return, after a prolonged absence, has been commemorated by Gregory Nazianzen, who compares the procession which welcomed him back, to the rising of the Nile. People strewed their garments in the way, and the honour thus done to him, it is said, resembled that paid to Agamemnon when he came back from Troy. Nine churches stood in the city of Alexandria, attended by crowds, so that children suffered from the pressure, and "some were carried home injured, though they did not perish."

Athanasius has been glowingly described by contemporaries, as he was in his life-time, as "virtue itself," as "the great enlightener," and as "the corner-stone of the Church." Also he has been pronounced haughty, hard-headed, narrow-minded, the author of broils, and the source of much unhappiness. Passing by extreme opinions, I must say that the more largely we study the history of his times, and the controversies in which he was engaged, and that the more minutely we look into his personal character, the higher will be our estimate of his worth. Even Gibbon, destitute of sympathy with the sentiments of this orthodox champion, cannot withhold a tribute of respect; and the German sceptical critic, Baur, expresses the opinion that "in modern times, though frequently charged with a passionate love for theological controversy, recent ecclesiastical and doctrinal historians are more and more unanimous in according to him a pure zeal for Christian truth."

A good many letters by Athanasius have been preserved; and a translation of several has recently appeared in a quarto volume edited by Dr. Wace and Dr. Schaff. The Festal Letters are full of warmth, vigour, and simplicity. A letter to the Bishop of Hermopolis (Ep. 49) is very noticeable. He had left his post at a time of persecution. " I fear," says Athanasius, " lest in flying for your own sake you prove to be in peril in the sight of the Lord." " You have caused us grief instead of joy, groaning instead of consolation." " There are some buzzing in your ears, advising you to hide. If they had read the Divine word they would not have so advised you. Moses and Jeremiah did not listen to such counsel. Gird yourself, so as not to leave us alone in the struggle. "[1]

It was a practice with Alexandrian patriarchs to issue " Festal Letters."[2] Those written by Athanasius

---

[1] *Select Library of Nicene and Post-Nicene Fathers*, vol. iv., pp. 557-560.

[2] Some are translated from the original Syriac in the thirty-eighth volume of the Oxford Library.

attained great celebrity. They regulated festivals in other places. So long as he lived, he riveted public attention; and to the end of life was *contra mundum*, rocklike, in resisting Arianism—" very courageous, not afraid, nor dismayed." A milder spirit marked his later days. Basil called him "the Samuel of the Church." His movements were "flights," and he bore the name of Barak —lightning flash. Banishments he endured with patience, and through life was free from all fear but a fear of God.

He was followed in the patriarchate by Cyril, who played a noisy part in Church councils, as will be found on an after page. In his day orthodoxy was in the ascendant, and before it heathenism and heresy sunk prostrate in the dust. The image of Serapis was dashed in pieces. Pagans were terrified, but no judgment followed; and this strengthened Christian faith. A magnificent cathedral rose in place of an old pagan temple, and when Cyril preached in it men clapped their hands, and women waved their handkerchiefs. Monks followed him as a body-guard. Hypatia—who had endeavoured to rival his popularity—was now denounced as an enchantress, and being attacked by a mob under Peter, Cyril's lesson-reader, she fell dead in the street under murderous blows. Cyril zealously opposed Nestorianism, but his spirit and conduct in supporting Church dogmas will not bear close scrutiny.

Neale gives Dioscorus, Cyril's successor, a bad character. His palace was disgraced by public dancers, and the too celebrated Irene was notoriously entertained as the patriarch's concubine.[1] The same historian touches, in connection with Alexandria, the development of Nestorianism there in the first half of the fifth century, and follows it through proceedings at the Council of Ephesus. Alexandria came into connection with that Council, and was subjected to its decisions.

II. In an outlying district of Alexandria lay the see of Ptolemais, occupied from A.D. 375 to about 430 by a remarkable man named Synesius. He had been a friend of Hypatia, and had sympathised in her philosophical principles; after his adoption of Christianity, he continued to manifest Neoplatonic tendencies. For some time, as a country gentleman, he continued fond of field-sports; but, at the same time, was fond of books, public-spirited, a moral man, and married to a lady whom he loved. He gained the good

---

[1] Neale's *Patriarchate of Alexandria*, p. 279.

opinion of Christian people, and, strange to say,
entered the priesthood whilst a disbeliever in the
doctrine of the resurrection. He said : " I never will
believe that the soul is born together with the body.
I will never teach that the world is destined to perish ;
the resurrection, as taught by the Church, seems to
me a dubious and questionable doctrine. I cannot
yield to the prejudices of the vulgar." His mode of
quoting Scripture was very odd. " I do not remember," he would say, " the exact words, but I feel
sure that somewhere in the Bible God is represented
to have spoken so and so." His letters and poems
indicate that inconsistent opinions influenced his
mind, and some might doubt whether he was a
Christian at all ; yet, most wonderful, neighbouring churchmen persuaded him to accept the see
of Ptolemais. It was no uncommon thing in
those days for unsuitable men to seek ecclesiastical
preferments ; here was a case in which one con-
scious of his unfitness was pressed to accept a
sacred office.

Gibbon notices Synesius as having been a disciplinarian. " The Bishop," he says, " exhorted the
clergy, the magistrates, and the people to renounce
all society with the enemies of Christ, to exclude
them from their houses and tables, and refuse them

the common offices of life and the decent rites of burial."[1]

This unique prelate gives an amusing account of an episcopal visitation, when mothers held up to him their uproarious babies, children screamed, women shrieked, and men groaned. His correspondence shows him to have been out of sympathy with his work; but to his honour be it said that his treatment of a worthless governor manifested moral dignity of the noblest kind.

I have said thus much respecting this remarkable man, because the incongruities of his case, with his life and character, throw considerable light on the age in which he lived,—Pagans and Christians, the orthodox and heterodox, were mixed up together in manifold ways, and mutually operated on one another's characters,—remembering this will help us in solving some ecclesiastical perplexities in the sixth century. Christendom, and the secular world surrounding it, were so different then from what they are now, that knowledge of our own times does little to aid us to understand what was going on at that period.

Before quite leaving the neighbourhood of Alex-

---

[1] *Decline and Fall of the Roman Empire*, vol. ii., p. 180.

andria, there is another notability to be mentioned—a striking contrast, in point of character, to the amiable Synesius. I refer to the contemporary patriarch of the renowned African city. Theophilus was his name, and the historian Tillemont justly says his theological knowledge was celebrated in the Church; but he proceeds to remark, "Woe to him in whom the knowledge which puffeth up is stronger than the charity which edifieth." Few men have had less charity than this famous prelate, the implacable enemy of Chrysostom. "There is little," it has been truly said, "to point the moral of his life. It is the deterioration which too great power can produce in one whose zeal in the cause of religion, although in itself genuine and active, is not combined with singleness of heart." Socrates gives Theophilus a bad character—" violent, cunning, and malicious." [1]

We are now on the edge of the dark ages—all the darker for the brilliant light which preceded and followed. As we approach the new crisis, the remark suggests itself that the period just before premonished what was to follow. When we take in all which has been told, surely we must see that a deteriorating

---

[1] Socrates, *Eccl. Hist.*, v., c. 16; vi., c. 9. Theophilus figures in the proceedings against Chrysostom at "the Oak." See Alice Gardiner's *Synesius of Cyrene*, chap. v.

change was at hand in the sixth century. The old Roman civilisation was advanced in decay, drawing its last breath, and the Gothic foe stood knocking at the gate. Had primitive Christianity retained its strength, had apostolic zeal, holiness, and faith been in the ascendant, pagan inroads would have been made in vain ; but the Church, as to the mass of its professors, was becoming weaker every day in faith, prayer, and holiness. If we could reckon the two populations, the old Romans and the young Goths, we should find the last stronger than the first. What was likely to follow but the deterioration of Christian influence on its beneficent side ? Synesius complains of "wandering bishops, deprived of their sees in times of trouble, and who refused to return when allowed to do so."[1]

Synesius was far from a perfect character, but it has been remarked that, without seeking to represent him as more of a philosopher or more of a Christian than he actually was, it is fair to consider him as an honest though sometimes erring man. " He was led, in later life, to adopt habits and phrases to which in his youth he had been a stranger, but never relinquished his grasp of those principles

---

[1] Gardiner's *Synesius of Cyrene*, p. 139.

which had first made life to have a meaning for him."[1]

In his latter days he was plunged into great trouble by one named Andronicus, Civil Governor of Lybia. The story of the two furnishes an original illustration of Church and State at war with one another. Andronicus was tyrannical and cruel; Synesius resisted his abominable designs. Andronicus increased the taxes that he might replenish his exhausted exchequer. He seized wealthy citizens, and tortured them with thumb-screws, gloating over their sufferings, as well as rejoicing over his own gains. If the Bishop befriended a sufferer, the man in power resented it by superadded oppression and cruelty. Synesius excommunicated the official: this made matters worse. Tempted to resign his episcopate, he resisted temptation and called on his brother bishops to help him in the execution of his sentence. Synesius so far succeeded; but something like civil war ensued. Moreover he lost two of his children, and suffered from illness; at the end he prepared to enter a hermitage.

III. Hippo Regius, in Numidia, on the North-West African coast, was not a city comparable with some

---

[1] Gardiner's *Synesius*, p. 166.

we have visited in the East; but Cicero mentions it as a noble and illustrious municipality. Plains to the north were dominated by mountains, whose lower slopes are still covered with chestnut trees. Hippo was destroyed by Vandals, and on its ruins there now stands the town of Bona. An aqueduct remains which conveyed water from the mountain to this city, of which Augustine became bishop. We can picture him, slender, with a slight stoop, the hue of his face betokening Numidian descent. He said, "A bishop may be allowed to wear costly raiment, but it does not become me, the son of poor parents." He commonly dressed in a black habit, with a leathern girdle, and sat daily at table with his monastic brethren, saying he had "never found any men better or worse than those who dwelt in a monastery."

He lived on vegetables, and encouraged free conversation at table, but always excluded what could be considered as scandal. He would preach five days in succession, sometimes twice a day. He bountifully relieved the poor, and is known to have melted down church plate for the redemption of prisoners. We fancy we can see and hear him in church, occupying the ambo, or pulpit, whilst the clergy sat round him on stone benches, some employed in noting down his discourses. The laity listened standing. They repaired to him for advice in settling disputes ; and he would apologise for injustice, innocently done, saying, " Often in strait places the hen treads with all her weight upon the chickens whom she warms —but she is not the less their mother."

Augustine was a great preacher, not like Chrysostom or any oratorical Greek ; nor are his homilies of the same class as those of Ambrose, whom he admired so much. Augustine's, however, are at times mystical, and so far resemble the Milan bishop's ; but they have a character of their own, and no doubt his thoughtful hearers came to be moulded after their teacher's pattern. Let me select a discourse of his on Matt. xii.—Blasphemy against the Holy Ghost. The leading idea is that *final impenitence* is unpardonable sin—a truth, however, which is scarcely the lesson of that passage. The sermon is long, and the treatment indicates need of thoughtfulness on the hearers' part, in order to apprehend its drift and point. Altogether it makes a demand on *sustained* attention to the end. Such attention was indispensable in order to a full apprehension of the preacher's design. It does not resemble Chrysostom's oratory, and presents a contrast between patristic and present preaching.

Next to theological treatises and sermons, Augustine's letters are of value for understanding his opinions as well as his spiritual life ; for acquaintance with the man himself no biography can be so satisfactory as his correspondence. " No controversy of his age was settled without his voice, and it is in his letters that we chiefly see the vastness of his empire, the variety of subjects on which appeal was made to him, and the deference with which his judgment was received. Inquiring philosophers, puzzled statesmen, angry heretics, pious ladies, all found their way to the Bishop of Hippo." [1] In many of his letters I have been deeply interested. At the same time I must confess he often dwells at inconvenient length upon points of controversy important in his own day, but unknown or forgotten in ours.

When Augustine reached his seventy-second year, he thought it wise, as most men who live so long should do, to seek for assistance, and if possible a successor. The record of this Hippo election is full of amusement.[2] The person thought suitable was a priest named Heraclius, who had preached occasionally in Augustine's church, but not in Augustine's hearing. One Sunday in September, A.D. 426, the basilica was crowded from end to end. After explaining the

---

[1] Preface to translated letters.
[2] Augustine's Letters, CCXIII.

important step about to be taken, the Bishop put the question to the vote; immediately the congregation twenty-three times over shouted: "Let us give thanks to God; let us give praises to Christ." "O Christ, hear us; prolong Augustine's life," were words repeated sixteen times. "You for our father; you for our Bishop," were uttered eight times. Then Augustine more fully explained what he wished to be done respecting Heraclius, adding, "You see that the notaries of the Church gather up what I say and what you say; my words and your acclamations do not fall to the ground." Again there followed cries, "O Christ, hear; prolong Augustine's life." At last six times the people shouted, "You for our father; Heraclius for our Bishop." It appears that this repetition was a traditional Roman practice. It obtained, we are told, when the Senate elected Tacitus to succeed Aurelian in A.D. 275, the people then exclaiming, ten and twenty times, "We do not make you a soldier but an Emperor."

The Vandal invasion of Africa happened in the fifth century. Cities, villages, churches were destroyed, and Hippo, with its fortifications, was not spared. In the midst of devastation Augustine lay on his deathbed. As he saw his end approach, he requested those who lived in the house not to enter his chamber except with his physician, that at other times he might be left alone to hold communion with God. He ordered the penitential Psalms to be written in large letters and affixed to the wall opposite his bed. In loneliness of meditation he spent the last six weeks of life.

He died August the 28th or 29th, A.D. 430.[1]

---

[1] In the ante-Nicene period, Carthage under Cyprian contained a large and prosperous population, but at the period we have reached, connected with Augustine, the city was destroyed. With regard to Augustine's sermons, they must, to a large extent, have been extempore, and we have brief reports of them. The same may be said of those by Chrysostom.

CHAPTER VI

WESTERN BISHOPS

WE turn to those we find in France during the fourth century, and call to mind at once a difference, in point of extent, between these sees and those we are familiar with now in our own country. A French bishop of the fourth century was, in many instances, more like a clergyman of some large parish than like a prelate now, in charge of a little kingdom.

The first here coming under our notice is Hilary of Poictiers, born between A.D. 315 and 320. He was married and had a daughter, and was chosen to preside by the citizens of the place whilst he was still a layman.

Banished by the reigning Emperor for three years, he was separated from his flock all that time; and one wonders what became of those poor sheep in the wilderness. Absent from France, and writing to his Majesty, we find him saying, "To thee, O

Constantine, do I proclaim, what I would not have addressed to Nero, thou art warring against God and the Church, overthrowing religion, tyrant as thou art." Hilary's theological opinions were, in one respect, broad and kind, but at the same time, in reference to some Church and State questions, intensely bitter. He treated semi-Arians with courtesy and kindness, while he violently treated Arians of a decided stamp. He has been regarded by critics under very different aspects. Augustine pronounces him "an illustrious doctor, a keen defender of the Catholic Church"; and Jerome speaks of his style as resembling the flowing Rhone, and of his character as a noble tree in the world's great garden. Daille judges this bishop with severity, while Dorner is an enthusiastic admirer. Erasmus thought him dangerously curious. Gibbon sympathetically quotes these words from Hilary : " It is a thing equally deplorable and dangerous, that there are amongst us as many creeds as opinions, as many doctrines as inclinations, and as many sources of blasphemy as there are faults among us, all because we make creeds in an arbitrary way." [1]

---

[1] Hilary, *Ad Constantium*, i., 4, 5. It is very odd to find Hilary saying that, after his baptism and he had been some time in his diocese, he had never heard the Nicene Creed (*De Synodis*, c. xci.).

Hilary's exile ended A.D. 360, and he spent three years on his homeward journey to Poictiers. He died in A.D. 368.

Hilary, a namesake in the fifth century, was Bishop of Arles, and seems to have resembled him in decision of character; for, we are told, *quicquid vult, valde vult.* Arles was a city of great magnificence, as its Roman remains at the present day abundantly testify. Ecclesiastically it was important, claiming as it did authority over a large part of Gaul. Hilary held a council at Vienne, where he deposed a priest named Chalcedonius, who appealed to Rome; and Leo, Bishop there, interposed on his behalf—an interference with Hilary's rights which the latter said he would not allow. Forthwith he crossed the snowy Alps on foot to protest against Leo's interference. This typified what often happened afterwards. France protested against Rome, but Rome would not listen to France. Hilary of Arles was not suspected of sympathising with Arianism, but he was charged with leaning towards Pelagian opinions.

In the fourth century Martin, Bishop of Tours, appears prominent amongst Gallic prelates. "Yet we have no works written by him, nor any account of his being influential in Church councils or eloquent as a preacher. Notwithstanding, he remains, undeniably, the one prelate who has made a very deep impression on France, and a large part of Christendom beyond the limits of his adopted country."[1] The story of dividing his cloak with the beggar is amongst the most popular legends of the Church, and a picture of the Bishop on horseback, sword in hand, cutting the mantle in two and giving half to the shivering suppliant, is familiar to every one. Some incredible legends about him, the Duc de Broglie regards as external representations of his spiritual conflicts against passion and sin. Notices of him by Sulpicius attracted much attention, especially that of his presence at a banquet given by the notorious Emperor Maximus at Treves. A cup of wine offered to the Bishop by that criminal usurper, instead of being returned to royal hands, was by Martin passed on to his attendant presbyter. The story is often told as a specimen of priestly arrogance; but Cardinal Newman reads it thus: " The Emperor wished him first to taste, and then to pass it to himself with the *blessing and good auspice* which a bishop could convey; but he *saw through the artifice*, and instead of handing the cup to the Emperor, passed it to his

---

[1] Dr. Cazenove's *Life of Martin* (S.P.C.K.).

own presbyter, as being higher in true rank, as Sulpicius says, than any other, even the most noble who were there assembled."[1] Whether or not Martin saw through "the artifice," it is quite plain what he thought of the dignity of the priesthood. It should be remembered, however, that he disapproved of the conduct of other bishops on important occasions. He subsequently declined attendance at ecclesiastical assemblies because he found them unprofitable.

There is a legend of St. Martin worth relating. Once the devil appeared to him clothed in royal robes and decked with gems, announcing that he was Christ Himself, come to pay him a visit before the second advent. The Bishop replied that he could not believe his visitor till he saw him show *the mark of the nails*. Dr. Newman, in his *Church of the Fathers*, makes this application of the vision : " Christ comes not in pride of intellect or reputation for philosophy. These are robes which Satan now wears. Many are abroad, and more are issuing from the pit. They display precious gifts of mind, beauty, richness, depth, originality. Christian, look hard at them, with Martin, in silence, and ask them for the print of the nails."

The case of Priscillian will come before us on a

---

[1] Newman's *Hist. Sketches*, ii., p. 193.

future page. He was accused of heresy before a secular tribunal, which Martin of Tours opposed, not on any modern ground of civil and religious liberty, but because he condemned civil interference with religious matters. Afterwards we meet with him at Treves, where he refused to sign a document involving what he disapproved. He afterwards declined to attend Church synods, and confined himself to episcopal duties at home. His funeral was attended by two thousand monks. After his death Roman booksellers declared no books were in such demand as Martin's *Biography* and *Dialogues*.

Before I leave Gallic ecclesiastical notabilities of the early period now touched upon, there is one, not a bishop, who here demands a passing notice— Vincentius Lirinensis, monk of a monastery on the shores of the Mediterranean, who died about A.D. 450. He wrote a book entitled *Commonitorium*, in which he laid down as a law of Christian belief the threefold authority, *Quod ubique, quod semper, quod ab omnibus, creditum est*. About sixty years ago this dictum was on every English theologian's lips, either for acceptance or for rejection. The *Tracts for the Times* gave it publicity,[1] and "Tractarians," as they were then

---

See *Records of the Church*, Nos. xxiv. and xxv.

called, fought valiantly in support of this principle. The Church's *authority* was maintained to be necessary as a support of theological teaching. No doubt the *ipse dixit* of Vincentius Lirinensis was generally adopted by Gallic believers in the fifth century. The right of private judgment must have been out of the question at that period.[1]

From Gaul we proceed to Lombardy, where we meet with Ambrose, Bishop of Milan. It is difficult to form an adequate conception of his character and influence. The story of his election to the episcopate is curious. A vacancy occurred, and a crowd assembled to choose who should fill it, when a child in the throng cried out, "Ambrose is bishop! Ambrose is bishop!" The cry was attributed to a Divine impulse. Ambrose was at the time Civil Governor, a difficulty overcome by the inspired decision. Basil called it an episcopal translation by God Himself. It is an original illustration of the alliance between Church and State.

Augustine's description of Ambrose, as he appeared at the time of Augustine's conversion, makes the Milan archbishop visible to us. We see him

---

[1] I have more to say about Gaul in a chapter on Incipient Nationalities.

in a cloister or under a verandah sitting silent and reading intently, yet accessible to his flock, "whose weaknesses he served." "That man of God," says his young admirer, "received me as a father, and showed me an episcopal kindness on my coming. Therefore I began to love him not only as teacher, but as friend. I listened to his preaching, testing his eloquence, whether it corresponded with his fame. I delighted in the sweetness of his discourse, while I opened my heart to the eloquence of his speech, and, by degrees, to the truth he uttered."[1]

Ambrose came into collision with the civil power. An Arian bishop had occupied a church from which Catholics ejected him. Justina, an Arian, mother of Valentinian, the Emperor, demanded the restoration of it to former occupants. How the building came into the possession of Arians I do not know. At all events, Ambrose declared that the church belonged to Christ, and must not remain in heretical hands. He would not, in this affair, submit to secular control. "Palaces," he said, "belonged to the Emperor, but churches belonged to the Lord and to His servants."

The orthodox party supported the Bishop, and

---

[1] Augustine's *Confessions*, v., 13.

joined in resisting secular interference. When imperial officers entreated Ambrose to interfere and repress popular violence, he declined to do it, and told his sister that he wept amidst the uproar, and prayed no blood might be shed; if it were, he wished it might be his own, not only for the sake of his flock, but for the sake of the heretics too.[1] He avowed as his maxim that "priests bestowed temporal authority, but did not assume it"; "nor," he might have added, "submit to it." He said they had a dominion of their own in the midst of personal helplessness. "When I am weak then am I strong."

Theodosius I., who occupied the imperial throne from 375 to 395, came to reside in Milan, and there was brought into contact with Ambrose. A Jewish synagogue at Acquileia had been burnt down in a riot, and the Emperor commanded it should be rebuilt at the expense of those responsible for the disturbance. Ambrose resisted this, and, inspired by anti-Jewish prejudices, thought perhaps there was more cause for approval than censure in the destruction of an edifice belonging to the race that crucified our Lord. After Theodosius had given his order he attended church, when Ambrose took

---

[1] *Epist.*, xx.

occasion to point with displeasure at his Majesty's proceeding. "So, my Lord Bishop, you have been preaching at me!" exclaimed the royal listener when the preacher left his pulpit. "I have not been preaching *at* you, but *for your good*," was the reply; to which Theodosius rejoined, "Well, my order about the Bishop's rebuilding the synagogue was a little too severe, but that is set right."

What afterwards happened is more remarkable. The people of Thessalonica quarrelled with their magistrates, and became rebellious. Tidings of their conduct—which included the crime of murder—reached Milan, and exasperated his Majesty, who retaliated by authorising a massacre of citizens. News of this reached Ambrose, who reproached the Emperor when he came to church, and forbade his participation in the Lord's Supper. Abashed by the Bishop's rebuke, Theodosius made no resistance, but submitted to discipline. Eight months elapsed; when Christmas came, he was restored, and re-approached the altar.[1] We are told that he felt he had committed a great fault in the sight of God, and determined to confess it before the people.

---

[1] This story is related by Theodoret (*Hist.*, v., 18), but is doubted by some critics, I think without sufficient reason.

"You allow your temper to act the judge," said Ambrose, " and permit passion instead of reason to pronounce sentence; you must make a law which shall render such hasty orders as yours null and void. Let thirty days elapse before a sentence of death or confiscation be executed." The Emperor consented. Then laying aside his regal robes and decorations, he entered church, and, falling prostrate on the pavement, smote his breast, saying, " My soul cleaveth unto the dust, O quicken me according to Thy word."[1]

After reading this memorable scene between the Archbishop and the Emperor (the latter meekly submitting to the faithful reproof of the former) it is touching to learn that Theodosius expired in the arms of Ambrose, commending to his care two orphan sons. There was a wonderful fascination in the Bishop's influence. He wrote a catechism for a pagan queen, who was so touched by it that she started at once to see his face and receive his

---

[1] Schaff in his *History of Christian Church*, iii., gives a good sketch of Ambrose, with original authorities. The chief works of Ambrose are the *Hexameron* in six books, on the days of the Creation; a book on Paradise; several about Cain and Abel, Noah, Abraham and Isaac, and other subjects. He was greater in administration than authorship.

blessing, but when she reached Milan he was gone. Ambrose expired on the evening of Good Friday, A.D. 397, immediately after receiving the Lord's Supper.

I must not conclude my notice of Ambrose without referring to an incident which has been a subject of animated controversy in our own day.

A church was about to be consecrated at Milan, and for this purpose a deposition of saintly relics was deemed desirable, according to ideas of that day. Ambrose gave orders that the pavement in a neighbouring church should be dug up with a hope of finding what was wished, though *why the particular spot was selected* does not appear. A vision is mentioned, but not on sufficient authority. Skeletons were found of an extraordinary size. Names previously unknown were given to the remains, and miracles were said to be wrought in those who touched them; a blind man laid his hands on the pall covering the relics, and was believed to have thereby recovered sight. There was difference of opinion as to the genuineness of these relics. Arians denied the orthodox report. The case now became a party question.

The man saying he had received his sight was

cross-examined, and the case engrossed general attention; but nobody—as far as I can discover—inquired into the origin of the marvellous discovery. Why was a particular grave opened? The fourth and fifth centuries abounded in credulity; nobody can read the twenty-second book of Augustine's *De Civitate* without seeing that.

The *Lausiac History*, by Palladius, Bishop of Helenopolis, abounds in tales picked up amongst Egyptian hermits. When demand for the wonderful was made, the demand was abundantly supplied. Palladius tells a story of some woman who was taken for a mare, until a spell on the eyes of her friends was miraculously removed. The *Lausiac History* is quoted by Sozomen, and Socrates makes special reference to the author. After detailing stories of monks, he tells us "there is a specific treatise on the subject by the Monk Palladius, who was a disciple of Evagrius, in which all these particulars are minutely detailed."[1] The credulity of that age was marvellous.

---

[1] Socrates, *Eccl. Hist.*, iv., 23.

CHAPTER VII

EPISCOPAL ROME AND ITS CATACOMBS

314—604

WHEN Constantine established the Church in connection with the Empire, Sylvester was Bishop of Rome. He had been exiled to Soracte, and then reinstated in his episcopal position. Platina, historian of the Popes, says the Emperor granted to those who presided over the see that "they should wear a diadem of gold, set with precious gems," a tradition, probably, which sprang up in after times.

Bishop Julius (A.D. 337—352) welcomed Athanasius to Rome, when he came there during his exile. His successor, Liberius, was accused of heresy, according to Jerome's report, and Athanasius says of him that he gave way, and, from fear of death, subscribed an Arian confession.[1] The fall of this

---

[1] *Historia Arianorum*, p. 41.

bishop was unquestioned till the fifteenth century, when a controversy arose on the subject, which would lead us astray from our subject, did we attempt to follow it.

Damasus was candidate for the see in 367, and the contest occasioned riotous proceedings, the rival candidates being supported by armed adherents. It is curious to find that Theodoric the Goth, an Arian, was requested to take part in the unseemly strife ; he decided in favour of Damasus. Peace was not secured by that decision. Charges were brought against the new bishop by two deacons, who, however, were condemned as false accusers. Scandals at that time attracted the notice of Ammianus Marcellinus,[1] who satirised the Ecclesiastical Court. "Considering," he remarks, "the wealth of the city, they who covet such things, having obtained these honours, are justified in pursuing them, even though it be with contention, for they will be enriched with the gifts of matrons, and will ride, sumptuously clad, in chariots, and make profuse entertainments, vying with regal banquets." But the writer candidly adds that "at the time, such a case was exceptional, and the Romans might wisely follow the habits of pro-

---

[1] *Hist.*, XX., xxvii., 3.

vincial pastors, who by plainness of attire and preparations for their dinner-table commend themselves to God by their religious simplicity." Light is incidentally thrown on the character of Damasus by a letter found in the correspondence of a distinguished contemporary, Basil the Great. He deprecates sending his brother, Gregory of Nyssa, on a mission to Rome, whilst Damasus was bishop there. These are his words: "His conference" (*i.e.* Gregory's) "with a mild and benignant man might be very valuable, but not with one so exalted" (namely, Damasus), "raised above the earth, and seated on high, therefore unable to listen to any one speaking truth; and on lower ground, how can it be well to send a man altogether unaccustomed to flattery?"[1] The Bishop of Rome then ruled the provinces of middle and lower Italy, with the islands of Corsica, Sardinia, and Sicily.

The next Roman bishop claiming notice is Leo the Great, A.D. 440—460. He was a strict disciplinarian, and to his clear oversight and unremitting energy, between one and two hundred letters of his, still preserved, bear ample testimony.

---

[1] Basil had no love for Damasus, treated him as an equal, not recognising the supremacy of the Roman see, and spoke of "Western superciliousness" (Ep. ii., 215-239).

We have seen what kind of man Hilary of Arles was. He came[1] into collision with Leo. But Leo gained the ear of Valentinian III., and obtained from the Emperor a letter speaking of Peter's merits and Rome's dignity. Valentinian said that "Leo's commands would be valid throughout Gaul, even without imperial sanction, for what in the Church can be beyond the authority of such a pontiff?" Leo responded, "Your empire is given you not only to rule the world, but to defend the Church."[2] It is a blot on the name of Leo that he vindicated the persecution of Priscillian, and employed force as well as argument against the Manicheans.

In writing to the Bishop of Thessalonica, Leo is seen pushing authority East as well as West. "Our care extends over *all the Churches*, for nothing less than this is required of us by the Lord, who committed to the Apostle Peter the primacy of apostolic

---

[1] See page 228 of this volume.

[2] "Nothing can exceed the ecclesiastical authority which is recognised as belonging to the Pope, in the constitution of Valentinian, which accompanied Leo's letter into Gaul, in the year 448, on occasion of the conflict between Leo and Hilary of Arles (*Leo Mag.*, Ep. xi.)."—*Dictionary of Christian Biography*, art. "Leo I.," vol. iii., p. 655. That Valentinian was much under Leo's influence is proved by Leo's letters in A.D. 440 (Ep. liv.—lviii.).

dignity as a reward for his faith, grounding the universal Church on him as its foundation; in fulfilment, then, of this obligation of solicitude which lies upon us, we would share it with those who are joined with us in a common office, and we appoint as our vicegerent Anastasius, our brother bishop, following the example of our predecessors, whose memory we honour, and we have adjured him to be on the watch to prevent any unlawful presumption; and we admonish you to give him obedience in matters connected with ecclesiastical discipline."[1]

Ambrose and Hilary may be said, through their own claims, and by their own submission, however qualified, to have raised a scaffolding for the papal structure, but the chief corner-stone was laid by Leo himself. On his birthday, as the date of his consecration is termed, he preached a sermon maintaining that Peter was chief of the Apostles, and that he was the channel through which grace flowed to his brethren. Then followed the assertion that Roman bishops were Peter's successors; that they, like him, held a mediatorial place; moreover, that as the metropolis of the empire was Rome, so the Church in that city through him became Mother of Christendom.[2]

[1] I adopt the translation in Gore's *Leo the Great*, p. 104.
[2] Serm. ii., 2, iii., Epistle X.

No man but a strong one operating on minds in harmony with his own could have secured obedience to claims so unfounded and so unreasonable.

One incident in Leo's episcopate has been magnified. Tradition says: "Attila, 'scourge of God,' when he was making havoc in that country, saw two venerable persons, supposed to be the Apostles Peter and Paul, standing by the side of the Bishop, whilst he was speaking to the fierce warrior." Veritable history informs us that when the warrior was approaching Rome an embassy from the city was sent to avert his vengeance. Ambassadors were graciously received, and it is added that the Bishop was one of them, who by his striking appearance made a favourable impression as he entered the barbarian's tent. Topographers endeavoured to decide where the interview took place, fixing on a spot near the charming Lago de Garda, in "Virgil's country, within sight of the very farm where Tityrus and Melibœus chatted at evening under the fig-tree."[1] By the payment of a ransom Rome was saved from Attila's soldiery.

During the Roman bishopric of Felix III. (A.D. 483—492) a strife arose respecting the Alexandrian

---

[1] Hodgkins' *Italy and her Invaders*, vol. ii., p. 178.

see, still more from a Monophysite controversy during the Chalcedonian Council. The Eastern Emperor Zeno (A.D. 474—475 and 477—491) proposed his Henoticon, or plan of union, between Eutychians and Nestorians. This was offensive to Rome, and its bishop threatened with excommunication all who adhered to the Eastern patriarch. Later Roman prelates took part in the conflict.

The fascinating Theodora, wife of the Eastern Emperor Justinian, brought under her influence Vigilius I., Bishop of Rome (A.D. 537—555). She sent an emissary to the Western capital to bring over to her by force that humiliated prelate, and this clever agent actually seized his Holiness as he was officiating in the Church of St. Cecilia, and conveyed him to Constantinople. It is said that at the passage of Vigilius down the Tiber people followed the Bishop with curses, and also pelted him with sticks and stones, using this exprobation, "Mischievous hast thou been to the city of Rome, and may mischief go along with thee." Pelagius I. immediately succeeded, and is accused of causing calamities which befell Vigilius.

In following these pontiffs we have passed by the fall of both Roman City and Empire in the fifth century. That catastrophe belongs not to Church history, but we may quote what Augustine tells us in his *City of God*, how places of Christian worship became refuges for the besieged :—

"Thither did such of the enemy as had any pity convey those to whom they had given quarter, lest any, less mercifully disposed, might fall upon them. And, indeed, when even those murderers who everywhere else showed themselves pitiless came to these spots where that was forbidden which the licence of war permitted in every other place, their furious rage for slaughter was bridled and their eagerness to take prisoners was quenched. Thus escaped multitudes who now reproach the Christian religion, and impute to Christ the ills that have befallen their city; but the preservation of their own life—a boon which they owe to the respect entertained for Christ by the barbarians—they attribute not to our Christ, but to their own luck. And they ought to attribute it to the spirit of these Christian times, that, contrary to the custom of war, these bloodthirsty barbarians spared them, and spared them for Christ's sake, whether this mercy was actually shown in promiscuous places, or in those places specially dedicated to Christ's name, and of which the very largest were selected as sanctuaries, that full scope might thus be given to the expansive compassion which desired that a large multitude might find shelter there."[1]

Gregory the Great became Bishop of Rome in A.D. 590. He appointed stations for Lent solemnities and other great festivals, on which occasions we find him riding on horseback, escorted by deacons and other attendants, from the Lateran to St. Peter's and St. Maria Maggiore. He was ceremoniously robed by archdeacons, and then conducted to the choir, preceded by incense-bearers and men carrying seven candlesticks. Psalms were sung as he reached his seat behind the altar, and he himself habitually preached on chief occasions. I remember once noticing, in the Church of Nereo ad Achilles, a part of Gregory's 20th homily engraved on the back of an episcopal chair.

Thinking of him as resident in Rome, no visitor to the city can omit walking to St. Gregorio, where stood the Bishop's residence. Our forefathers inspired his pity as he thought of the little boys in the Forum, offered for sale as slaves, who, as he said, might from *Angles* be transformed by Divine grace into *angels*.

The interest which Gregory took in the conversion

---

[1] *De Civitate Dei*, i., 1.

of Britain was very great, and cannot fairly be set down to the credit of earthly ambition, intent upon extension of authority and rule: whatever we may think of his ecclesiastical position from a Protestant point of view, it is only fair to recognise his missionary zeal, manifested by the interest he took in Augustine's proceedings. As to Gregory's theological opinions, I may add he believed that for some minor transgressions there is a purgatorial fire previous to the final judgment.[1] As to his regard for literature, he has been accused of burning a library of heathen books, but Tiraboschi[2] has defended him against that charge, though Eichhorn[3] quotes language of Gregory showing his neglect of human learning.

Looking at Gregory as incipient Pope, we are reminded of his correspondence with John the Faster, Patriarch of Constantinople. John assumed the title of Ecumenical Patriarch. Gregory said the title was "foolish, pestiferous, and profane—a sign of Antichrist's approach." Yet what was wrong at Constantinople was soon after right in Rome. "Peter's successors," said Gregory, "had not claimed ecumenical authority, though they might have done."

---

[1] *Dial.*, iv., 39. [2] Vol. iii., p. 102. [3] Vol. ii., p. 443.

Gregory's account of the apostolic authority claimed for his own see is strange enough. "It is," he says, "in three places—Antioch, Alexandria, and Rome. Peter was at Antioch seven years. In Alexandria he was represented by Mark. In Rome he died. *Therefore* the three sees are one, and the three bishoprics are one in Him who said, 'I am in My Father, and you in Me, and I in you.'"[1] In contrast with this wonderful assumption, Gregory called himself " Servus servorum Dei." It should be added that, though *he* objected to the title "*Ecumenical*" assumed by his Eastern brother, that title was adopted by subsequent Bishops of Rome.

The development of patriarchal power under Gregory appears reaching a point only short of its later supremacy. There can be no doubt control over the West was then claimed, and conceded to a great extent. Episcopal power in Europe was enhanced not only by what might be called ecclesiastical prerogative, but further by the bestowment of property on a so-called successor of the Apostle Peter. The Bishop became a large landholder, having estates in Italy, Sicily, and elsewhere. Waggons by road and corn-ships by sea conveyed to his barns load after load of rich grain.

---

[1] Ep. xlvi.

Gregory has left behind him eight hundred letters, which throw light on his affairs. It may be gathered from them how much of business he had to superintend, how many churches and monasteries were under his control. An interesting incident appears. A bishop took possession of a Jews' synagogue and made it a church. Gregory decided that the building could not be restored to its rightful owners now it was consecrated, but the value of it was to be paid to them in money. Touching Gregory's letters, historical justice claims the remark that subserviency to the great, the flattery of princes, and connivance at crime where it ought to have been rebuked have been fully proved against him over and over again. An instance of it appears in his correspondence with Queen Brunhilda. She is truly designated as "one of the Jezebels of history"; but Gregory expresses joy on account of her "Christian spirit,"[1] no doubt because of her liberality to the Church.

Gregory accomplished three results which became

---

[1] The view taken of Gregory's character (*Hist. of the Later Roman Empire*, by Bury, vol. ii., pp. 151-158) is, I think, on the whole, just. The Bishop's political and military policy was effective. His conduct in relation to the accession of Phocas to the Eastern throne, and the way in which he wrote to Brunhilda, are indefensible. Yet when, as Mr. Bury remarks, "we

main props of papal power—*i.e.* exemption of monasteries from episcopal control, freedom of priests from civil jurisdiction, and effective administration of Peter's patrimony.

Notice may here be taken of Gregory's authorship. The best known work of his is a Commentary on the Book of Job. " One who treats of Holy Writ," he says, " should be like a river which sometimes overflows its banks, and then returns to its own channel."[1] The Bishop's exposition has no banks at all. It overflows in one vast deluge of allegorical renderings. His book on pastoral care was translated into Greek by order of the Emperor, and into English by the pen of our good Alfred. The work is fourfold, to use the author's words, " that it may approach the reader by ordered steps : first, how a man should enter into office ; secondly, how he should live afterwards ; thirdly, how he should teach as well as live ; and fourthly, how a teacher ought to take care that his life and teaching do not puff him up." Many of

---

take into account the ideas of that age, in which heresy was looked on as the deadliest sin and religious zeal as efficient to cancel many crimes, it is hardly to be wondered that Gregory treated Brunhilda with respect." This, however, admits that he did not rise above the opinions and habits of his age.

[1] Introductory Epistle, ii.

Gregory's instructions are admirable, and it is astonishing how a man who wrote so well on pastoral care could compose the *Dialogues* which bear his name.

At the time of Gregory's death, ecclesiastical Rome was on the high road to supremacy. As we trace the steps we find nothing like them in the world's history. They are not matched by any in Sparta or Athens. The gradual growth of Rome's empire was fostered by military conquest and senatorial wisdom. It culminated under Cæsar Augustus. What followed down to the time of Constantine's reign served to place the imperial city above all others in the world. The city, by politics and war, prepared for its spiritual supremacy. This mother city of mankind was made by Roman bishops to be mistress of Christendom. The process required time. The city was not built in a day, nor was the supreme authority of its Church.

When in Rome many years ago I selected the Catacombs of Callistus for examination, and having reached them on a beautiful afternoon was admitted into a garden, instead of entering through the Church of St. Sebastian. With my guide I descended several steps, carrying a lighted taper, and presently found myself in a narrow winding passage with a number of recesses cut in the walls. They are generally arranged in three tiers, one above another. Some are long, sufficiently so as to receive a common-sized corpse. Others are short, pronounced to be graves for children ; but, more probably, as Rochette thinks, unfinished graves. Among openings of unequal size are small square ones containing cups. Some have a little vessel represented on the border, others with part of the slab broken away have dust and bones remaining inside. Many are covered with tiles and left vacant. I noticed sarcophagi with sculptures of boys squeezing grapes. The passages widened and bent confusedly, so as to defy attempts to make out the topography. Some openings had been blocked up with stones. Ascents and descents and passages one above another bring into view frescoes and classical monuments, ornamented with a dove and a shepherd watching his flock. There are excavated chapels, containing rude representations of the marriage at Cana, the healing of the paralytic, and the casting of Jonah into the sea. One sees confused figures of peacocks, sea-horses, dolphins, and other objects, with Christians kneeling down to pray by martyrs' graves.

The establishment of Christianity commenced a new era in the history of the Catacombs. Subterranean pagan interments came to an end, perhaps gradually. Damasus repaired and decorated these chambers of the dead, constructing new staircases for pilgrims, as well as searching after remains of martyrs. This excitement did not last long, and between A.D. 375 and 400 subterranean interments were only one in three. The taking of Rome by Alaric so affected Catacomb burials that scarcely an instance at that period is recorded. But pilgrims flocked in crowds, and the Church must have been excited and increased in consequence.

Jerome[1] tells us: "In Rome, whilst engaged in literary pursuits, I was accustomed, in company with others of my own age and actuated by similar feelings to my own, to visit the sepulchres of Apostles and Martyrs, and often to go down into the crypts, dug in the earth's heart, where walls on either side are lined with dead bodies, and where the darkness is so intense that one almost realises the prophet's words, 'They go down alive into Hades,' though here and there a scanty aperture, ill deserving the name of window, admits scarcely light enough to mitigate the gloom which reigns around; and as we advance with cautious steps we are forcibly reminded of Virgil's words, 'Horror on all sides, even the silence terrifies one's mind.'"[2]

---

[1] Born about 345, died 420. [2] *In Ezechiel*, c. xl.

There is a famous pictorial representation in the chapel pertaining to the cemetery of Marcellinus and Peter. It represents a half-circular table, at which persons are seated, with a matron-like looking lady placed at each end. A smaller table stands in front, with some eatables placed on it, with a servant near, apparently waiting for commands. A tall vessel is placed in front of the group, and on the wall at the back are two inscriptions, one with the words " Irene, da calda " (" Peace, give me hot water"), and the other " Agape, misce mi " (" Love, mix me some wine "). Some have supposed this picture depicts an agape, or love-feast, such as early accompanied the Eucharist, or Lord's Supper, but afterwards became a usage by itself, and at last a scandal, so as to cause its being abolished. Other critics regard the picture as intended to represent something quite different, *i.e.* a funeral supper, which seems to me an improbable explanation.

We find in the Catacombs at the period under review representations of Noah's Ark and the dove with an olive branch in its mouth, also of Abraham offering up Isaac, Moses on Mount Sinai receiving God's law, the prophet Jonah swallowed by a whale, Daniel in the lions' den. Conspicuous amongst such representations is a portrait of our blessed Lord, with a noble head and flowing locks, and a countenance some think fashioned after that of Jupiter. All these bear witness to the fact that many Romans of later times were different from their fathers under Cæsar Augustus. The Church had degenerated, but it still was free from many beliefs and practices which prevailed in after ages.

A large collection of Catacomb slabs, without date, evidently from their character and writing belong to an early period. Many inscriptions are rudely carved and badly spelt, showing the ignorance of survivors and the poverty of buried friends.

Catacombs of the fourth century form a distinct class from earlier ones. A monogram of Constantine belongs to that period, and near it we meet with a stream of water, said to have been used for baptism. The Catacomb of St. Ponziano contains a more perfect baptistery. One of the most interesting relics is a sarcophagus representing Christ and Peter, the former on the right, the latter on the left side of a column, surmounted by a bird—no doubt a memento of the cock-crowing. At the back there is a view of a church and baptistery such as belonged to that period, —the first oblong and barn-like, having a blank wall, gable ends, and a sloping roof; the second of circular form, with a curtain hung in the doorway.

The Catacomb of St. Agnese is near the church of that name. The passages in it are lined with *loculi* —recesses fitted in some cases to receive two bodies, in others only one. Names of consuls in the year A.D. 336 occur in this part. A palm of victory is scratched on the mortar, and remains of glass phials are found near, which some suppose belonged to a martyr's memory. A square chamber occurs in the same place, with an armchair hewn out of the rock, said to have been used by a catechist who there kept school. Another apartment just by is reported to have been a chapel, and bears marks of altar and credence-table. The roof represents Christ sitting between the Old and New Testaments.

It is common with Roman Catholics to search in the Catacombs for what may seem to confirm their views of faith and worship. On the other hand, Protestants apply themselves to finding learned reasons for refuting their opponents. But this is not the way to improve a visit into these subterranean regions. Do not plunge into controversy as you walk amidst these memorials of the past. It appears that at the period when the Catacombs were used as sepulchres, typical representations of Christianity were in the ascendant; and ideas and practices were developed in forms which should have startled early Christian believers. Such and such things are said to have a tendency to prepare for superstitions which followed; therefore in early days good people *should* have foreseen the consequences, and avoided what was sure to prepare for them. Very true to a certain extent, but the fact is, they *were not foreseen*, for want of what we have learned from subsequent history.

CHAPTER VIII

LATIN DIVINITY

"GOD hath made of one blood all nations of men for to dwell on all the face of the earth." There is a family likeness throughout the human race; yet with resemblances there are differences. Studying the literature of past ages, we soon discover habits of thought which may be classified according to distinctness of race and individual idiosyncrasies. The fact strikes us in reading patristic theology. Greek Fathers of Alexandria manifest a way of thinking different from Latins at the decline of the Empire. Clement and Origen can never be confounded with Gregory and Augustine. Not only do their languages differ, but habits of thought also differ. Western theology and Eastern theology are easily distinguishable—the earlier is more ideal and speculative, the later more energetic and practical. This we shall see as we proceed.

The Latins of Rome and Hippo have a way of looking at things, distinguishable from that of Greeks in Alexandria. Topics of different kinds arrest and absorb attention.

Easterns were foremost in a desire to penetrate mysteries of the Divine nature. Western theologians, while not standing so far off as never to engage in what was dear to Oriental thinkers, addicted themselves chiefly to the study of Divine government, and its relation to human activity.

We meet at the head of Latin Christian authors, when chronologically arranged, one, however, who largely dwelt on modes of instruction such as were distinctive of the Oriental class. Ambrose, Bishop of Milan (A.D. 374—397), was, as we shall see hereafter, much more distinguished as an ecclesiastical administrator than as a doctrinal divine, but he largely addicted himself to mystical interpretations of Holy Writ though I should question whether he could fully enter into Origen's method of treating it. He made Basil his model, and, indeed, sometimes did little, if anything, more than render into Latin what he found in writings of that Greek expositor.

Ambrose was ascetic, as well as mystical. Six of his works, covering more than three hundred pages, closely printed, in double columns (Migne's Edit.), are devoted to the subject of virgins and widows. He has six books on the sacraments, two *De Penitentiâ*, and three *De Officiis*.

Augustine, who stands at the head of Latin divines, claims more particular attention. We have seen something of his history. Now we turn to his writings.[1]

He has left a treatise "on the Trinity," full of subtle criticism touching Arianism and other errors. Twelve of its fifteen divisions contain Scripture proofs bearing on the subject, and the rest are chiefly employed in answering objections. He tells us he began it when young, and finished it when old; this shows that throughout life he never lost sight of that which absorbed the attention of Oriental Fathers.

As to sacraments, Augustine seems to have been decidedly Catholic in doctrines respecting the Church and Baptism; on the cardinal points of Latin orthodoxy he follows the older African theologians

---

[1] It is worth noticing that in England, after the Reformation, high churchmen were drawn to the Greek Fathers, and Puritans to the Latin, especially Augustine. Much the same difference occurred in the Tractarian controversy between Puseyites and Evangelicals.

in a symbolical theory of "the supper." This is Dr. Schaff's opinion, but I question whether Augustine was what is generally understood by the word *symbolist*.[1] He distinguished, I think, between the outward sign and the inward grace, and considered that those who did not believe in Christ so as *to abide in Him*, had no share in the blessing of Holy Communion.

Augustine is most eminent in that department of study which relates to the moral condition of mankind and Divine purposes respecting them. Some factors in his system are found in earlier writers, but his views mainly resulted from a study of Scripture under the effect of his own experience. The turning-point in his history occurred in a change he experienced at Milan.

The first time, many years ago, I visited that city, the story of his conversion, as he relates it, followed my thoughts with a strange fascination. I passed a little garden with fruit trees. I could fancy I saw the young man and his friend Alypius, the former apart, tearing his hair, beating his forehead, clasping his knees, and throwing himself on the ground "under a certain fig-tree," when he heard a child chanting "*Tolle, lege*" ("Take up and read"). Augustine

---

[1] Schaff's *Hist. of Christian Church*, vol. ii., pp. 498, 499.

opened his New Testament, and read, " Not in rioting and drunkenness, not in chambering and wantonness, not in strife and envying" (the words pointed to his past life), "*but put ye on the Lord Jesus Christ*, and make not provision for the flesh." "No further words I then read," he says, "nor needed I, for instantly, at the end of this sentence, by a serene light let into my heart, the darkness of doubt fled away."[1] It was *a sudden conversion*, and the suddenness had no little effect on his theology afterwards. He saw at once how he had sinned, and how he could be saved, not by his own righteousness, but by putting on the Lord Jesus, and that God had been beforehand with him in this change. He was in his thirty-second year when he thus became a new creature in Christ Jesus.

Augustine before his conversion, and whilst leading an immoral life, had not been indifferent to philosophical speculations. Very imperfectly acquainted with Greek, he was not altogether ignorant of Neoplatonic opinions. Manicheism seems for a while to have had a great hold on his thoughts, though he does not appear to have gone deeply into that subject. We find nothing in what Augustine wrote as a

---

Augustine, *Confessions*, viii., c. 29.

Christian theologian at all resembling the lucubrations of Alexandrian divines, though he was far from confining himself to strictly religious thoughts.

The distinctive elements of his creed were that Divine predestination and a human acceptance of the gospel, under the influence of the Holy Spirit, constituted the basis of individual salvation. A touch of philosophical realism may be recognised in Augustine's idea of the essence of humanity being folded up in Adam—a belief not accepted by Origen and other Greeks. Augustine worked out his ideas to the full extent of their consequences. We are struck with his boldness in avowing conclusions he could not resist. He walked with unfaltering steps into dark mysteries, and with open eyes gazed on awful wonders. In after-life sometimes the dialectician was mastered by the saint; and, stepping back from the edge of a fathomless abyss, he would turn to the effulgent throne of love, saying, "Let God be true, and every man a liar." He wrote, "If there be no grace of God, how doth He save the world?" Again, "If there be no free will, how doth He judge the world?" In two of his works he held that human freedom is consistent with Divine foreknowledge and predestination.[1]

[1] Ep. 214; Wiggers, i., p. 136.

Schemes of metaphysical thought, especially of a Neoplatonic order, had occupied his attention, and this fact must be taken into account when we study his opinions. He had been changeful in his course of thinking, taking up and laying down from time to time metaphysical theories; this fact should be remembered throughout the study of his theological opinions. We cannot think of his Christian life without remembering his previous and subsequent mental habits. Especially should we bear in mind his strong convictions of Divine rectitude in the government of the world, and of the deep sinfulness of mankind.[1] Nor should we forget that what would appear to many decided contradictions he could reconcile to his own satisfaction; for his mental acuteness made him wonderfully dexterous in handling an argument. I may add that in striving to understand some of his writings, and Neander's explanations of them, one is often perplexed.

In the course of time, after Augustine's conversion, a change occurred in his opinions. It is thought by some critics his views of predestination underwent

---

[1] It is remarkable that the maxim, "Sub justo Deo quisquam nisi merentur, miser essenon potest," is said to be found in Augustine's writings. Quoted by Hallam in his *Literature of Europe*, iv., p. 237. He gives no reference to Augustine's published works.

alteration. At one period—about the year A.D. 394 —he wrote a book entitled *De Vera Religione et de Libero Arbitrio*; and afterwards came out his exposition of difficult passages in Paul's Epistle to the Romans. It was called *Explicatio prepositionum quarundam de Epistola ad Romanos*. His principles at one period respecting Divine election were that it was *conditioned* by Divine foreknowledge of individual faith. In proportion as Augustine "learned to place a higher value and dignity on faith, and belief on *authority* came to be refined and transfigured into an idea of *living faith*, in the same proportion it became clear to him that faith pre-supposed an entrance of Divine life into the soul."[1] According to this representation, Augustine *at one time* based Divine election on the *foresight* of a believer's trust in God. But afterwards he believed Christian faith was an inspiration on the part of Heaven, and that a Divine purpose was an original cause of individual salvation.

Dr. Hampden remarks that we find in Augustine " no exact theory of Divine and human agency in their relation to each other. His opinions are so qualified

---

[1] See Neander's *Church Hist.*, translated by Torrey, vol. iv., pp. 304-311.

in some instances, and so unqualified in others, that different conclusions have been drawn from them by Jansenists and Jesuits."

The speculations of Augustine were taken up and carried out by mediæval schoolmen, and wrought into a system preserving main characteristics of the African Father's theology. Predestination, regarded as the sole primary cause of all our actions, as they are moral and Christian, as they have any worth in them or any happiness, was asserted in that theology in the most positive manner. "But *reprobation*, as it implies a theory of the moral evil of the world," Dr. Hampden remarks, "I think I may confidently say is no part of the system. The term, indeed, is derived from the schoolmen, and so far they are chargeable with having perplexed theology with the disquisitions arising out of it."[1] The sins of the schoolmen ought not to be visited on Augustine. "But if there must be a theory, the schoolmen were so far right that they simply endeavoured to trace the Divine goodness as manifested by nature and revelation to its primary cause in the Divine Being." The predestination insisted on by Augustine was a predestination in reference

---

[1] Hampden's *Bampton Lect.*, p. 181.

to goodness, not evil. It may be thought reprobation is *implied* in what he says; but it is not just to assume that such an implication was consciously accepted and defended by him. People are liable to inconsistency, and spiritual instinct will often incline a theologian to resist a conclusion which opponents may logically draw from his premisses. Augustine says a great deal I should not accept, but he distinctly declares God is not the author of sin in the reprobate.[1]

There was another controversy in which Augustine was engaged. His anti-Pelagian works form a considerable portion of his writings. Bede says: "Pelagius, a British monk, spread far and near the infection of his perfidious doctrine against the assistance of Divine grace, being seconded therein by his associate, Julianus of Campania, whose anger was kindled by the loss of his bishopric, of which he had been deprived."[2] It is known from his writings that Pelagius was shocked by prevalent ungodliness and immorality, even among professed Christians; and this, I think, led him to resolve true piety into moral endeavours, the absence of which he saw plainly, in many who were proud of their orthodoxy.

---

[1] *Opera*, vol. ii., p. 934.   [2] *Eccl. Hist.*, i., chap. x.

Pelagius quoted Jerome as favourable to his views; but this was going too far, for though Jerome's tone of remarks with reference to Pelagianism in a dialogue he wrote on the subject[1] was much milder than that of Augustine and others, the system was treated by him as heresy, under the Church's ban. Jerome was not like Augustine, but reduced election to a foresight of human choice, though he did not endorse Pelagianism.

The controversy touching Divine grace and the human will took a new turn in the South of France, where, on its sunny shores, extreme views entertained by the two leaders were considerably modified by certain thinkers. John Cassian, founder and abbot of a famous monastery near where Marseilles now stands, had, in his youth, come under the influence of Chrysostom's teaching, and felt strongly the importance of moral obligation, and the duty of insisting upon this, in all religious teaching. Being convinced that we are saved by grace, he was no less convinced that men are free agents, and individually responsible. The system of Cassian has

---

[1] *Dialogue c. Pelag.*: Hier., *Opera*, ii., pp. 693-806. "Pelagius was at first on friendly terms with Jerome, but disagreements soon arose between them, and Jerome became his vehement opponent."—Robertson's *Eccl. Hist.*, ii., p. 144.

been called semi-Pelagian, because it blended with the opinions of Augustine some ideas which were held by his antagonist.

In concluding this notice of Augustine, let me add a sentence from a famous book written by William Tyndale at the Reformation period: "Augustine complaineth in his days how that the condition and state of the Jews was more easy than the Christians under traditions, so sore had the tyranny of the shepherds invaded the flock already in those days."[1] The lynx-eyed reformer discovered in the writings of Augustine a proof that superstitions in worship, preparatory to later ones, culminating in mediæval Christendom, began in the fifth century, and attracted the notice of Augustine.

In the year A.D. 529 a council was held at Orange, a city on the Rhone, retaining still an old Roman arch, not far from Avignon. Bishop Cæsarius presided on the occasion, and it was decided that the sin of Adam injured the soul, not the body only—that grace disposes us to pray, that good thoughts are gifts of God, and that we have no merit of our own. This doctrine has been denominated semi-Augustinianism; and it is said by a critic

---

[1] Tyndale's answer to the *Dialogue* of Sir Thomas More.

who has carefully consulted the decrees at Orange that it would be difficult to point out one of them not borrowed, *word for word*, from Augustine, or from those who followed him, in controversy with Pelagians or semi-Pelagians. The gist of the canon is "that evil is not the result of predestination, but it is God alone who inspires us with faith and love."[1]

In looking at Augustine's theology, we must regard it, at one time in connection with habits and opinions he had previously held. When a man changes his convictions, he may still be influenced by old habits of thought and feeling. We cannot conceive of Origen, with his early experience and character, passing through such a change as Augustine did. Origen's experience and character in childhood and youth had prepared him for a *gentle transition* into a state of spiritual thoughtfulness, sentiment, and action, such as we discover in his after-life. But the mental struggles and the immoral indulgences of young Augustine were only natural antecedents to a *passionate* conversion,

---

[1] *Dict. of Christian Antiq.*, vol. ii., p. 1462; also Smith's *Christian Biography*, vol. i., p. 378. See also *Council of Orange*, and Schaff's *Hist. of Christian Church*, iii., pp. 865 *et seq.*

and his spiritual life, his terrible conflicts, indeed all his exceptional experience, gave characteristic form to his theology afterwards. In like manner, when we contemplate the early days of Chrysostom, we see how impossible it was that he should traverse such a course of thought and feeling as Augustine encountered.

At another controversy of those days I can afford but a glance. Manicheism, in some form or other, had long troubled the Church. It was a sort of Gnostic outgrowth,—in its *metaphysical* aspect a developed contrast between light and darkness, good and evil; in its *moral* aspect resembling Buddhism, ascetic, with reverence for life in every form. It taught the essential evil of matter—that it was the hotbed of sin, the curse of the world. Manicheism had led Augustine astray, and its mischievous influence is a burden bewailed in the *Confessions*. Leo the Great carried on a war of extermination against this heresy. He authorised a diligent search through Rome for its abettors, and discovered a number of people implicated in its maintenance and diffusion. He attacked it in one of his sermons, declaring " all other heresies, however justly to be condemned, have yet a hold, each in its way, upon some elementary truth ; but in

Manicheism there is nothing which, from any point of view, can be regarded as tolerable."[1]

The *Divine Word* so absorbed the thoughtfulness of the Church in the earlier centuries that the redemption of men, though the consequence of His Incarnation and death, received comparatively little distinct attention. Christians, however, pondered the words of Paul in his Epistle to the Colossians: "Having forgiven you all trespasses, blotting out the handwriting of ordinances that was against us, which was contrary to us, and took it out of the way, nailing it to His cross; and having spoiled principalities and powers, He made a show of them openly, triumphing over them in it."

Calvary thus comes within view, as a battle-ground where Christ was victorious. The Fathers, in fluctuating and perplexing ways, employed this figure to denote the accomplishment of redemption, through means devised by the great enemy to prevent it. The idea entertained was that the wisdom of God overreached the subtlety of Satan. In the wilderness, on the mountain top, and on the temple wing at Jerusalem Satan's cunning found in the Lord a wisdom which baffled it. The agony in the garden

---

[1] Quoted in *Leo the Great* by Gore, p. 43.

and the death on the cross were facts of a different order from Christ's temptation and His defeat of the tempter; yet Irenæus and Origen, amongst ante-Nicene divines, like those who followed, did not adopt the true conception. The sacrificial character, the reconciling power, the vicarious aspect of the Atonement more or less dropped out of sight. Yet Fathers ascribed salvation to the blood of Christ, and Leo the Great, though not free from influences of an old prevalent conception, distinctly states that "in Christ's death an *oblation*—a *true sacrifice* for sin—was offered to His Father."[1] Such a theory of the Incarnation and Atonement as is propounded in the *Cur Deus Homo*, so far as I am aware, was, in the sixth century, unthought of, and waited for its elucidation by Anselm. It is remarkable with what tenacity the old patristic notion of Christ's death kept its hold on theological minds, so far as the subject interested them. The way in which the Fathers wrote upon the efficacy of our Lord's sufferings can be scarcely called *a theory of the Atonement* at all. They confined their thoughts to a victory over Satan by Divine wisdom defeating satanic purposes.

When we proceed to the doctrine of *justification*,

---

[1] Sermo lix., 5; Ep. cxxiv., 2; lxiv., 23.

held by Western divines, we ask, What did they mean by the word? They speak of its grace and say that it comes by faith—but how? Some evangelical critics have picked out passages, in order to show that Latin Fathers held Protestant views on the subject. Cited words here and there may *seem* to support what such critics maintain; but, when the whole range of patristic teaching at the time is surveyed, citations fail. Take Augustine, and you may find passages which read as though they meant what Reformers did; but turn to *De Gratia Christi* and other works, and you discover the author speaks of the grace whereby we are justified as identical with an *infusion* of God's love. He contends that God not merely forgives in this gracious act, but imparts love through the Holy Spirit. He defines justification as being *made* just, "*justi efficimur*," and speaks of it as perfect in martyrs, but not in ordinary believers.[1] At the Council of Carthage (A.D. 418) it was decreed against Pelagius, "Whosoever shall say that the grace by which we are justified through Jesus Christ our Lord avails *only* to the remission of committed sins, and not as an aid against a future commission of them, let him be anathema."[2]

---

[1] Wiggers' *Augustinianism*, p. 172. [2] Canons iv., v., vi.

Passages in Augustine and other Fathers have been supposed to agree with Luther's doctrine of Justification; but the more I reflect on theological opinions divided by centuries, the more I am persuaded that habits of thought in the *fifth* and in the *sixteenth* centuries considerably differ on this subject. A broad resemblance as to *salvation by grace* may be traced in ages far apart; but the *precise* apprehension of minor distinctions developed in a long succession of inquiries is found to vary. There may be substantial unity of *religious* faith, with considerable diversity of *theological* apprehension.

The future state did not largely occupy the thoughts of Nicene thinkers, West or East, from what may be called a *theological* point of view. Some regarded deceased believers as passing through a purifying process, and Augustine, commenting on the words "saved so as by fire," remarks it is not impossible something of this kind may occur in a future state, and goes on to speak of the dead as benefited by the almsgiving of Christians. Gregory was probably the first to lay down the doctrine of a purifying fire before the last day; but this fell short of the Romish theory of purgatory.

Let me add a word respecting the change which came over the patristic tone of thought respecting the end of the world. Tertullian and Lactantius had no idea of a long duration before that momentous event. Tertullian expected a millennium after "the second coming," and thought that the New Jerusalem awaited saints after their resurrection. Lactantius speaks of the false prophet and of Christ's appearance to judge the world; also of a renewed earth and the loosing of Satan. "Perhaps," he says, "some one may ask, When shall these things be?" He answers, "The amount of the years as reckoned varies considerably; yet *no expectation exceeds the limit of two hundred years.*"[1] It was a general impression that the world, even with the gospel in the midst of it, was in a hopeless state, and that it needed a clean sweep of all things as they are. Heresies and persecution made Christians feel they were in the midst of war, which would not cease till the Captain of salvation came to end the strife. But when imperial patronage took the place of persecution, a change came over patristic forecasts; and when we read the twentieth chapter of the *City of God*, written by Augustine, we find ourselves in a new atmosphere of thought. Prison doors are shut, and a bishop sits on a throne. The Bishop of Hippo now says that, "although God is always

---

[1] *Div. Inst.*, vii., 25.

judging the world, it is reasonable to confine attention to the last judgment." The millennium seems to fade in the fifth and sixth centuries.

Two things strike me as I read patristic literature. Ante-Nicene Fathers had an indomitable will, and conquered the difficulties of persecution. Nicene Fathers inherited their ideas of the invisible. They looked at a world above and beyond the present.

The Boyle Lecturer for 1863 remarks: " I have lately read in the records of our Arctic discoveries how during the long weeks of the outward voyage—while the crew, with little occupation in hand, were divided between regrets for the homes they were leaving and interest in the strange objects to which they were advancing—it was observed that, according to the complexion of each, they would fix themselves abaft or forward: the one class wistful and melancholy, glancing backward on the receding waters; the other sanguine and alert, gazing with unblanched cheek on the gulfs before them, and scanning with ardent gaze every opening of new incidents and features. Hope was at the prow; at the stern were listlessness and despondency."[1] We may employ that

---

[1] The Rev. C. Merivale, B.D., *The Conversion of the Northern Nations*, p. 114.

picture as an illustration of the difference between the regrets with which worldly people look upon the world they are to leave before long and the expectations which open in the future before a Christian.

Many a believer in the fifth and sixth centuries resembled the boatmen sitting at the prow, full of hope, and those at the stern, who were absorbed in regrets. The following words, written by Ambrose, express the thoughts of some Christian contemporaries : " We shall go where there is a paradise of joy,— where Adam, who fell among thieves, has forgotten to weep over his wounds ; where the thief rejoices in the Kingdom of Heaven ; where are no clouds, no thunder, no lightning, no storms of wind, no darkness, no night ; where neither summer nor winter will vary the seasons ; where no cold, or hail, or rain, nor the need of sun and moon and stars, shall be known ; but God alone shall be the light thereof."[1]

---

[1] *De Bono Mortis*, 12.

CHAPTER IX

RELIGIOUS WORSHIP

GOING back to notices of this in ante-Nicene times, we find that the Lord's Supper was a central service. Of public worship but little can be gathered from patristic writings. Socrates the Historian reports alternate chants, witnessed by Ignatius in a vision of angels, which became an authority for Church singing.[1] Consecration of bread and wine at the Lord's Supper by the president, and the distribution of these elements by deacons, are noticed in the Apostolical Constitutions written at the end of the third or beginning of the fourth century.[2]

The third century had altars in churches; representations of them exist in Ravenna, and in the same city are pictures of priests in fifth-century

---

[1] Socrates, *Eccl. Hist.*, vi., 8.
[2] Palmer's *Origines Liturgicæ*, i., 11.

robes—the alb being an ancient tunic, the chasuble a hooded cloak, the cope an upper vestment, and the pallium an oblong blanket hanging on the shoulders. In short, familiar garbs we find appropriated for ecclesiastical uses. Commonly church dress was white, but colour prevailed in Constantinople. We read of Tyrian priests wearing a heavenly crown, and "a sacerdotal garment of the Holy Ghost"—whatever that may mean.

This is noteworthy—secular edifices were turned to sacred uses. The basilica where civil business had been transacted was now employed in sacred service. The oldest church in Rome, illustrative of this fact, is San Clemente—modernised now to some extent, but still preserving its basilican form. This edifice, architecturally, brings before us a place of worship where wealth and importance had opportunity for display. A basilican plan, with an altar in advance of the eastern wall, and the bishop's seat behind, still, if I rightly remember, indicates that an administrator of the Holy Supper did not officiate in front of the table, but behind, not with back, but with face towards the congregation.

Liturgies are of early date, but the exact period when they originated is a question too minute to be discussed here. Four of such formularies seem to have existed: the Oriental, the Alexandrian, the Roman, and the Gallican. The Oriental included forms bearing patristic names, such as Basil and Chrysostom. The Alexandrian was attributed to Cyril, and the Roman to Gregory I. These resembled each other, and we find in them mention of the kiss of peace, the exhortation "Lift up your hearts," a hymn of praise with angels and archangels, intercession for the Militant Church, and supplication for rest and peace on behalf of souls departed in God's faith and fear.

There are no liturgical books dating from the ante-Nicene age, nor is there proof of any having existed before the fourth and fifth centuries.

The Council of Laodicea prohibited the public use of hymns by private individuals, although singing commenced at an early period, being introduced in the East by Ambrose, which gave rise to Ambrosian chants. Kneeling in prayer seems to have been a primitive practice, but standing was enforced in the fourth century. Epiphanius, Augustine, and Jerome commended kneeling, but not on Sundays, when standing upright was thought to typify our Lord's resurrection. It became in early days a practice for women to cover their heads when engaged in devotional service.

Psalmody originated amongst the Jews, and was hallowed by that touching example, "When they had sung a hymn they went out to the Mount of Olives." The fourth Council of Carthage made a rule that a singer should not enter upon office without the bishop's knowledge, and by appointment of a presbyter. Choirs are of early origin, the most celebrated being attributed to Gregory the Great. Congregational singing does not appear to have been practised at an early period; and this we do not wonder at, recollecting how limited was the ability to read, and how difficult it would have been to provide hymnbooks for singers.

Worship was no doubt affected by national habits. I remember, one Sunday in Egypt, seeing people in a Coptic church folding their feet under them without shoes, which were piled up by the entrance door. National habits now control the conduct of Copts in their worship; and, I infer, the practice just noticed may be thus accounted for,—not, however, forgetting the words addressed to Moses from the burning bush: "Put off thy shoes from off thy feet, for the place whereon thou standest is holy ground."

Ceremonialism carried to extremes might be seen at Nola in Campania, about the end of the fourth century. An Aquitanian named Paulinus, to be noticed hereafter, lived there, that he might be near the tomb of Felix, a martyr who suffered under the Decian persecution. Paulinus built a church over the spot, adorning it with paintings, and he also wrote a poem in memory of the confessor.

Arians at Constantinople excited emulation by their singing, and Gregory Nazianzen composed verses for worship. Anatolius, Patriarch of the Eastern capital, wrote in the fifth century a Christmas hymn beginning with the words:—

"A great and mighty wonder
The festal makes secure,
The Virgin bears the infant,
With virgin honour pure."

Another hymn, on Christ's calming the stormy sea has been well translated by Neale.

"Fierce was the wild billow,
Dark was the night;
Oars labour'd heavily,
Foam glimmer'd white;
Mariners trembled,
Peril was nigh;
Then said the God of God,
'Peace! it is I.'

"Ridge of the mountain wave,
Lower thy crest!

> Wail of Euroclydon,
> Be thou at rest!
> Peril can none be—
> Sorrow must fly—
> Where saith the Light of Light,
> 'Peace! it is I.'
>
> "Jesu, Deliverer!
> Come Thou to me:
> Soothe Thou my voyaging
> Over life's sea!
> Thou, when the storm of death
> Roars sweeping by,
> Whisper, O Truth of Truth!
> 'Peace! it is I.'"

Hymns for Latin worship were numerous, Hilary and Ambrose taking the lead. The former wrote one beginning "Lucis largiter splendidi," and also a pentecostal opening with the words " Beata nobis gaudia." Such was the fame of Ambrose that chants of praise bore his name. The most celebrated relic of his muse is his "Te Deum Laudamus." Prudentius, Fortunatus of Poictiers, with Gregory of Rome, were distinguished hymn-writers.

The monophysite Peter of Antioch is said to have been the first who introduced the Virgin Mary's name into Church prayers. Churches were dedicated to her, and the first which bore her name was the basilica of Liberius, Bishop of Rome, rebuilt after the Council of Ephesus.[1] Justinian invoked her aid for the prosperity of his administration.[2] Those about the person of Narses affirmed that he was accustomed to pray to the Mother of God, and never engaged in war without seeking a sign of her approval.[3] Stories were told of divinely wrought images of our Saviour sent down from heaven.[4] Rogation days with processions and litanies began in the fifth century.

During the first six centuries there appeared, in addition to the Lord's Day, festivals, of which it is sufficient to notice Easter, Whitsuntide, and Christmas. Easter, in memory of our Lord's resurrection, was the crown of them all.

The time for celebrating Easter differed for a while in Eastern and Western Christendom, till it became fixed for both on the Lord's Day next after the full moon of the vernal equinox. The great week, as it was called, in the fourth century corresponded with the fifteen days of the passion and resurrection weeks combined. Whitsuntide, in commemoration of the Spirit's descent on the day of Pentecost, followed fifty days afterwards, when houses were decorated

---

[1] *Patrol.*, c. xxviii., 31.
[2] *Cod. Just.*, i., 27.
[3] Evagrius, iv., 24.
[4] *Ibid.*, iv., 27

with green boughs and flowers. Christmas began to be observed in the fourth century.[1]

In reviewing the progress of ceremonialism between the first and the sixth century, we are struck with its advance. For instance, nothing could be more simple and beautiful than the institution of the Eucharist. "And as they were eating, Jesus took bread, and blessed it, and brake it, and gave it to the disciples, and said, 'Take, eat, this is My body'; and He took the cup, and gave thanks, and it gave them, saying, 'Drink ye all of it, for this is My blood of the New Testament, which is shed for many for the remission of sins.'" In the time of Justin Martyr the Holy Supper was administered in accordance with that narrative. But in the time of Gregory the Great, to use the words of Bona, in his description of liturgical services, "there is no ceremony of the Church of which more frequent mention is made in liturgies, ancient and modern, than burning of incense during a celebration of the Christian sacrifice."

With regard to images in Christian worship, I may remark that Eusebius reproved Constantine for wishing to have a statue of the Saviour; and

---

[1] In what I have said here, I follow Bingham and Riddle.

Epiphanius tore in pieces a painted church curtain. In the fifth century there were reputed miraculous pictures of Christ, the Apostles, and the Virgin Mary. Even so early as Tertullian's time, mention is made of a communion cup representing a shepherd bringing home a lost sheep.[1]

---

[1] See on these subjects Bingham, Riddle, and an article on "Images" in Smith's *Dictionary of Christian Antiquities.*

CHAPTER X

INCIPIENT EUROPEAN NATIONALISM

THE state of Christendom for the first three centuries can with advantage be treated as a whole, but not afterwards. The division of empire East and West partly accounts for this, but not entirely. Gothic invasions had much to do with it. Wave after wave from the North broke on the South, settling, some in smaller, some in larger pools, to be flooded and lost in after-tides of population. Where the invaders were Christianised, often more in name than fact, Churches rose, which became national. After the establishment by Constantine, authority of law and endowments of property converted nascent communities, so that they became political and ecclesiastical powers. They cannot be properly called *national* till after the sixth century, but they were preparing for it.

It is important to bear in mind that certain barbarous races, in the transition stage, were gradually blended with elder Roman people. Of the greater part of the earth little or nothing was known. The extent of Roman conquests formed the boundary of geographical science. Earlier and later comers under imperial dominion had been enrolled in Roman armies, had fought with the old state legions side by side; some even had shared in dignities and emoluments. It has been remarked: "They come down upon the country which is to be their prey in successive expeditions, like billows tumbling one over the other; they sweep through it; then, like waves, they retire; and then, again after an interval, they return. By violence or by treaty they gain possession and occupation of some territory, and take their place as landed proprietors amidst the old tenants and institutions of the soil."[1]

Turning to Germany, we find there were probably at an early period, Christian people amongst the inhabitants exerting influence over pagan neighbours. Some, with an apostolic spirit, might undertake missionary work, and go out proclaiming the Gospel to heathen tribes. Legends to that effect have been

---

[1] Newman's *Essays*, iii., p. 289. Dean Merivale has a striking lecture on "The Conversion of the Northern Nations," Lect. VI.

preserved. We reach something like firm footing when we meet with the fact that Athanasius spent a year of exile in Treves on the Moselle, no doubt exerting a Christian influence.

Under the Church of St. Paulinus, outside the city of Treves, the church in itself of no antiquity, there is a crypt, with very ancient sarcophagi, lately discovered, bearing names belonging to Roman senators. They are said to have been Christian martyrs. Large iron nails are shown, reported as having been used in their crucifixion—upon which report no reliance whatever can be placed; but it is not improbable, as tradition says, that there were martyrs at Treves under Diocletian.

That there were Christians at Worms at an early date we know from inscriptions. Moreover, it may be inferred Christianity spread along the banks of the Rhine, as is shown by Christian inscriptions of the fourth and fifth centuries at Bingen, Boppart, Rudesheim, and other places. We can hardly doubt that, by the end of the fifth century or the beginning of the sixth, Christianity prevailed in several Rhenish towns.[1]

In Augsburg, Ratisbon, and other places we find

---

[1] Baring Gould's *Church in Germany*, pp. 9, 10.

Christian converts, and Severinus was connected with Cologne, as Bishop in that city. Gibbon,[1] who had a keen eye for the picturesque, relates an interview between a monk bearing the name of Severinus and Odoacer, the Gothic chieftain. The lowness of the door would not admit the lofty stature of Odoacer; he was obliged to stoop; but in that humble attitude the saint could discern the symptoms of his future greatness, and addressing him in a prophetic tone, "Pursue," said he, "your design; proceed to Italy; you will soon cast away this coarse garment of skins, and your wealth will be adequate to the liberality of your mind." The barbarian, whose daring spirit accepted and ratified the prediction, was admitted into the service of the Western Empire, and soon obtained an honourable rank in the guards.[2]

One figure in Germany comes out distinctly— Ulphilas, "Moses of the Goths," as he is called. Sozomen[3] relates how a stag, chased by a party of Hunnish sportsmen, led them through a lake into a land peopled by tribes whom they attacked and conquered. The vanquished tribe fled and disappeared, and the victors sent to Constantinople

---

[1] *Decline and Fall of the Roman Empire*, chap. xxxvi.
[2] *Ibid.*, chap. xxxvi, vol. iii., p. 333.
[3] Soz., *Eccl. Hist.*, vi., 37.

messengers asking for admission to the Eastern Empire. Ulphilas was one thus sent. In the Eastern metropolis he was educated and converted. After this he became a church reader. That led him to his study of Scripture, and the immortalising of his name as the first Gothic translator of the sacred volume. It is said, he omitted in his version of the Old Testament books recording wars, which he feared might foster the military propensities of his race. A manuscript of his work, in silver letters on purple parchment, is well known as *Codex Argenteus* in the Royal Library at Upsala. The silver letters of the *Codex Argenteus* are said to be impressions of silver leaf, resembling titles on the backs of books bound in vellum or leather; but I find the editor of *Gothic and Anglo-Saxon Gospels* remarks: "On looking minutely at our accurate facsimile, I saw variations which could not have occurred if metallic letters had been used. The word at the end of the third line of our facsimile is abbreviated to make it accord with the preceding line." Another scholar says: "I may add that the *Codex* has evidently been ruled throughout with double lines for writing; single lines would have been sufficient for stamping." In A.D. 341 Ulphilas became a bishop, and is generally called an Arian; I find he was present at a synod in Constantinople in A.D. 360, where a modified Arian creed was adopted. Many denominated Arian were rather anti-Athanasian than anything more; they believed in Christ's true Deity, but did not adopt the Nicene definition of it.

We possess, in the *Codex Argenteus*, quite as early and genuine a monument of the Gothic language as our Greek and Latin codices supply in the case of any classical author. "It is seven centuries more ancient than the Scandinavian *Edda*, five older than the German *Nibelungen Lied*, three older than the poem of our Cædmon. We may trace in it the very foundation of our mother tongue."

II. Theodoric, an Ostrogoth, educated in Constantinople, ruled a district in North Italy in A.D. 395 —an incipient nationality which was nipped in its early growth. It is difficult to give it an appropriate name. Honorius, on the division of the old empire, removed his court from Rome to Ravenna, and when Theodoric took possession of the city in A.D. 489, he held an undefinable position as a centre of Western rule. Like other Goths, he is called an Arian, and it is curious to couple this fact with his influence in the election of Damasus, Bishop of Rome.[1] He

---

[1] See page 240 of this volume.

cleverly separated Gothic soldiers from native Italians, reserving the former for foreign war and employing the latter in home civilisation. Ambassadors to Ravenna admired his wisdom, magnificence, and courtesy. By marriages he united himself and family to Frankish, Burgundian, and other powers; he also cultivated the affection of Roman senators and people. He visited the old-world capital, and there won popularity. But though he established a sovereignty which lasted his own time, his institutions were not enduring. A coherent national Church did not follow as the result of his enterprise, but an orthodox succession of bishops continued in Ravenna. The religious element survived the political. Epiphanius, Bishop of Pavia, comes before us in Theodoric's history as a faithful Christian counsellor, constraining him to acts of mercy, which he exemplified in his own conduct; for Epiphanius crossed the snowy Alps, braving the cold March winds, to secure the release of captives ransomed by Theodoric's gold.

The successors of Theodoric's political rule disappeared after the siege of Ravenna by Belisarius in 539, when it became subject to governors who ruled in the name of Byzantine emperors. The same territory afterwards became "Estates of the Church." This gave Papal Rome its title of the

"Holy Roman Empire." The title lasted for a thousand years, and then ended under Napoleon Bonaparte.

Nobody who has visited quaint old Ravenna but must have been spellbound while passing from one church to another in its silent streets. Domes, columns, arches, take one back nearly fifteen hundred years; they stand now as they did then. Two of the Arian churches built by Theodoric still exist— S. Apollinare Nuovo and S. Spirito. The first has a row of columns in the nave supporting arches, above which are rich mosaics representing twenty-two virgins, each carrying a crown. The second, with a west-end vestibule, is adorned with coloured marbles. It was originally Arian, but afterwards consecrated by an orthodox archbishop, named Agnelles. As an instance of authorship in his case, may be quoted the following passage, "Where I could obtain no information, I have composed the life myself, by the help of God and prayers of my brethren."[1]

The churches at Ravenna reaped revenues from State sources; but Theodoric differed from subsequent authorities in granting toleration to others than

[1] *Muratoris Scriptores Rerum Italicarium*, vol. ii., p. 62.

the orthodox, until Catholics offended him ; then he became their persecutor. Theodoric died in A.D. 526, and the kingdom did not long survive its founder. Dark shadows fall over his last days. He put to death Boethius, the philosopher, and also the father-in-law of Boethius, named Symmachus ; the former, it is said, without a fair trial, the latter without any trial at all.

The name of Boethius, associated with Ravenna (A.D. 470—526), has been enrolled amongst Catholic saints ; works on the Holy Trinity and the person of our Lord are attributed to him ; but Boethius, author of the well-known *Consolatio Philosophia*, and put to death by Theodoric, was a different person. Hallam, in his *Literature of Europe*, speaks of him as "the last of the ancients, and one who forms a link between the classical period of literature and that of the middle ages." The historian describes him as, in elevation of sentiment, equal to any of the philosophers, and as mingling a Christian sanctity with their lessons. Boethius "speaks from his prison in the swan-like tones of dying eloquence." His *Consolation*, interesting though it be, has no place in the theological history of the Church.[1]

---

[1] Hallam's *Literature of Europe*, vol. i., p. 2

Contemporary with Boethius was Cassiodorus, Minister of State to Theodoric, and he is worthy of passing notice for piety and learning. He was a genuine patriot, and adapted himself to Theodoric's court only so far as it enabled him to alleviate the misfortunes of his countrymen. When famine visited the north of Italy, he lightened the burdens of taxation, and relieved the sufferings of the poor. Weary through the troubles of his age, he retired to a monastery, and established a community for promoting literature and philosophy. He strove to elevate the taste and habits of ecclesiastical orders, and endowed a monastery with his own library, enriched, as it was, with classical and sacred MSS. Under the auspices of Agapetus, Bishop of Rome, he sought to provide chairs (or professorships, if these modern terms may be used) " for the culture of general learning in connection with theology." He was a voluminous author, and amongst his works we find an *Ecclesiastical History* and *Expositions on the Psalms*, also *Comments on the Canticles and the Apocalypse*.

III. France now requires attention. The Council of Arles, in A.D. 314, is a proof of the eminence which that city had reached so early, when Bishops of Marseilles, Autun, Rheims, Bordeaux, and Rouen were present, showing how many episcopal cities existed in the country at that period. The place of their assembly had then attained importance, both as a Roman settlement and as a seat of Christianity. The museum there still contains early monuments, exhibiting, in bas-relief, Christ with saints carrying palms of victory : Pilate and Mary Magdalene are also represented.

Cardinal Newman, with some imagination, says of Gaul: " About that time it was as cultivated and happy as Asia Minor after its three centuries of peace. The banks of the Rhine are said to have been lined with villas and farms; the schools of Marseilles, Autun, and Bordeaux vied with those of the East, and even with that of Athens ; opulence had its civilising effect upon their manners, and familiarity with the Latin classics upon their native dialect."[1]

In our notice of Gaul at the fall of the empire, we should bear in mind how much of Roman architecture, civil and sacred, remained in that country. At Vienne there existed a forum, an amphitheatre, and pagan temples, some of them at the period now under consideration being employed for Christian uses.

---

[1] Newman's *Historical Sketches,* iii., p. 121. I think the colours are here laid on too thickly.

Arles and Nismes are famous, in our day, for churches which were originally heathen structures. Notably on the slope of the Vernégues there is still such a church. "Circular-domed edifices, raised by the Romans as mausoleums, were imitated by the Christians in their circular baptisteries, while the pillared hall, lighted by a clerestory, was exactly copied in the nave or large vessel of the Christian church."[1]

We now reach the reign of Clovis, or Clodovich, as some call him (A.D. 465—511), of the Merovingian line of kings—tall and stately, with long, shaggy locks falling over his shoulders. Gauls were of the Philistine type, body and mind. From affection or policy—perhaps both—Clovis married Clotilda, a Catholic lady, who persuaded him when going to battle to seek help from the God she worshipped. Clovis yielded to her fascinating influence, and fought with success a battle which led to the Gaulish throne. He then declared himself willing to adopt the Christian faith, and "any political reasons, which might have suspended his public profession, were removed by the devout and loyal acclamations of the

---

[1] Macgibbon's *Architecture of Provence and the Riviera*, pp. 35, 78, 94.

Franks, who showed themselves alike prepared to follow their leader to the field of battle or to the baptismal font." Clovis was followed by three thousand Franks. His so-called conversion produced little or no effect on his character, beyond what was ceremonial.[1] Gregory of Tours informs us, Clovis suggested to the King of the Ripuarian Franks the murder of his father, and when the murder had been committed Clovis mounted the vacant throne.[2] As an example of strange mingling of what he learned from the Bible with his own battle-loving temperament, I may mention that Clovis delighted in the imprecations of the Psalms, and adopted the words, " Thou hast given me the necks of mine enemies, that I might destroy them that hate me." He wished he had been in Jerusalem at the crucifixion, that, at the head of his valiant Franks, he might have avenged the Saviour's injuries.

It is here significant to notice two men elected to Gallic episcopal office in the fifth century, Avitus and Sidonius Apollinaris,—the first a literary layman ; the second a country gentleman living in a Roman villa, amidst " lakes, cascades, and nightingales,"

---

[1] Gibbon tells the story in his *Decline and Fall of the Roman Empire*, vol. iii., p. 387.
[2] Gregory, ii , 27.

chosen Bishop of Clermont, and then Archbishop of Bourges. "If one-tenth of his writings be deducted," says Ampere, "the remainder would leave us in doubt whether he were a Christian." Sidonius must, however, have possessed winning qualities, for the public voted him the title of *saint*; and the Church declined to canonise him, *only* because he wrought no miracle.

In the fifth century we meet with Prosper of Aquitaine, a distinguished priest at Marseilles, who issued three editions of his Chronicle, bringing it down to the storming of Rome by the Vandals. Ecclesiastical affairs chiefly occupy his attention. "The destinies of the spiritual power seem closely related to the destinies of the past; and even beyond the frontiers of Italy, and at a time when imperial rule was, to all appearances, destroyed for ever, the clergy persistently and earnestly believed in the perpetuity of the empire."[1]

When we dwell on the condition of Gaul at the period under review—especially on the deep ignorance of the lower classes, and the prominence given to ceremonial worship, through which religious impressions must have been chiefly conveyed—we see

[1] Masson's *Early Chronicles of France*, p. 7.

how the effect of existing theological controversies was confined to the clergy. As we ponder what is said by Hilary, and other Gallic divines on the orthodox side, we see how little even educated laymen, supposing they met with and read the discussions, could enter into subtle arguments such as those on the Trinity. As to the unlettered class —by far the majority—how utterly unintelligible to them would be the reasoning on both sides!

Salvian throws light upon the social condition of France, in the neighbourhood of Marseilles. Local brigands, domestic slavery, and the property of large estates in the hands of corrupt aristocrats, he describes at length. He gives a deplorable account of Gaul in his own time, the fifth century. He was married, though a priest, but adopted the habits of monastic life, and obtained such distinction as to wear the title of Episcoporum Magister, and was renowned as monk and scholar. He wrote a book on *The Government of God*, in which he gives a lively picture of social life in Gaul, painting the character of laity and clergy in dark colours, but excepting from his charges of immorality the Gallic monks.

Generally with regard to the condition of France, I may say that account ought to be taken of the shattered condition in which we find Roman civilisation at that time; the imperfect influence of Christianity on people who professed to embrace it; the old pagan habits of thought, feeling, and conduct which lingered throughout the land; and the extent to which faith, worship, and conduct in the Church had been corrupted in the fifth and sixth centuries.

Cities on the Loire adhered to Clovis. Arian Burgundians submitted. Visigoths resisted, but were overcome. He gained victories which made him the first of Frankish sovereigns, and, indeed, founder of the French Church. That Church included different races, and the word "church" must not be taken with reference to the Franks in the modern sense. After the extinction of Arianism, Franks, in the mass, followed Catholic priests and Catholic worship. Political and religious laws being bound together, subjects of Clovis would come under this double dominion, leaving no right of private judgment, or very little.

Clotaire, in A.D. 558, was a successor to Clovis. He married Radegonda, daughter of a Thuringian prince, who is glowingly described by Alban Butler, in his *Lives of the Saints*. She would have preferred a life of celibacy, and the Franks said their king had espoused a nun. Clotaire bears a wretched character, and is charged with assassinating his wife's brother. She, in consequence, left her husband, was ordained a deaconess, entered upon a conventual life, and ultimately became an abbess. Her accession to that dignity is elaborately described, and she appears to have addicted herself to literary pursuits, and to have welcomed the visits of Vinatius Fortunatus, a French author, who is sketched in fantastic colours by M. Augustin Thierry, in his *History of the Merovingians*.

From the story of Fortunatus and Radegonda, as told by M. Thierry, no one would expect that Fortunatus could write a hymn on the Cross of Christ, rich in evangelical feeling; yet, as Archbishop Trench remarks, words in the composition indicate that the cross is the tree on which the vine of the Church depends for its tendrils and its fruit.[1]

---

[1] *Sacred Latin Poetry*, selected by R. C. Trench, p. 113, *De Cruce Christi*. The lines in the original are—

"Appensa est vitis inter tua brachia, de quâ
Dulcia sanguineo vina rubore fluunt."

The writer, probably, had in his mind words in the Vulgate version of the first Psalm: "Et erit tanquam lignum quod plantatum est sicus decursus aquarum, quod fructum suum dabit in tempore suo."

Chilperic, in A.D. 567, followed Clotaire next but one, and infamously treated his queen. He had a concubine, steeped in crime. What, at such a period, could occur but the state of things indicated by the historian Hallam, who says, "It would be difficult, as Gibbon has justly observed, to find anywhere more vice or less virtue"?[1] Gregory, in his *History of France*, written in Chilperic's reign, dwells on the miseries he witnessed, mourning over the sufferings of the Church.[2]

The state of France, consequent upon the dissolution of the Roman empire, must be taken into account in our estimate of religion at that crisis. Society had become thoroughly disorganised, and the Church struggled with peculiar local difficulties. For instance, political treason was no crime in the eye of existing law. The penalty for murder was only a small fine. In personal quarrels friends and relatives were sure to become involved. The freedom of people was entirely at the mercy of rulers. Thousands might be transported from one part of the country to another, on the authority of government, such as it was. Property in land could be seized for use by those who had no right to it. The life of an

---

[1] *Middle Ages*, chap. i., part I.   [2] Liber viii.

old Roman in the country was worth only half that of a Frank. "It is a weary and unprofitable task," says Hallam, "to follow changes, through scenes of tumult and bloodshed, in which the eye meets with no sunshine."[1]

Historical justice demands our recognition of what is recorded of ecclesiastial virtues. Six bishops, at least, are described as honouring their profession. Claudius of Vienne, in the fourth century, was a Greek and Latin author, who wrote a treatise on *Human Souls*, and composed verses condemning profane poetry; and without using the title he fulfilled the duties of a bishop. Simplicius, in the fifth century, after suffering imprisonment for conscience' sake, adorned his episcopate by humility and benevolence, and, having married, "brought up his children in the fear of God." Lupus of Troyes, in the same century, is called "father of fathers, bishop of bishops, and chief of all Gallic pontiffs." He liberated slaves, and made the poor his heirs. Perpetuus, a literary man, and Archbishop of Tours, protested against priestly immoralities. Remigius, contemporary Archbishop of Rheims, is described as an eloquent orator.

---

[1] Hallam's *State of Europe*, chap. i., part 1. Salvian paints a terrible picture of France.

Cæsarius of Arles, in the sixth century, laboured to restore ecclesiastical discipline.[1]

Gregory, Bishop of Tours in the last quarter of the sixth century, a well-known author, made a mark amongst historians; and, as a worthy ecclesiastic, braved the wrath of King Chilperic, declaring, "You must follow the teachings of apostles and the orthodox Church."

Religion in France depended much upon episcopal appointments. A right of choosing its own bishop was claimed by the diocese, but gradually it was denied and withdrawn. Large property was possessed by the Church. Some sees were richly endowed, and their wealth became the prey of kings and nobles; an episcopal throne fell to the highest bidder.

IV. There is no country where traditionalism has run riot to the same extent as it has done in Spain. It is asserted that the Apostle James—Santiago he is called—soon after the crucifixion, asked the Virgin Mary's permission to preach the Gospel in Spain; and having obtained it, went to Zaragoza, whither "angels then brought her on a jasper pillar," and there the pillar remains unto this day, an object of

---

[1] *Fleury*, xxxiii., xxxv. See also *Smith's Dictionary of Christian Biography*.

worship to thousands of Spaniards. Numerous Spanish authors maintain the genuineness of the legend. That the Gospel was preached at an early period in Spain there can be no doubt; and churches existed there before the Moorish invasion. Magnificent cathedrals, which now fill visitors with wonder, are of later date.

Spain is curiously connected with the story of Ravenna. Amalaric, grandson of Theodoric the Goth, was recognised sovereign of Gothic territories west of the Rhone; and royal treasure was sent from Ravenna to Narbonne, where Amalaric held his Court. He married Clotilda, daughter of Clovis. Clotilda was Catholic; Amalaric was Arian. Quarrels ensued between the families. The Frankish sovereign marched against Narbonne, and defeated the Goths, who fled to Spain. There they became established; and, strange as it seems, Levvigild, a Goth, became king of a territory south of the Pyrenees. Levvigild raised his son Ermenegild to the throne, and they reigned together, both being Arians. The son afterwards married an orthodox wife, and this exasperated the heterodox spouse of his father. She determined to make her daughter-in-law like herself; and, for that end, seized her by the hair of her head, and trampled her under foot. She succeeded so far as to force her victim to receive a fresh baptism from an Arian priest. Afterwards Levvigild's son, Ermenegild, renounced Arianism and professed orthodoxy, which act incensed his parents, and a furious quarrel ensued. The rebellious son was imprisoned and executed, dying an avowed Catholic. Legends relate that his dungeon was miraculously illuminated, and angels sang a requiem over his corpse. Levvigild had, by a former marriage, a son named Reccared, who succeeded his father. Reccared had been an Arian, but, after his accession, professed the orthodox faith, and persuaded a synod of Arian bishops to follow his example. The orthodox revolution proved a success.

Under the Goths an ecclesiastical establishment of prelates and provincial councils took place; also monasteries, with a record of miracles, began to appear. Absurd stories are told of a bishop's corpse placed on a bier being miraculously carried "up hill and down dale"; and of St. Fructuosus, who sought solitude, and was accompanied by a flock of crows which went before to guide him to his place of retreat. But Isidore is the man who appears with greatest glory in early Spain, both as saint and author. "O Great Isidore," exclaims St. Braulio "in thy works thou hast comprised the histories of thy country; the distinction of periods; the rights of the Church; the discipline of the priesthood; the laws, ecclesiastical and civil; the geography of climes and regions; the origin and nature of all things, human and divine."[1] Isidore was a diligent compiler, and "undoubtedly the greatest man of his time in the Church of Spain."[2] He was Archbishop of Seville for nearly forty years, and died in 636. "If we place the birth of Isidore about 560, we shall not be far wrong."

The Catholic Faith was declared the religion of Spain in A.D. 589.

---

[1] *Hist. of Spain and Portugal*, vol. i., p. 215. A work of extensive research.

[2] *Dict. of Christian Biography*, by Drs. Smith and Wace, article "Isidore."

CHAPTER XI

MONKS AND MISSIONS

ASCETICISM was floating in the air at an early period. We meet with a notable hermit in Antony, of the third century. The history of him is a work attributed to Athanasius, and his character is eulogised by Jerome after the following fashion: " Perhaps, at the close of *this little book*, some who are ignorant of his inheritance, who adorn their houses with marble and cover their estates with elegant villas, may ask, Why were all these wanting to this poor aged man? You drink out of a cup of gems; he was content with one which nature supplied,—the hollow of his own hands. You clothe yourselves in embroidered tunics; he was clothed in a garb such as your slaves would not wear. But, on the other hand, to this poor man paradise was opened; for you, rich men, perdition is prepared. He, though naked, was clothed in the robe of Christ; you, clothed in fine linen, lack the better raiment. Paul [the hermit], covered with a little dust, is about to rise to glory ; you, slumbering under marble sepulchres, shall be consumed with all your possessions. I entreat you who read these things that you would be mindful of Jerome a sinner, who, if the Lord would give him the choice, would much rather have Paul's humble clothing with his merits, than the purple robe of kings with their punishments."

Jerome was a scholar, employed by Damasus, Bishop of Rome, to revise the Septuagint version of the Old Testament ; and whilst so engaged became acquainted with a noble family represented by a lady named Paula, who had become a widow, and was filled with a longing to visit the Holy Land, and now the two resolved on a pilgrimage to Jerusalem. They did not travel together, but after separate departures she followed to Bethlehem, where she instituted a nunnery and he gathered a community of monks. A great change had occurred in Jerome's religious feeling, and this led to a decided turn in his course of life. Athanasius' visit to Rome and his story of St. Antony is connected by historians with the step now taken by Jerome and Paula. It was preceded also by the resolve of another lady, named Melania, who lost her husband and two or three children; after which bereavement she exclaimed, "I am the freer to serve Thee, my Lord, since Thou hast separated me from earthly ties." She departed from Rome, and left a little boy behind, saying, "God will take care of him better than I can do"—thus neglecting an obvious duty while yielding to a superstitious impulse.

When Paula and her virgins, and Jerome, with other friends, reached Bethlehem, she with her companions settled down in a nunnery, while he adopted as his permanent cell, a cave near that of the Nativity. Paula died in A.D. 403, but Jerome survived her seventeen years.

Epiphanius, Bishop of Salamis, visited Jerusalem, and there preached a sermon condemning the writings of Origen, then held by many Eastern Christians in great renown. Jerome, and Rufinus, at that time in the East, both decided ascetics, had been admirers of the distinguished Alexandrian; but now the former appeared to sympathise with Epiphanius, this displeased Rufinus, and the quarrel between the two was regarded by Augustine as a *magnum et triste miraculum*. After having vied with each other in admiration of the great critic and philosopher, they became rivals in the violence of their dislike to him. The controversy spread, and it continued to burn between the two scholars with increasing fierceness. Rufinus wrote against Jerome, and Jerome wrote an apology for himself in reply whilst at Bethlehem in the year 402. An account of both works may be found in the third volume of the *Nicene and Post-Nicene Fathers*, edited by Drs. Wace and Schaff. The two ascetic scholars had been close friends; now they appeared as excited foes; yet one is glad to find that in the midst of the strife Jerome wrote a friendly letter to Rufinus.

At Jerusalem, Jerome came in contact with Vigilantius, an early antagonist of superstitious worship, who maintained that honour rendered to memories and to graves of departed saints was superstitious, and therefore to be condemned; also he said that money sent for poor saints at Jerusalem by Christians in Italy and France had better have been kept in Europe. Moreover Vigilantius declared the hermit who spent his time in solitude was a coward, and that it would be good for priests to marry. Such opinions Jerome condemned as blasphemous; and Vigilantius returning to Europe, continued his war against superstition, and published a book on the subject in A.D. 403. It is said that the Bishop of Toulouse favoured the anti-monastic views of

Vigilantius, then beginning to spread in Southern Gaul. Jerome retained his indignation against the reformer, and plunged into controversy on the side of existing worship.

Jerome's character presents a great puzzle. Superstitious, ambitious, vain of his learning, impatient under reproof, and merciless in his castigations of an opponent,—better things are known of him. Amidst his haughtiness he wrote in a letter: " Because the Lord sets free the captive, and looks to the humble and the contrite, perhaps He may say to me also, lying in the grave of wickedness, ' Jerome, come forth.' All things are possible with God, and conversion is never too late. The thief from the cross entered paradise." Jerome's precepts differed from his conduct. " Whether you read or write, watch or sleep," he said, " let love sound a trumpet in your ears."

At the time when Jerome the monk lived and worked so hard, asceticism, of which he so largely partook, prevailed powerfully, East and West; and a not much noticed, but remarkable, instance of it may be here introduced. A Greek gentleman, named Nilus, after having held a high position in the Constantinopolitan court, determined upon leading a hermit-life, in the wilderness of Sinai—

near where the present monastery of St. Catherine stands—in awful solitude, under the matchless splendour of a sky which, once seen, especially at eventide, can never be forgotten. Nilus took with him a son, who fell into the hands of Arabs. They led him away captive, intending to offer him as a sacrifice to the morning star, but oversleeping themselves they found it was too late to accomplish their purpose. They sold him for a slave, after which he came into the hands of a bishop, who restored him to his father; and he was afterwards consecrated a Christian priest.

Amongst those who devoted themselves to an ascetic life in the West was Honoratus, a noble Gaul, who, after having visited Greece, settled in monastic life within a small island on the coast of France— the Riviera, now so fashionable a resort of winter visitors. The island, two leagues from Antibes, and bearing the name of Lerins, and St. Honoré, became his fixed abode; where, in A.D. 400, he founded a famous monastery, to which disciples flocked; and amongst the earliest was Hilary, who succeeded Honoratus as Abbot of Lerins and as Bishop of Arles. The place became a resort for such as forsook the world, amongst whom were zealous students who secured on its behalf renown for learning and piety.[1] Literary culture was a commanding pursuit in some of these monastic foundations, and to them the modern world is indebted far beyond what is generally acknowledged.

Whilst we have seen that asceticism yielded fruit in the East under different forms, we may add it was also variously developed in the West. We learn much of what went on through a like agency at that period in Ireland. John Cassian, educated at Bethlehem, and afterwards familiar with the monasticism of Egypt, is thought to have conveyed to the Green Isle, through his writings, a knowledge of his ascetic system. His ideas became an inspiration, leading to monastic modes of life, and to heroic endeavours for enlightening the minds and converting the lives of Western pagans.

The famous Irish monk known as St. Patrick, whose birth, as to exact date, is wrapped in mystery, was, at the latter part of the fourth century, an instrument of conveying Gospel truth to his benighted countrymen. I avoid attempts to unravel

---

[1] An interesting account of the monastery, and its extensive architectural remains, may be found, with ample illustrations, in Macgibbon's *Architecture of Provence and the Riviera*, a book well worthy the perusal of those who visit that fashionable neighbourhood.

the critical story of his mission, and confine myself to what he has himself written. "Whence has it come to pass," he asks, "that in Ireland they who never had any knowledge, and until now worshipped idols, have lately become a people of the Lord?"[1] Obscurities of expression occur in his reply, of which the substance appears to be that he fulfilled his mission by Divine help.

He commenced at Wicklow, and preached to some swineherds there. This brought him into collision with Druidical priests, and he visited Connaught, converted a king's daughter, and was so successful as to found the See of Armagh. He established monasteries, resembling those in Egypt; in fact, clusters of huts, shaped like beehives, and entered through low doors, sometimes not without crawling, the largest of such enclosures measuring about twenty-four feet by fifteen.[2] Columba followed Patrick in missionary work, and was educated at St. Clonard, where his labours commenced; and to him is attributed the foundation of three hundred churches. It is said, he made copies of the Scriptures, and spent forty years in Christian work. One

---

[1] *Confessions of St. Patrick.* See Stokes' *Ireland and the Celtic Church*, p. 26.

[2] Stokes' *Ireland and the Celtic Church*, Lecture IX.

beautiful monument of his missionary enterprise is the founding of a monastery at Iona, which, with its azure sea on a calm summer's evening, is a picture once seen never to be forgotten.

Adamnan wrote a life of Columba, dwelling on his prophecies and miracles. Incredible stories are related; but we can believe the community over which he presided was numerous; that meetings were held for deciding disputed questions; that the monastery was a harbour of refuge; and that hospitality was a virtue displayed to all strangers. One Sunday morning, as the matin bell rung, Adamnan lay, looking towards heaven with wistful gaze; and making efforts to utter a benediction, he passed away to the world of peace and joy.

But this early missionary Church in Ireland appears to have been powerless to civilise its own neighbourhood. Early promise in this respect was not accomplished. The savage custom of summoning women to fight, it is said, was rebuked; but there remains no good evidence that the Celtic missionaries sought to restrain tribal wars.[1]

---

[1] See, on the subject of early Christianity in Ireland, Stokes' *Ireland and the Celtic Church*; Olden's *Church of Ireland*, Second Period.

Columbanus, another Irish missionary in the sixth century, whose birth is dated A.D. 543, proceeded to the Continent, with twelve companions, and undertook a journey to the Vosges district. There lingers still a tradition, in the neighbourhood of Colmar and Munster,[1] that, at the date mentioned, some Scotchmen built huts with sods and boughs, and also employed themselves in tilling the land. It is to me a noticeable coincidence that at Ban de la Roche—not very far off—the memorable French pastor Oberlin laboured in modern times for the temporal and spiritual welfare of this parish. With my recollections of that pleasant spot, and of Oberlin's parsonage, I love to blend the story of Columbanus. It is pleasant to think of the two at work in the same vicinity, apart in time and form, but alike in combination of civilising and sacred toils.

Columbanus remained abroad, wedded to his native Celtic habits of keeping Easter and preserving the tonsure—a distinction which separated Irish from Gallic Catholics; and the breach between

---

[1] Wolf's *Country of the Vosges*, p. 214. Dr. Döllinger paints too bright a picture of Ireland in the sixth and seventh centuries. Irish missionaries abroad seem to have been much more effective than the Church at home.

them was widened by Irish reproofs of immorality occurring in the Burgundian Court under Queen Brunehild. Irish faithfulness offended her majesty, and the king sent the missionary away. Columbanus, availing himself of his freedom, visited a friendly prince, who conducted him to the Rhine, whence he proceeded to Switzerland and reached the Lake of Constance, where he settled for a while, at Bregentz, whence he proceeded to Italy.

Another Irish monk was St. Gall, who settled at the west end of the lake, seeking the conversion of the neighbouring inhabitants. He built a cell, which afterwards became the magnificent building still known by his name. Different times of keeping Easter, and other customs, kept the Irish from communing with foreign Churches.

In tracing monastic activity on missionary lines and for the sake of preserving the order of events and not interrupting the progress of the Irish enterprise, I have passed by a development which was Italian, and commenced by the famous Benedict of Nursia, born about A.D. 480, after the death of St. Patrick, and more than half a century before Columbanus entered the world. He was a man of a very different type from those Hibernian missionaries I have imperfectly described.

I some time ago made an excursion from Rome to Subiaco. Just by that town there is a deep gorge, with sloping sides of rock and foliage, reaching down to the river Arno, bordered by chestnut trees, amidst which, here and there, rose a tall cypress. The brow of the hill, on the side of the river nearest Subiaco, bears a far-famed monastery in which (very different then from what it is now) Benedict spent his early days, and prepared for his lifework, which really began at Monte Cassino, early in the sixth century. There he met the ferocious Totila, and was in the same place cheered by the visits of his memorable sister.[1] His conception of monastic life was altogether different from that of the men I have just described. Theirs was missionary work, preaching the gospel to heathens; but Benedict's was the improvement of Italy and Europe in civilisation, literary culture, social habits, and Christian life, according to ideas which obtained at that period. Benedict inaugurated a new era in monastic history. Rule and system took the place of local and accidental custom, and this reformer elaborated an institute which spread far and wide, playing a distinguished part in European civilisa-

[1] See articles "Benedict of Nursia" and "Sta Scholastica" in Smith's *Dictionary of Christian Biography.*

tion for ages afterwards. No one who has read Benedict's Rules but must admit his eminent genius and benevolent disposition. The Rules were adapted to the age, as shown by the fact that 1,481 Benedictine monasteries existed in the eighth century. His Rules provided hospices where travellers were welcomed and refreshed, after salutation, prayer, and a kiss of peace. Washing feet, and rubbing them with oil, are prescribed as parts of the welcome given ; also reading the Bible, or some other religious book, for the instruction of visitors. Benedictine monasteries were provided with sitting-rooms, dormitories, and kitchens, for sojourners, distinct from those used by members of the Order. Sometimes a few strangers were invited to the abbot's table.[1] In the unsettled mediæval age the institution was valuable beyond what is generally supposed.

We now come to our own country, to find it in a miserable condition. It is surprising, after Roman civilisation had existed here so long, after the British Church had attained importance sufficient to secure for it representatives at the Council of Arles, to discover that the British people had to a large

---

[1] See, in Smith's *Biog. Dict.*, article on Benedictus of Nursia just noticed.

extent sunk into a state of comparative barbarism and pagan ignorance.

There seems ample evidence to prove that the Romanised Celts, whom our Teutonic fathers found here, influenced materially the character of our nation. But the main stream of our ancestors was Germanic. Our language alone decisively proves this. Arminius, "the great Germanic hero and conqueror of the first century, is far more truly one of our national heroes than Caractacus; and it was our own primeval fatherland that the brave German general rescued from barbarism when he slaughtered the Roman legions, eighteen centuries ago, in the marshy glens between the Lippe and the Ems."[1]

The British Gildas, whose work is a rambling lamentation over the troubles of his country, has frequently been cited as to the influence of Christianity within our shores; but it appears to me that his authority is doubtful, since searching criticism has made it appear uncertain as to who he was and where he lived. His birth has been sought between A.D. 484 and 520, his death between 565

---

[1] Creasey's *Fifteen Decisive Battles of the World*, chap. v. Arminius broke the Roman yoke, and prepared for the liberties of England.

and 602. If the earlier be correct dates, then what he says of comparative prosperity would carry weight with it; but if the latter be near the mark, then he could only rest on old reports liable to much inaccuracy. However, we can rely on Haddon and Stubbs, who give a summary of authorities for the statement, that there existed a British Church, with edifices, clergy, and discipline, at the end of the fourth century. So general a conclusion is not all we want. Examinations have been made into architectural remains of sacred edifices containing Roman work; but, from what I have seen of some such relics, and what I have read respecting others, it seems likely that they belonged to buildings at a period when Britain was under Imperial rule. The history of England from the departure of the Romans to the mission of Augustine is wrapped in mystery.

It seems probable that the island relapsed into a state of more or less heathenism. We find that, early in the seventh century, the vestiges of British Christendom were confined to Wales, and a few other spots in the island. We find no clear notice of bishops in Britain between the early part of the fourth century, when the Council of Arles was held, and the arrival of Augustine. Pagan conquests of

Roman territory swept away the vestiges of Roman Christianity. It is remarkable what a religious blank is left in the history of our country between the fourth and the close of the sixth century. At the later period we find Ethelbert, King of Kent and Bretwalder, or overruler, of princes south of the Humber. He married a daughter of a Frankish monarch. This lady brought to England a Frankish bishop, who exercised his ministry in a little church near Canterbury. It is curious to find that the learned antiquary, Sir T. Duffus Hardy, gives reason for thinking that the Utrecht Psalter,[1] with the Athanasian Creed appended, once belonged to this same Bertha, and probably was bequeathed by her to the monastery of Reculver. Sir Thomas believed the handwriting in the Psalter to be of sixth or seventh century date, while the MS. gives further evidence of its great antiquity and costliness. It could have belonged only to some royal personage.

---

[1] "The Athanasian Creed and Utrecht Psalter" is a facsimile of the original, edited by Sir Thomas, and printed for private circulation. He favoured me with a copy, now on my table. I may here add that Pearson, Usher, Hammond, l'Estrange, and others are cited as authorities in support of the Latin origin of the Creed.

As monks were noted missionaries in Ireland and on the Continent, so now monks, headed by Augustine from Rome, brought Christianity back to this country at the close of the sixth century. Last summer, when at Ramsgate, I visited the reputed spot where he arrived, but tradition is so vague and the coast is so altered that I could reach no satisfactory conclusion as to the exact place where he disembarked. The spot on which the king met the monks from Rome is described as on "high ground, dotted with woods." The latter have long since vanished.

Dean Stanley gives this imaginary sketch of Augustine's arrival : " The Saxon king, ' the Son of the Ash-tree,' with his wild soldiers round, seated on the bare ground, on one side ; on the other side, with a huge silver cross borne before him (crucifixes were not yet introduced), and beside it a large picture of Christ, painted and gilded, after the fashion of those times, on an upright board, came up from the shore Augustine and his companions, chanting, as they advanced, a solemn litany, for themselves and for those to whom they came. He, as we are told, was a man of almost gigantic stature, head and shoulders taller than any one else. With him were Laurence, who afterwards succeeded him as

Archbishop of Canterbury, and Peter, who became the first Abbot of Saint Augustine's."[1] Such, it may be imagined, was the opening of a missionary commission, which brought a permanent reign of Christianity into our native land.

Augustine sent his companion Laurence back to Rome, and he returned to England in A.D. 601, with other monks, to strengthen the mission. Soon afterwards Gregory wrote to Augustine congratulating him on the success of his labours, pronouncing them "miraculous," adding, "Rejoice not at this, but rather rejoice that your names are written in heaven." Gregory authorised Augustine to establish twelve bishoprics in this country, and gave instruction as to applying ecclesiastical revenues for supporting the episcopate, the clergy, the poor, and the building of churches. It is curious to find him saying, "Those admitted to holy orders, and unable to lead a life of continence, ought to marry."

Gregory directed that heathen temples should not be destroyed, but stripped of idolatry and devoted to Christian worship. Arbours were to be constructed round such buildings, and commemorations

---

[1] *Historical Memorials of Canterbury*, p. 17.

held in them "with sober meals." The Bishop of Rome was a shrewd man, saying, "You cannot reach the top of a hill by one jump, but must ascend step by step."

He wrote letters both to King Ethelbert and Queen Bertha. The latter he compliments by comparing her to Helena, mother of Constantine, and exhorts her to confirm her husband in Christian faith.[1]

These letters belong to the opening of the seventh century. Augustine died in 604.[2]

It should be remembered that there had been in England a Celtic or Latin Church before Augustine came to fulfil his mission; but that Church had died out, and the Anglo-Saxons, for some reason, cherished an antipathy against it. The two races were antagonistic—Saxon opposed to Celt, Celt to Saxon. There seems to have been "a determination

---

[1] Bede is the only trustworthy author for the story of Augustine's mission to England. It is easy to speculate on the subject, and to give imaginary sketches of what was probable; but such imaginations must not be taken for history. It is remarkable how much solid information on the subject is afforded by the "venerable Bede."

[2] What I have stated is gathered from Bede's *History* and Gregory's *Epistles*.

in the Celtic Church not to attempt the conversion of the Anglo-Saxon race. The Celtic Church, after a time, returned to a sense of duty, although old prejudices lingered long in Wales and Cornwall." [1]

---

[1] Hook's *Lives of the Archbishops of Canterbury*, i., 12.

CHAPTER XII

ECCLESIASTICAL REVENUE AND OUTSIDE HELP

NOTICE has been taken of magnificent churches built by Constantine and his successors. Besides such benefactions we can enumerate other helps afforded from national resources. In the two centuries following the establishment of the Church, no less than eighteen hundred churches were added to the wealth of Christendom, as imperial gifts, increased by popular contributions. The three basilicas of St. Peter, St. Paul, and St. John Lateran had bestowed on them a rent-roll from the State amounting to £12,000. Such endowments were divided into four parts, for bishops, inferior clergy, the poor, and the maintenance of Divine worship.

Arbitration on pecuniary questions was entrusted to clerical persons, and then legally ratified. Money liabilities could be removed by episcopal intercession;

and, besides this, the privilege of sanctuary was transferred from pagan temples to Christian churches. The judgment of moral conduct depended largely upon the sacred order, and so did the decision of pecuniary disputes between Christianised citizens— buyers and sellers, tenants and landlords. The clergy had more than enough to do with such business between one citizen and another. Priests became consulting authorities in many secular matters, and civil law was often mixed up with religious advice. When we recollect how legislation was sought in ecclesiastical disputes, and matters of a pecuniary kind, requiring adjustment between one neighbour and another, came for consideration before the clerical order, one can understand how cases of conscience often became mixed up with pecuniary affairs, and how much secular business fell into clerical hands.

Let me here quote what Gibbon says on matters of this description :—

"Every popular government has experienced the effects of rude or artificial eloquence. The coldest nature is animated, the firmest reason is moved, by the rapid communication of the prevailing impulse; and each hearer is affected by his own passions, and by those of the surrounding multitude. The crisis of civil liberty had silenced the demagogues of Athens and the tribunes of Rome; the custom of preaching, which seems to constitute a considerable part of Christian devotion, had not been introduced into the temples of antiquity; and the ears of monarchs were never invaded by the harsh sound of popular eloquence, till the pulpits of the Empire were filled with sacred orators, who possessed some advantages unknown to their profane predecessors. The arguments and rhetoric of the tribune were instantly opposed, with equal arms, by skilful and resolute antagonists; and the cause of truth and reason might derive an accidental support from the conflict of hostile passions. The bishop, or some distinguished presbyter to whom he cautiously delegated the powers of preaching, harangued, without the danger of interruption or reply, a submissive multitude whose minds had been prepared and subdued by the awful ceremonies of religion. Such was the strict subordination of the Catholic Church that the same concerted sounds might issue at once from a hundred pulpits of Italy or Egypt, if they were tuned by the master hand of some Roman or Alexandrian primate. The design of this institution was laudable, but the fruits were not always salutary. The preachers recommended the practice of the social duties, but they exalted the perfection of monastic virtue, which is painful to the individual, and useless to mankind. Their charitable exhortations betrayed a sacred wish that the clergy might be permitted to manage the wealth of the faithful for the benefit of the poor. The most sublime representations of the attributes and laws of the Deity were sullied by an idle mixture of metaphysical subtleties, puerile rites, and fictitious miracles; and they expatiated with the most fervent zeal on the religious merit of hating the adversaries and obeying the ministers of the Church."

The representatives of the Christian republic were regularly assembled in the spring and autumn of each year, and those synods diffused the spirit of ecclesiastical discipline and legislation throughout the hundred and twenty provinces of the Roman Empire.

Whilst one cannot help recognising the spirit of these criticisms, the testimony thus borne to some of the preaching in the fourth century is not without use if we seek for shadows as well as lights in the oratory of the age. At the same time we are bound to remember, on the other side, the faithful appeals and reproofs addressed to false and inconsistent professors of Christianity at that period. Gibbon, while he tells us a part of the truth relative to the Church in the fifth and sixth centuries, does not tell the whole. He cleverly blends shadows with lights, or omits the whole altogether. Of faithful and salutary preaching he takes no account.

The study of historical origins, in ecclesiastical as in political matters, is deeply interesting, and forms an important chapter in what relates to *outside helps* conferred on Christianity, as we examine the rise and progress of what early occurred in Church history. Much attention has been paid to this subject, and it has amply rewarded, by literary results, thorough critical students. How much more we know on such subjects than our fathers did at the beginning of the last century! Take, for example, Stubbs' *Constitutional History of England*, and it will be found how much light has been thrown upon subjects which were enigmas to our forefathers.

We see in our account of Augustine's arrival what he did in England. It was the planting of slips from the great tree on the banks of the Tiber; and the culture of it in the county of Kent, then a distinct kingdom, was, if we may so speak, in the hands of Roman gardeners, who would bind and guide the young saplings as far as possible in Roman fashion.

There would be little of original British training in the young trees, which began to grow near the eastern coast, and were fanned by breezes from distant imperial heights. In plain words, what was done ecclesiastically at Canterbury was after an Italian type; but, by degrees, English influences would be brought to bear upon ecclesiastical business in general.

What had been distinct Anglo-Saxon kingdoms would and did become distinctly *Anglo-Saxon* Churches, and could not lay open to all such influences as floated round what was becoming the lordly Vatican. Moreover, be it remembered, that while Canterbury was converted by a missionary direct from Rome, Wessex was converted by Berinus from North Italy, East Anglia by a Burgundian priest, Northumbria and Mercia by missionaries from Ireland—men of a type different from Augustine, and such as we met with in our account of missionaries in the preceding chapter. Essex and Sussex were evangelised by Saxon priests, Chad and Wilfrid. It seemed as if the divisions of the Heptarchy were reproduced in the early British sees, and the fact must not be overlooked that the formation of Anglo-Saxon methods had largely to do with ecclesiastical work in our island, so many miles away from the

Vatican, when communication with it such as is common now could not exist.

Let me now directly quote from Dr. Stubbs, to whom I am mainly indebted for the information just given :—

"The development of the local machinery of the Church was in a reverse order to that of the State; the bishoprics being first formed, then the parishes; and, at a much later period, the archdeaconries and deaneries. The original bishoprics of the conversion were the heptarchic kingdoms; and the see was, in some instances, the capital. The kingdom of Kent formed the dioceses of Canterbury and her suffragan Rochester; Essex was the diocese of London; Wessex that of Dorchester or Winchester; Northumbria that of York; East Anglia that of Dunwich; the site of the original Mercian see is not fixed, but within a few years of the conversion, it was placed by St. Chad at Lichfield. In all cases, for a short time, the diocese coincided with the kingdom, and needed no other limitation; the court was the chief missionstation, and sent out monks and priests to convert the outlying settlements. There were as yet very few churches; crosses were set up in the villages, and on the estates of Christian nobles, at the foot of which missionaries preached, said mass, and baptised. The only officer of the bishop was his deacon, who acted as his secretary and companion in travel, and occasionally as interpreter. The bishop's house, however, contained a number of clerks, priests, monks, and nuns, and was both a home of retreat to the weary missionary and a school for the young. These inmates lived by a sort of rule, which was regarded as monastic, and the house and church were the monasterium, or minster. Gifts of land were, at this very early stage, bestowed both on the bishop's minster [or principal church] and on others, which, although under his governance spiritually, were less exclusively his own, having their abbots and abbesses with full powers of economical administration. These houses were frequently of royal foundation, ruled by persons of noble blood ; some of them contained both male and female votaries, and might be ruled by persons of either sex."[1]

"The maintenance of the clergy was provided chiefly by the offerings of the people ; for the obligation of tithe, in its modern sense, was not yet recognised. It is true that the duty of bestowing on God's service a tenth part of the goods was a portion of the common law of

[1] Stubbs, vol. i., p. 224.

Christianity, and as such was impressed by the priest on his parishioners. But it was not possible or desirable to enforce it by spiritual penalties, nor was the actual expenditure determined, except by custom, or by the will of the bishop, who usually divided it between the church, the clergy, and the poor. It was thus precarious and uncertain, and the bestowal of a little estate on the church of the township was probably the most usual way of eking out what voluntary gifts supplied." [1]

---

[1] Stubbs, vol. i., p. 227.

CHAPTER XIII

SEPARATION BETWEEN EASTERN AND WESTERN CHRISTENDOM

THE fact becomes prominent at the period we have reached, and the steps by which it arrived at its completion in the sixth century require our attention.

1. A precedence on the part of the Roman Church far short of what it afterwards attained may be dimly discerned at an early period. It has been justly remarked in a recent publication: " Rome had probably a larger Jewish population than any other city of the West, and here, too, a Christian Church was formed, if not by an Apostle, at least in the lifetime of many Apostles. It was inevitable that the Church in the capital of the world, when it came to be an important body, should exercise a dominant authority over Churches of the neighbouring cities. Such was in fact the case, though its

predominance was not at once recognised."[1] "A dominant authority," as the words are here employed, appears too strong a term for expressing the fact, but it may be said that, from the foundation of Christendom, the Church in the metropolitan city of the world could not but be in a prominent and influential position. So long as the Emperor reigned West and East, ruling Italy and a large part of Europe, also, by degrees, more and more of Asia and the north of Africa; the Church in the imperial city could not but be looked up to as a mother, though not a mistress. While one Emperor reigned East and West, a superior position would be occupied by the Christian community in the world's capital; when there came to be two Emperors, one West and the other East, that would produce a marked difference.

2. The altered political condition of the world, during and after the time of Constantine in particular, especially the removal of an Emperor from Rome to Constantinople, would make a separation between West and East, such as would tell effectively on the ecclesiastical position of communities in the two empires. "Of those who bore a title of Emperor,

---

[1] *Church Hist.: Early Period*, by Cheetham, p. 109.

one ruled in Constantinople, and, more and more absorbed in the cares and calamities of the Eastern sovereignty, became gradually estranged from the affairs of the West. Nor was it till the time of Justinian that any attempt was made to revive his imperial pretensions to Rome. The Western empire lingered for a time in obscurity among the marshes of Ravenna, till at length, in the sixth century and afterwards, the faint shadow of monarchy established there melted away, and a barbarian assumed the appellation of Sovereign of Italy. Still, of the barbarian kings, not one ventured to fix himself in the ancient capital, or to inhabit the mouldering palaces of the older Cæsars. The internal government of the city retained something of the old republican form, which had been permitted to subsist under the Emperors, and it was counted as a territory o the Holy Empire."[1]

3. Ecumenical Councils distinctly told on a division of Christendom into East and West. I have sketched sundry details touching those assemblies, and we cannot fail to be struck with the absence there of Western bishops. Theological discussions, equally interesting, one might have thought, to both

---

[1] Milman's *Latin Christianity*, vol. i., p. 81.

parties, took place, and were keenly contested between opposite divines; but Western representatives are distinguished by absence, as Eastern are by their presence. Decisions reached on these occasions were held to be binding East and West, yet the West had little or nothing actively to do with the conclusions reached at such gatherings. Orthodox divines in the West were by no means wanting in zeal and energy as upholders of our Lord's true and proper Divinity. They wrote, as we have seen, on this vital subject; it is only the large absence of such divines from the so-called Ecumenical Councils that I am now thinking of, as illustrating the fact of marked distinction between what we may call the two old Christendoms. The heterodoxy of Arianism appears much more prevalent and fierce in the East than in the Western division. Europe was not free from this contagion, but, assuredly, it affected Asia to a more alarming extent.

4. Bishops of Rome and Constantinople gradually come to the front in collision with each other on certain points. This is not to be wondered at; they were now rival dignitaries, and would naturally look at certain questions from their own local and personal standpoints. The greatest dignitary of the West, tracing his ecclesiastical descent from Clement

of Rome, who touched upon apostolic times, does not surprise us in his assumption of superior dignity, whatever we may think of his official pretensions and however we may condemn his ecclesiastical ambition. He would naturally look back to the early history of his see, and appreciate the honour conferred on his Church by the Epistle of Paul to the Romans. Though this would not justify Rome's ecclesiastical assumptions, it makes us less surprised at them. The rivalry between the opposite capitals is too intricate a subject and too fertile in opposite assumptions to be discussed fully in a volume like this.

5. But I may mention that the residence of the Emperor being removed from the Western capital, it left a vacancy in the latter for a new kind of rule; potent in its spiritual effect as the old, if not more so, though of a different kind. Gregory the Great recognised Patriarchs of Alexandria and Antioch as equals, because successors to St. Peter and sharers in the one chair of the same founder. He rebuked John the Faster, Patriarch of Constantinople, for assuming the title of "*Ecumenical Bishop.*" He said such an assumption was proud, foolish, and an imitation of Satan. The popedom, as it came to be called, was a form of sovereignty

new in the history of mankind, and the shape which it ultimately assumed could scarcely be imagined at the moment under review; but indefinite scope was now left for aspirations such as had never been previously awakened. Might not a new sort of sceptre now be wielded over the world, tempting to human ambition, while it promised spiritual benefits to mankind? What thoughts, what desires, might then enter the mind of a Leo, and afterwards the mind of a Gregory, who can tell? To suppose the aspirations of such men were all base, or all noble, would be equally unreasonable.

6. Then, further, imperial authority, in much of its old form, being shifted from West to East, at the same time the Patriarchate of Constantinople was opening fresh forms of aspiration and attainment. Asia Minor, Thrace, Pontus, to mention no other country, were coming under a new Oriental sway; and at the Council of Chalcedon all that magnificent dominion was within ecclesiastical reach of the new chief Eastern prelate. On him new powers were being conferred, and though representatives of Rome were present at Chalcedon, they could not prevent the augmentation of Eastern influence. No doubt proceedings there gave a lift from *without* to the Patriarch of Constantinople,

and he soon extended from *within* his augmented authority, by doing what he could to repress the ambition of rival prelates at Antioch and Alexandria. The checking of these Eastern rivals by the ambition of their favoured brother, who now reached the Eastern primacy, served to strengthen and increase his influence, and to bring him more on a level with the pontiff in Italy. That pontiff was to him an object of envy. But mark, how what now took place really operated to the disadvantage of the Eastern bishop. It provoked the jealousy of Orientals to see one of their own order thus lifted up above the rest; so they actually repaired to Rome, and sought from the bishop there his sympathy and aid under this new emergency. He was only too glad to take their part, and to condemn the treatment they had received from their superior. Athanasius had fled from East to West in the day of his adversity, and now irritated Easterns were imitating his example.

"Very soon after the Council of Chalcedon, Leo, Bishop of Rome, appointed a resident legate to Constantinople to watch over Papal interests, and to communicate with the Vatican on matters of importance.

"For the next hundred and thirty years the disputes respecting the equality of the two sees, as well as the limits of their jurisdiction, were carried on, with little interruption perhaps, but with less violence. But in 588, at a synod called at Constantinople respecting the conduct of a Patriarch of Antioch, John, surnamed the Faster, who was then Primate of the East, adopted the title of Ecumenical, or Universal, Bishop. It appears that this title had been conferred on the patriarchs by the Emperors Leo and Justinian, without any accession of power; nor was it, in fact, understood to indicate any claim to supremacy beyond the limits of the Eastern Church. But Gregory could not brook such assumption in an Eastern prelate, and used every endeavour to deprive his rival of the obnoxious title, and at the same time to establish his own superiority. He failed in both these attempts—at least his success in the latter was confined to the Western clergy, and to the interested and precarious assent of the discontented subjects of the Eastern Church."[1]

7. Mutual rivalry and jealousy helped to widen differences between Western and Eastern capitals. A Roman bishop had jurisdiction over ten suburban provinces, and his was the only Western diocese

---

[1] Waddington's *History of the Church*, p. 195.

that could put in a plea for direct apostolical succession. That plea arose from the pretended episcopate ascribed to Simon Peter. However invalid in itself, much was thought of such a pretension by traditionalists at the time. The position of Roman bishops as *subjects* became gradually effaced by their growing power as rulers. Leo I. was really founder of Rome's subsequent spiritual power; and an epistle of his, addressed to the Emperor Flavius, claimed a right to settle theological disputes both in the East and in the West. So early began the claim of œcumenical sway on the part of Western primates. After Leo came Gregory the Great, at the close of the sixth century. He may be counted chief founder of the popedom, and by his claim of supreme power in the universal Church drove off fellowship on the part of Eastern dignitaries. The two communions became totally separated.

This separation between East and West may be regarded as confirmed and augmented by the use of distinct languages. The Greek tongue was predominant in the East. Leading Greek Fathers were Easterns. Origen, and Athanasius, to mention no others, had left behind them treasures of their thoughtfulness in the tongue of Plato and Aristotle; and theological works handed down from such authors were favourite subjects of study on the part of those who stood forward as later representatives and teachers of Eastern Christendom; while Tertullian and Cyprian, Ambrose and Augustine, were guiding lights of Western divines. Difference of language after the Nicene age became more and more a factor in the distinction between Eastern and Western Christendom.

Much more might be added upon the subject of this chapter, but limited space forbids our pursuing it. In closing, it may be remarked that, on the side of the West, the larger and more important influence on the modern world of such men as Augustine and Jerome, not to mention others, is apparent enough; that missionary labours on the part of Irish monks, in their own country, on the Continent, and in England, take the lead in our existing Church literature in this department; that the influence of these memorable Western believers and teachers on posterity as factors—evangelical, social, and religious—amongst a large class, is, at the present day, very considerable; and that it would be easy to supply a chapter on this peculiar branch of history, full of animating illustrations,[1] cannot be doubted.

---

[1] See Kurtz's *Church History*, vol. i., pp. 254, 262, 308, 309.

CHAPTER XIV

THE BORDERLAND OF CHRISTENDOM

LEGENDS relative to the introduction of the gospel amongst outside heathen would naturally arise in Churches planted within the period to which this history belongs, and notices of them occur in the literature of the first six centuries. Indeed, what we find respecting Christian progress on the edge and outside imperial boundaries, in works written by early authors and those who immediately followed, consists chiefly of traditions they had heard from the lips of fathers and mothers, who loved to repeat what they had listened to in their own childhood. A few relics may be introduced in approaching the close of this volume.

In an early chapter[1] mention is made of the way in which Iberians became acquainted with the facts

---

[1] See p. 102.

of Christianity. To legends related in that part of
our history another of later date may be introduced,
touching the same or a kindred branch of the Gothic
race. Theodoret, a Christian chronicler of the fourth
century, informs us how the famous John Chrysostom
took a deep interest in the welfare of numerous races
who touched on a region, not out of reach by
Christians under Constantine, and selected some of
them acquainted with the Gothic tongues. After
having had them ordained as presbyters and deacons,
such persons as now indicated were provided with
a church for missionary uses, and many people
on the borderland, by such instrumentality, were
reclaimed from heathen and idolatrous worship.
Chrysostom himself visited such missionary Churches,
and addressed the people by help of an interpreter.
He exhorted other Christians in the city to engage
in similar efforts, and thus deliver their neighbours
from errors and superstitions in which they had
been entangled. It would seem that Arian ideas
had laid hold of such people, and that it was the
endeavour of Constantinopolitan Christians to bring
them back to the enjoyment of primitive Christianity.[1]

Mention is made of a man living at that period

---

[1] Theodoret, *Eccl. Hist.*, v., c. 30, 31.

named Gainas, ferocious, proud, and tyrannical, of Scythian race, who had under him military forces, composed of Roman infantry and cavalry. This Scythian and his soldiers had imbibed Arian opinions, and they requested the Emperor to set apart a building in which he and his soldiers might worship God in their own way. Chrysostom urged his majesty to make no concession. An interview with Gainas followed on the part of the Bishop, and this seems to have had a salutary effect. For Gainas, we are told by the historian, heard of Chrysostom's approach, and remembering his ministerial fidelity, travelled a long way to meet him; and when he saw the Bishop, this soldier placed his right hand on his eyes, and drew his children round his knees, in token of reverence and affection.[1]

It may be added, from later history as to the borderland in other directions, that many more illustrations may be gathered in the way of lights and shadows than we have space for in this volume.

An interesting legend of conversions in India during Constantine's reign has been preserved by the historian Socrates.[2] Meropius, a Tyrian philosopher, visited the East, and took with him two youths. A

---

[1] Theodoret, *Eccl. Hist.*, v., c. 32, 33. [2] *Eccl. Hist.*, i., c. 19.

treaty between the Romans and the people visited having been recently broken by the latter, these travellers in India found themselves in imminent peril. People of the country seized the strangers, and killed the philosopher who brought them. The boys were sent as slaves to an Indian sovereign, and he, pleased with their appearance, made one his secretary and the other his cup-bearer. The monarch died soon afterwards, leaving a wife and an infant son, whereupon the queen made the two young men tutors of her child; hence there sprang up an attachment between the child and his preceptors. The strangers, so promoted, became persons of importance; and Frumentius, one of the two, being acquainted with Christians in the neighbourhood, joined the latter in religious worship, and having built a house of prayer, instructed the Indians in gospel truths.

When the royal youth attained his majority, and felt able to undertake his own affairs, Frumentius resigned them into his hands, and requested permission to return to his native country. But the king and his mother desired the continuance of his service, and entreated him to remain in the country; he, however, as well as his brother, was bent on departure. The brother hastened to visit his parents, while Frumentius went to Alexandria, where Athanasius had just been raised to the episcopate. The visitor expressed a strong desire that efforts should be made for the conversion of India, and he begged Athanasius to send missionaries there. The Bishop became interested in the youth, and responded to his desire for India's evangelisation. Frumentius entered Holy Orders, and having been ordained presbyter, accepted episcopal office in India. We are told that the new bishop, aided by Divine grace, "performed various miracles, healing diseases, both soul and body, of many amongst the people."

The Church took root in Persia so early as the fourth century, but at that period it suffered from persecution on the part of fanatical magians, and also through wars on the side of the Empire. In that century, Sapor the Great carried on a fierce contest against Christianity during thirty-five years, when, it is said, sixteen thousand clergy, monks, and nuns altogether were put to death. The number, no doubt, was exaggerated. At length persecution ceased, and toleration followed. The destruction of a fire temple in 418 A.D. by a professed Christian brought on a fresh persecution of Christianity, which was carried on fiercely during thirty years. The generosity of a Mesopotamian bishop redeemed a multitude of Persian prisoners, and this noble act secured for a time a better feeling on the part of the persecutors. In 498 A.D. the Persian Church initiating a policy of toleration, the country continued in peace and prosperity for many years. But in the middle of the seventh century Christianity was crushed in Persia by the victories of Mohammedanism.

Mohammed made his appearance and accomplished his mission in the seventh century. Driven from Mecca, he returned to conquer it, and there consecrated an old heathen kaaba as a temple for his religion. At the time of his death all Arabia had accepted his doctrine and engaged in his form of worship. It spread far and wide, and became established in Persia; also in Egypt, Syria, and Spain. It restricted worship to prayers, fastings, and ablutions, and rejected such teaching as Christianity enforced on the great truth of man's redemption. Wherever it made way it quenched belief in the truths of Christianity. But it did good, wherever it took effect, by sweeping away idolatry: thus it came into contact with image worship, which was now becoming prevalent, particularly in some parts of Europe.

The inroads it made upon Christianity in the South of Europe were immense. Spain came under its influence to an almost incredible extent. Not only did the sword win victory on the battlefield, but we are told youths of the highest rank entered Moorish schools, and enthusiastically engaged in the study of the Arabic language and literature. Mutual persecution was the terrible result in that magnificent peninsula. Mementoes of the strife still fascinate the traveller through that region. Moorish architecture in ruins, and Christian cathedrals in cherished magnificence, make impressions which can never be forgotten by travellers in Spain.

Mohammedanism was beginning to make its appearance in the Eastern Church, but not to the same extent of architectural destruction as in the West. There the position assigned in churches to sculptured figures and other material mementoes of Christ was beginning to transform Christian worship into something which resembled what was seen in heathen temples. Simple pictures of Christ and the saints were the nearest approach in the East to what was becoming common in the West, where people might be seen on their knees praying at the feet of sculptured figures.

Looking at Christianity as it appears in the New Testament, it fills us with astonishment to find controversies in the fourth and fifth centuries such as are recorded in this volume. Shadows are seen crossing the lights so as to bewilder students who pursue inquiries respecting clerical orders and the observance of rites and ceremonies.

At the time now noticed a contrast comes out between the absence of endeavours for the conversion of heathen on the part of Eastern Churches and the work carried on by Western missionaries.

In a preceding chapter, under the title of "Monks and Missions," some account has been given of what was done by Columba and others. What they did is worthy of remembrance, and makes a bold mark of difference between them and those on the Eastern border of Christendom. Zeal for the propagation of the gospel shines much more brightly in the West than in the East.

N.B.— On conversion in Persia (noticed p. 355 of this volume), see Socrates' *Eccl. Hist.*, viii., c. 8.

CHAPTER XV

THE DIVINE LAWBOOK OF THE CHURCH

THE Church's main foundation rests in the teaching of Holy Writ, and approaching the close of this imperfect delineation of lights and shadows of early Christendom, that fact comes prominently within notice. Inspired writings were recognised by early patristic writers as a Divine law, to which they were bound to make appeal, not only for settling controverted questions, but as the supreme guide of thought and conduct.

Eusebius brings before us the Old and New Testament as the Church's lawbook. There had been, as noticed already, a fearful destruction of Scriptures under the Diocletian persecution; next came a distinct recognition of Divine oracles as the Church's guide. A letter of Constantine to Eusebius, and the course adopted by Eusebius, in reference to Holy Writ, here claim attention.

Constantine wrote to Eusebius saying that in the city which bore his name, *Constantinople*, a multitude of people had attached themselves to the Church; that this influx of believers was on the increase, and consequently, not only were more churches needed, but copies of Holy Writ, as well. He directed Eusebius to have prepared fifty copies of the Divine volume, to be written by scribes well instructed in penmanship. He said orders had been issued to the governors of provinces to furnish everything needful for such a work; and with this communication authority was given to Eusebius to employ a couple of royal carriages for conveying the books, when finished, to his Majesty's hands. These copies were intended for churches in the new capital, and were "to be executed with care and carried out with diligence." All showed what earnestness the Emperor threw into the movement. Eusebius states, he fulfilled this charge, without giving particulars of the way he did so. It may be inferred, however, that a Greek Bible was issued for public use, with books of the Hebrew Canon, including the Apocrypha as appendix. The catalogue quoted by Eusebius differs as to the Book of Esther, and there is nothing to show what place he assigned to it. All books of the New Testament now received were added in the list sent, with the exception of the Apocalypse, which, perhaps, was added as an appendix,[1]—the Constantinopolitan Bible including New Testament as well as Old, with the Epistles of Paul; and the latter not, as in an Alexandrian list, immediately next to the Book of Acts.

Eusebius, in his *Ecclesiastical History*, supplies a catalogue of New Testament contents.[2] First he places the four Gospels, next to them the Acts of the Apostles, then come fourteen Pauline Epistles, and next the First Epistle of John and First of Peter; after "these books," as he calls them, the Apocalypse is noticed, with an intimation that he intends to set forth judgments passed on this portion of Holy Writ. He, in due course, speaks of objections made to the Apocalypse. Some thought the style of composition seemed unlike what we find in the fourth Gospel. Its authority appeared questionable, from internal indications, and from absence of external evidence. Eusebius felt doubts respecting it. He speaks of Paul's Epistles, without noticing the Epistle to the Hebrews; and afterwards cites portions of it, as if it was written by Clement of Rome. He notices

---

[1] Eusebius, *Vita Constantine*, iv., 36.
[2] *Ecclesiastical History*, iii., c. 24.

seven Catholic Epistles, so-called, but makes no use of that ascribed to Jude, and the second named after Peter, with the second and third named after John. The Apocalypse is rarely quoted by Eusebius.

I should attribute importance to his testimony for two reasons: first, that he was a more skilled and careful literary critic, from his large acquaintance with historical documents, than most Fathers were likely to be. His *Ecclesiastical History* shows how extensive must have been his studies in that direction. The second reason for regarding him as a superior judge, is that he appears to have been free from theological and ecclesiastical partisanship, consequently less biassed on such a subject as that before us.

No question as to inspiration and authority of Holy Writ came under discussion at Nicea, but a council held at Laodicea in the middle of the fourth century took up that subject carefully. The Laodicean council was a small gathering from the neighbourhood of Lydia and Phrygia, assembled about A.D. 363. The members laid down, as law for Christian worship, that psalms composed by private persons were not to be read in church, nor any book admitted but canonical ones. A list of such was added; but this list is considered to be of later date, and to carry

Ch. XV] THE DIVINE LAWBOOK OF THE CHURCH 363

with it little or no authority. Indeed, the proceedings of so small an assembly were of little importance, and it included unorthodox members.

Councils claiming ecumenical character have been noticed, but they did not take up the canonicity of Scripture, which was obviously a practical matter requiring attention in their debates, and would have afforded employment far more appropriate and profitable than some questions on which they spent their time.

The *Apostolical Constitutions*, forming a body of early ecclesiastical laws, to which no specific date can be attached, contains the following rule, which may be referred to about the fifth century: " Let the reader," it is said (that is, of the assembly), " standing upon some elevated place, read the books of Moses, Joshua, Judges, Kings, Chronicles, and those of the return from captivity (Ezra and Nehemiah), in addition to Job, Solomon, and the sixteen prophets. As readings are made two at a time, let another chant David's hymns, and the people chant in response the close of each verse. After this, let the Acts of the Apostles be read, and the Epistles of Paul, our fellow-worker. After these books, let the deacon or presbyter read the Gospels, which we, Matthew and John " (so runs the document), " gave to you, and which the fellow-workers of Paul, Luke and Mark, having received, left to you. And whenever the Gospel is being read let presbyters and deacons and all the people stand in complete silence, for it is written, ' Be silent and hear, O Israel.' " Unless the Book of Esther be omitted, the Canon of the Old Testament here given is exactly that of the Jews. As to the New Testament, Catholic epistles are probably included in the Acts.

"In the works of Chrysostom, a synopsis of the Old and New Testament has been preserved which is probably genuine, and certainly a Syrian catalogue of Chrysostom's time. In this the contents of the Old Testament are described somewhat indistinctly. The enumeration of the historical books contains only those of the Hebrew Canon (except Esther, though reference is made to the Maccabean war). Ecclesiasticus (the Wisdom of Sirach) is added to the moral books, and the Psalter is reckoned among the prophets. In the synopsis itself, Esther, Tobit, Judith, Wisdom, and Ecclesiasticus are analysed without any note as to their character.

"The order in which books of the New Testament are cited is remarkable: the fourteen Epistles of St. Paul, the four Gospels, the Acts, and three of the Catholic Epistles—James, 1 Peter, and 1 John. The quotations in Chrysostom's voluminous writings confirm the same canon. He never uses the Apocalypse nor the four Catholic Epistles."[1]

From these public documents, as they may be termed, we proceed to notice what can be gathered from individual Fathers with regard to their use of Scripture.

We have seen the place and influence of Athanasius at Nicea, now let us listen to what he says of canonical literature in his thirty-ninth Festal Letter: " As I am about to speak of Divine Scripture, I shall use for the support of my boldness the model of the Evangelist Luke, and say as he does, 'Forasmuch as some have taken in hand to set forth in order for themselves the so-called Apocrypha, and to mix it with the inspired Scriptures, which we most surely believe, even as they delivered it to our fathers, who, from the beginning, were eye-witnesses and ministers of the Word, it seemed good to me also, having been urged by true brethren, and having learnt from the first, to publish the books which are admitted in the Canon, and have been delivered to us, and are believed to be Divine, that if any one has been deceived he may condemn those who led him astray, and he

---

[1] *The Bible in the Church*, p. 174.

who has remained, pure from error, may rejoice in being again reminded of the truth.'"[1] Athanasius then enumerates the Old Testament books as twenty-two, corresponding with our recognised list, but including as well the Book of Baruch. Then he gives the four Gospels, the Acts, the seven Catholic Epistles, the fourteen Epistles of Paul, and the Apocalypse of John. These, he says, are "fountains of salvation, so that he who thirsts for salvation may satisfy himself with these oracles. Let no one add to these, nor take anything from them." Athanasius mentions "Apocryphalas" distinct from these canonical works.

Gregory Nazianzen says to his flock at Constantinople, "That you may not be cheated by strange books, receive this my approved enumeration;" and his list of the Hebrew Canon specified, includes twelve historical, five metrical, and five prophetical books. Esther is omitted, and Ruth is counted as a distinct work. In the New Testament Gregory enumerates four Gospels, the Book of Acts, fourteen Pauline Epistles, and seven Catholic ones.[2]

---

[1] *The Bible in the Church*, p. 159.
[2] Quoted by Westcott, *ibid.*, p. 166.

Cyril of Jerusalem writes: "Learn from the Church what are the books of the Old Testament and the New; and I pray you read nothing in the Apocrypha. Read the twenty-two books, but have nothing to do with apocryphal writings."[1]

Thus Athanasius and Cyril lay down the canonical law of Scripture. At the same time the Alexandrine authorities make use of the Apocrypha.

We must now look westward. The Roman Church in the fourth century occupied a position of much power and influence. It craved a wide —a world-wide leadership, and had really more scope for influence and rule after the imperial throne had been shifted from the banks of the Tiber to the Sea of Marmora. The new city left behind it that power of organisation and far-spreading rule which the old city retained and exercised. Though neither Jerome nor Augustine lived in Rome at the end of the fourth century, they were undoubtedly factors of Latin authority. Jerome was pre-eminently so as translator of Holy Writ into Latin, a language then becoming, more and more, a vehicle of intercommunication throughout Europe and the civilised world. Wherever Latin

[1] *The Bible in the Church*, p. 168.

was intelligible, there, within reach of all who could read, the Vulgate version was a fact of immense importance. But Jerome's inclusion of the Apocrypha in his Bible was a serious drawback on its value ; he, however, explained distinctly that apocryphal additions to Esther, David, and Jeremiah had no place in the Hebrew Canon, and, consequently, were not to be used as part of Canonical Scripture.

Jerome attested the canonicity of the Apocalypse, saying: "In the Isle of Patmos, where he was banished by the Emperor Domitian, John, one of Christ's disciples, witnessed the Apocalypse, containing infinite mysteries of the future."[1] The Apocalypse, in some cases, was not read *publicly* from difficulties in the interpretation. Jerome says, "We accept the Apocalypse, by no means following the present custom, but the authority of ancient writers."[2]

Augustine's attention was particularly fixed on the canonicity of Scripture. Before his conversion he had imbibed Manichean errors, and had, like other members of that sect, become acquainted with apocryphal Gospels and Acts, which, of course, he repudiated after his adoption of orthodox Chris-

---

[1] *Adv Jovinian*, i., 26.   [2] *Ep. ad Dard.*, 129, § 3.

tianity. Subsequent to his wonderful change he took part in a council held at Hippo, A.D. 393. The decisions of that council are lost; its statutes were considered and revised by the Council of Carthage in 397. In his important treatise on *Christian Doctrine* he takes up the subject of canonicity, and lays down the principle that Christians are to follow the authority of as many Catholic Churches as possible. "He will be the wisest student of Scriptures," was his conclusion, "who shall have first read and learnt those books which are called canonical. For the rest, he will read with greater security, when furnished with faith in the truth; as there is danger lest they preoccupy a mind as yet unstable, and instil ideas contrary to what is sound understanding by perilous fictions and fancies."[1] Augustine's object was to mark distinctly those books which had ecclesiastical authority. His decision in this respect did not essentially differ from that of Jerome. The decree at Carthage in A.D. 419 was a confirmation and renewal of that published in the same place twelve months before.

I may here add a word on the subject of this

---

[1] *De Doct. Chr.*, ii., 12, 13.

chapter, respecting Hilary, Bishop of Poictiers. He flourished in the latter part of the fourth century, as stated already. In a prologue to his Commentary on the Book of Psalms he followed Origen closely, and gave a free rendering of the Old Testament list of authors. He reckoned twenty-four books in the Old Testament, according to the number of Greek letters, by the addition of Tobit and Judith—the Roman alphabet of twenty-three letters being comprised between the Hebrew and the Greek—"because," he adds, "it is in these three letters being comprised between the Hebrew and the Greek."

The recognition of *Canonical* Scripture, and its gradual acceptance during the three centuries after the Nicean Council included within this volume, though often overlooked, claims a distinct and prominent place in ecclesiastical history. It set up the Divine light for all Christendom.

At the Council of Carthage, A.D. 397, at which Augustine was present, a decree was ratified which determined the list of "Canonical Scriptures" in accordance with his opinion. It is decreed that nothing except the Canonical Scriptures be read in the Church under the name of Divine Scriptures. The Canonical Scriptures are Genesis, five books of Solomon (Proverbs, Ecclesiastes, Canticles, Wisdom, Ecclesiasticus), Ezekiel, Tobias, Judith, Esther, Esdras (2), Maccabees (2); of the New Testament, the four Gospels, Acts, thirteen Epistles of St. Paul, the Epistle of the same to the Hebrews, Peter (2), John (3), James, Jude, Apocalypse.

Note.—Let the Transpontine (Roman) Church be consulted about the confirmation of that Canon. Also let it be allowed that the Passions of Martyrs be read on the celebration of their anniversaries.[1]

---

[1] Westcott, *Bible in the Church*, p. 188.

CHAPTER XVI

HOLY CATHOLIC COMMUNION

THE Rev. F. D. Maurice asks, Is there a Catholic Church? and proceeds to answer the question by a discussion as to its principles and constitution, its doctrines and institutes. To confine oneself to this aspect of the title is to overlook the personal element altogether. The Church has its laws given in Scripture and illustrated in history. It has also an aggregate of persons, amongst whom are found those "who are redeemed from amongst men,"[1] "called, chosen, and faithful."[2] It is not merely an Institute, but a *Company*. "Church" signifies an aggregate of *persons* as well as a system of doctrine and a collection of institutes.

In the New Testament we have histories and epistles, and in the Apocalypse letters, addressed to

---

[1] Rev. xiv. 4.   [2] *Ibid.*, xvii. 14.

Ephesus, reproving the Church there for leaving her first love; to Pergamos, for holding the doctrines of Balaam and the Nicolaitanes; to Sardis, because it had a name to live while dead; to Laodicea, because it was lukewarm, neither hot nor cold.

Something different from any such local communities is indicated by St. Paul: "There is one body, and one spirit, even as ye are called in one hope of your calling; one Lord, one faith, one baptism, one God and Father of all, who is above all, and through all, and in you all."

Paul says Christ "gave some, apostles; and some, prophets; and some, evangelists; and some, pastors and teachers; for the perfecting of the saints, for the work of the ministry, for the edifying of the body of Christ: till we all come in the unity of the faith, and of the knowledge of the Son of God, unto a perfect man, unto the measure of the stature of the fulness of Christ: that we henceforth be no more children, tossed to and fro, and carried about with every wind of doctrine, by the sleight of men, and cunning craftiness, whereby they lie in wait to deceive; but speaking the truth in love, may grow up into Him in all things, which is the Head, even Christ: from whom the whole body fitly joined together and compacted by that which every joint supplieth, according to the effectual working in the measure of every part, maketh increase of the body unto the edifying of itself in love." [1]

The Apostle here describes, not only a system or order of *things*, not simply an *institute* of law and government, remaining to be worked out, more or less imperfectly, by an aggregate of persons, but a community of souls, knit together by spiritual sympathies, and constituting a unity, spread over the earth, perpetuated through ages, permanent and stable, yet ever growing by virtue of its common life in Christ. There is vital coherence, a common belief, sympathy one with another—the whole making increase, love being the ligature which binds the parts together.

What Paul describes, Hooker, in his *Ecclesiastical Polity*, defines, as that "Church of Christ which we properly term *His body mystical*": "Only our minds, by intellectual conceit, are able to apprehend that such a real body there is; a body collective, because it containeth a huge multitude; a body mystical, because the mystery of their conjunction is removed altogether from sense. Whatsoever we read in Scripture concerning the endless love and the saving mercy which God showeth towards His

---

[1] Eph. iv. 11-16.

Church, the only proper subject thereof is *this* Church. Concerning this flock it is that our Lord and Saviour hath promised, 'I give unto them eternal life, and they shall never perish, neither shall any pluck them out of My hands.' They who are of this society have such marks and notes of distinction from all others as are not objects unto our sense, only unto God, who seeth their hearts, and understandeth all their secret cogitations ; unto Him they are clear and manifest." The distinction between the one Catholic Church and those local Churches which appear in the New Testament is recognised by Hooker as obvious. "In St. Paul's time the integrity of Rome was famous, Corinth many ways reproved; they of Galatia much more out of square in St. John's time, Ephesus and Smyrna in far better state than Thyatira and Pergamus."[1]

It is difficult to fix upon a right word to express the distinction now brought out. Hooker uses the word "*mystical*," but "mystical" comes so near to mysterious that it suggests the idea of what is unintelligible. To call organised Churches, each or altogether, "*visible*," and to denominate actual believers, which organised bodies do not envelop, as

---

[1] Hooker's *Ecclesiastical Polity*, III., i., 15.

"*invisible*," would imply that believers might really exist without giving manifest proofs of it—a thing incredible. Notwithstanding, the use of the word "invisible" is most common in our ecclesiastical phraseology. Perhaps it is best to employ the word "spiritual," to mark off "the Holy Catholic Church" from what is *formal*, remembering that "the form of godliness" does not of *itself* exclude "the power."

"Having the form of godliness and denying the power thereof" is what we are warned against; and yet this implies that, under the form, the power may, does, and ought to operate. A globe of glass envelops the burning lamp, and at the same time preserves and diffuses the illumination.

The history of the first six centuries should be studied in the light of the seven epistles, at the commencement of the Apocalypse. When we find in St. John's days such an account of inconsistency, false doctrine, unholy practice, all dishonourable to the name of Christianity, can we wonder at anything recorded in the preceding sketch of early Christendom? For within the Churches described by the searcher of hearts were faithful souls who worked for Christ and endured persecution for His sake and held fast His name, who kept the word of His patience, and who, notwithstanding much inconsistency, were offered refined gold and white garments by Him who stood outside their door knocking for entrance.

There was, then, in the first century *a Church within the Churches*, on which rested the patient, loving eyes of Him who died upon the cross for the salvation of souls—a Church which, amidst an outward fellowship, including unworthy members, was in reality united to the spiritual communion described by the Apostle Paul in his Ephesian letter. And as in the first century, so in the second and third, there was a Church within the Churches, composed of a multitude which no man can number, redeemed out of many nations, tribes, peoples, and tongues. In the midst of heathen pollution they did not defile their garments, but walked with Christ the Lord, in white, for He counted them worthy. They passed through persecution, but as there were pauses in the beating storm, and the sun broke out after the rain, then the faithful had peace and rest; being edified, and walking in the fear of the Lord, and in the comfort of the Holy Ghost, they were multiplied. In tempestuous seasons they were afflicted and tormented; they wandered in deserts, and in mountains, and in dens and caves of the earth,[1] yet they had continued communion with Christ, and among themselves. "Then they that feared the Lord spake often one to another: and the Lord hearkened, and heard it, and a book of remembrance was written before Him for them that feared the Lord, and that thought upon His Name. And they shall be Mine, saith the Lord of hosts, in that day when I make up My jewels; and I will spare them, as a man spareth his own son that serveth him."[2]

Thus under varied circumstances the spiritual Church preserved its identity, and retained its power, and exerted its influence. Each member was a light shining in a dark place, until a better day, as regarded liberty and scope of action, dawned upon them; a day, however, which brought with it new temptations, for whilst it favoured the form of godliness, it saw so many who, by their real character and actual life, denied the power.

In looking at the shadows which dimmed and the lights that glorified early Christendom, we may distinguish between shadows from *without* and those which arose from *within*. The spiritual Catholic Church cannot be made responsible for early heresies.

---

[1] Heb. xi. 38.   [2] Mal. iii. 16, 17.

Gnostics, Ebionites, Judaising teachers, were really *outside* the border; and they in their assaults were vigorously repelled by many who were within. Heresies injured the harvest of good seed sown by Christian hands; but some of the tares did not long continue to grow to any great extent amidst fields tilled by faithful hands. Gnosticism and Ebionitism were shortlived. Evils, however, did arise in orthodox Christendom: innovations, rivalries, lax and misguided discipline, perversions of Divine rites, worldliness, with manifold inconsistencies of conduct.

When we turn to the lights in contrast with the shadows, we have on record the lives and writings of such men as Clement of Rome and his namesake of Alexandria, Ignatius the Martyr, Irenæus the Advocate, the learned expositor Origen, and the indefatigable Cyprian, who sealed the truth with his blood. We have, moreover, a consistent body of truth maintained in the Apostolic Creed, and in the writings of individual Fathers, who stimulate us by their examples, whilst they instruct us by their works. Social worship is illustrated by ante-Nicene sermons, prayers, and hymns. Reaching the age of Constantine, we have the Nicene Creed, and a goodly array of Nicene names—the Gregorys, Chrysostom,

Augustine, Basil, and many more. Later come the missionary labours of Augustine, who planted the Church of England in the then remote Western world, and of others who propagated the gospel round the Mediterranean shores, and far away in Eastern climes. When we look upon these lights amidst surrounding darkness, can we doubt the existence of a Holy Catholic Church in the midst of a sinful world?

CHAPTER XVII

ON THE EDGE OF THE DARK AGES

A NUMBER of lights and shadows have passed before us in this second part of our imperfect history, and now a few instances of men less known, but characteristic of the period when they lived, may be appropriately noticed.

I begin with Servian, a man by no means of good report, whom we meet with in the days of Chrysostom. The latter had left him as Bishop of Gabala, in Syria, where he became celebrated, but is said to have behaved ungratefully to his patron. Chrysostom forbade his preaching in Constantinople, and Servian, in consequence, left the city, till he was recalled by the Empress, who managed some kind of reconciliation between the two. Resentment lingered in the breast of Servian, who influenced those around him and organised a strong and troublesome party against the popular preacher. They managed to rake up something against him in his earlier days at Antioch; and this contemptible feud shows how much folks in those days were like our own. This Servian turns up again at Constantinople, where he ventured to preach against the Bishop, and was driven out of the city by friends of the latter.

A curious case—in its relation to our own times—occurs in connection with the name of Eligius, who was created Bishop of Noyon in A.D. 640. Dr. Robertson, in his Life of Charles V.,[1] mentioned him as an example of mediæval preachers, who told their hearers "they satisfied every obligation of duty by a scrupulous observance of external ceremonies." It has been shown by Dr. Maitland[2] that this statement is untrue, and that a sermon by Eligius is found in his works which really seems as if it had been written in anticipation of what Robertson has ventured to assert. This case illustrates ignorance and carelessness amongst historians a century ago in relation to the dark ages. A namesake of Robertson in our own time shows how noted Eligius was for his piety and faithful preaching. He was

---

[1] *Charles V.*, by Robertson, ii., p. 29.
[2] *The Dark Ages*, pp. 103 *et seq.*

a goldsmith, and devoted his wealth to religious and charitable purposes, so that poor people used to flock round his doorway for relief, and while working at his craft kept the Scriptures within reach for frequent perusal.[1]

Taking a general view of the clergy at the opening of the middle ages, it must be remembered they were under obligation to remain unmarried. "The general aim of the canons, enacted during this time, was to prevent clerical wedlock, altogether if possible, to extend the prohibition to inferior grades of the ministry, to debar the married from higher promotion." The result was that the enforcement remained impracticable; amongst men in holy orders, gross immorality followed as a natural consequence. The clergy were prohibited from having women in their houses except they were near relatives; and the issue of forbidden marriages were declared by law incapable of inheriting property.

At the same time, and partly as a necessary result, wealth went on increasing in the Church. Sin was supposed to be expiated by the bestowment of money, and at the same time priests were exempted from the authority of lay tribunals. Bishops were

---

[1] Robertson's *Church History*, iii., p. 35.

not required to give evidence in court. But their authority went on increasing in many respects. They engaged in secular business, and were eligible for state offices. All clerical patronage was in episcopal hands; but builders of churches had rights of presentation.

In new Western kingdoms clerical orders became of great importance; where new kingdoms arose as an effect of conquest, clergy became mediators between vanquished and victorious. They also had great influence in the framing of laws. Their exclusive possession of learning gave them power and influence such as in our day can scarcely be conceived. They had no doubt an immense amount of power for doing good, and it is but a righteous amount of charity to believe that in a multitude of cases they did what was in their power. When we think of wild barbaric hordes conquered by military force and brought into service for civilised life, we see what openings, to an immeasurable extent, thereby arose for usefulness on the part of clerical orders in acts of civilisation. Their religion taught them kindliness and charity, and we cannot justly doubt that many of the beneficed orders were instruments in building up institutions for national well-being, and in promoting the amenities of private life.

At the point we reach in the present chapter the historian finds himself on the edge of a period very different, on the whole, from that now left behind. Many things doubtless remain as before, but many old fashions are either left or greatly altered; new objects appear on the foreground. Hermits in their ancient modes of life diminish in number. We see no longer numerous recluses living apart from other people on the banks of the Nile and under the sunshine of an Oriental sky. Here and there hermitages are met with, few and far between. In Provence and Languedoc, it seems, there existed the strange practice of burying alive, in a solitary cell, some pitiable creature; the door walled or nailed up, with the seal of a bishop's ring upon it. Immediate starvation did not follow, as the poor incarcerated victim was allowed a daily provision, let down in a basket.[1]

But as hermitages became few, monasteries multiplied. The institutes of Bernard of Nursia became numerous, and preserved from otherwise inevitable destruction the learning and wisdom of an old world. All over Italy, France, Germany, and Europe libraries

---

[1] Smith's *Dictionary of Christian Antiquities*, article on "Hermits."

were collected and preserved by monks, affording welcome to weary travellers and help to diligent students. Much, and more than we can calculate, passed away with the old-world learning, but abundant intellectual wealth was preserved, which is ours and our children's after us.

Missions to the German nations were chiefly carried on by monks. "They planted colonies in lonely places, where towns soon grew up, as at Fulda, St. Gall, Eichstadt, and Fritzlar, and with the knowledge of religion they spread that of agriculture and civilisation among the people. Through the employment of monks in missionary labour, ordination was largely introduced to their ranks, as a necessary qualification for religious duties.

"In some cases, sees were filled up with monks from flourishing abbeys — an arrangement most natural, because learning was chiefly cultivated in monastic societies. Thus Strasburg received its bishops from Munster, in Alsace; Spires from Wissenburg; Constance from Reichenau or from St. Gall. The reputation of sanctity continued to wait on monkish orders. The term *religious*, which had been specially applied to the monastic profession by a council at Orleans as early as A.D. 549, became more and more restricted to it."[1]

The dark ages decidedly set in, with augmenting gloom, during the seventh century. Then papal authority, under Gregory the Great, reached a point it had never done before. It lost nothing under his immediate successors; on the contrary, Roman Catholicism advanced. But the Lombard kingdom did not, at that period, maintain cordial relations with it. Spanish bishops influenced the choice of Spanish kings—the most eminent of the former at that period being the famous Isidore of Seville. Ildefonso, Bishop of Toledo, burned with zeal for maintaining the perpetual virginity of our Lord's mother. France, plunged into troubles of its own, could do but little in the Church's service. But in the seventh century saints appear conspicuous amongst French sovereigns. The Irish Church saw palmy days, and Roman religious customs prevailed in Britain. Amongst our forefathers, Bede and Cædmon were burning and shining lights.

During the whole of this period, image-worship in the West, and reverence for pictures in the East, went on increasing, till idolatry spread far and wide

[1] Robertson's *Ecclesiastical History*, iii., pp. 215, 216.

all over Europe. The sunset of early Christendom was followed by a wintry-night sky, in which, through the mercy of Him who rules day and night, star after star appeared, until the morning of the Reformation dawned, and the dense mediæval gloom rolled gradually away.

INDEX

Adamnan, 320.
Aetius, 138.
Agape, 78.
Alexander, Bishop of Alexandria, 136.
Amalaric, 309.
Ambrose, 34, 146, 153; on Virgin, 166; made Bishop, 232; in connection with Theodosius I., 234, 236; his death, 237; an ascetic, 260; his chants, 285.
Ammianus Marcellinus, 135.
Anathema, 177.
Andronicus of Lybia, 220.
Anicetus, 57.
Anobius, 93.
Antoninus Pius, 112.
Antony, 83, 84, 312.
Apocryphal Gospels, 18, 360, 368.
Apollinaris, 58.
Apostles' Creed, 141.
Apostles, Prophets, and Evangelists, 27.
Appion, 17.
Arethusa, 185.
Arianism, 132, 142, 144, 148, 189, 261, 352.

Aristotle, 51, 65.
Arius, 133, 136, 138.
Arnobius, 124.
Arnold, Dr., 91, 99.
Artemas, 89.
Asceticism, 83, 312.
Asclepediorus, 86.
Athanasius on Antony, 83; at Alexandria, 133; at Nicea, 136; on Divinity of our Lord, 142; accused of murder, 144; exile, 149; made Bishop, 211; his letters, 213, 365; visit to Rome, 313.
Atonement, doctrine of the, 274.
Augustine on the Virgin, 166; his doctrine, 193; became Bishop, 221; as preacher, 222; his death, 225, 330; his description of Ambrose, 232; his conversion, 262; creed, 264, 271; in controversy, 268; quoted by Tyndale, 270; on justification, 275; *City of God*, 277; decrees, Canonical Scriptures, 370.
Aurelian, 113.

Baptism, 39, 41, 161.
Barnabas, Epistle of, 10
Basil, 163, 201, 260.
Basilicas, 281.
Benedict of Nursia, 322-324.
Bernard of Nursia, 385.
Bingham, 34.
Blandina, 121, 122.
Boethius, 297.
Brahmanism, 1.
Buddhism, 1.
Butler's *Analogy*, 66, 67.

Canon of Scripture, 21, 366.
Caractacus, 325.
Cassiodorus, 298.
Catacombs, 126; of Callistus, 252; of St. Ponziano, 256; of St. Agnese, 257.
Celsus, 45, 65, 66.
Chilperic, 306.
Christmas, 287.
Chrysostom, 156; elected Archbishop 191; a child, 185; his doctrine, 193; his preaching, 194, 222; his letters, 196; last days, 198; visiting Churches, 352; his works, 364; forbids Servian preaching, 381.
Church of the Holy Sepulchre, 182.
Claudia, 103.
Clement of Alexandria, 10; the *Didaché*, 29; his hymn, 34; on Baptism, 40; on Christianity, 58; persecuted, 59; Alexandrian school, 68.

Clement of Rome, 11; *Recognitions* and *Homilies*, 15; Epistle of, 36, 72; on the Apostles, 112, 379.
Clementinus, 11, 15.
Clerical orders, 384.
Clonard, St., 319.
Clotaire, 304.
Clotilda, 300, 309.
Clovis, 300.
Codex Argenteus, 293.
Coliseum at Rome, 117.
Columba, 319, 358.
Consecration of Bishops, 67.
Constans, 148.
Constantia, 132.
Constantine, reign of, 84; gospel under, 100; built churches, 130; on idolatry, 130; laws enacted, 131; baptised, 132, 145; opening of council, 136; banquet, 139; edict of toleration, 140; Nicene Creed, 144; death, 145; Church and State under, 147; his sons, 148; faith of, 151; portrait, 156; his mother, 156, 182; churches built by, 332; letter to Eusebius, 360.
Constantine II., 148.
Constantius, 148.
Cornelius, Bishop of Rome, 101.
Corpus Inscriptorium, 115.
Councils, 33; Carthaginian, 34; at Arles, 95, 130, 298, 326; at Nicea, 133, 135, 362; at

Ancyra, Rimini, and Seleucia, 149; canons of, 157; at Constantinople, 163, 176; at Ephesus, 163, 167, 286; at Chalcedon, 172, 346; at Orange, 270; of Laodicea, 282, 362.
Creeds, Nicene, 141; Apostles', 141; Athanasian, 327.
Cyprian, 35; on baptism, 40; his writings, 46; his home, 78; on Church government, 80; his death, 82, 123; assembled a council, 95.

Damaris, 69.
Damasus, 240, 253.
Decius, 106, 113, 117.
Demetrius of Alexandria, 62.
Didaché, 29.
Didymus, 211.
Diocletian, 110; edict, 114; persecution, 140, 159, 359.
Diognetus, 12.
Dionysius, 58, 69, 184.
Discipline, ecclesiastical, 45.
Donatists, 95, 131, 161.

Easter, 130, 161, 286, 321.
Eastern Christendom, 350.
Eastern theology, 259.
Ebionism, 30, 46, 379.
Ebrard, 28.
Edict of toleration, 130.
Eleutherus, 57.
Ephrem the Syrian, 208.
Epicureans, 104, 105.
Epiphanius, 165, 295, 314.
Epistles, Barnabas, 10; Clement, 11; Pauline, 26; Ephesus, 27; Corinth, 27; Titus, 29; Corinthians, 46, 72; Romans, 47, 72.
Ermenegild, 310.
Ethelbert, 327, 330.
Euripides, 65.
Eusebius, 70, 86; on Churches, 97; on Aurelian's reign, 113; on Polycarp, 118; on Justin Martyr, 120; on Constantine, 129, 139; on New Testament, 361.
Evagrius, 187.

Fabricius, 146.
Fasting, 161.
Faustinus, 16.
Faustus, 16.
Felix III., 244.
Flavius, 349.
Fortunatus, 305.
Frumentius, 354.

Gainas, 353.
Gall, St., 322.
Gallienus, 113.
Geoffrey of Monmouth, 105.
Gibbon on Priscillianists, 153; on Athanasius, 212; on Synesius, 216; on Hilary, 227; on preaching, 332.
Gnosticism, 46, 54, 58, 75, 379.
Gospel, of Mary's Nativity, 18; Thomas, 18; Nicodemus, 18; doctrines of, 25.
Gregory the Great, 247; his theological opinions, 248; his letters, 250; his death, 252; founder of Popedom, 349.

Gregory Nazianzen, 159; on councils, 162; invited to Constantinople, 188; at Athens, 201; his verses, 284; on Hebrew Canon, 366.
Gregory Thaumaturgus, 53, 100.
Gregory of Tours, 123.
Grote, 19.

Hadrian, 112.
Hampden, Dr., 266.
Hegesippus, 58.
Hengstenberg, 28.
Henry VIII., 105.
Herbert (George), 83.
Heresies, treatise on, 53.
Hermas, Shepherd of, 14.
Hilary of Arles, 228, 285, 317.
Hilary of Poictiers, 226, 370.
Homer, 73.
Homilies, 15, 17, 67.
Honoratus, 317.
Hooker, 170, 374.
Hosius a Spaniard, 137.
Hypatia, 215.

Ignatius, Bishop of Antioch, 12; letters of, 30; on the Eucharist, 43; Christianity at Antioch, 94; Epistles of, 115; martyrdom, 117.
Incarnation, 174.
Inspiration of Gospels, 5.
Irenæus, 2, 30; on baptism, 41; his treatise on Heresies, 53; his doctrine, 57; on truths of gospel, 93; writings of, 379.
Jerome, 3; meaning of "angel," 28; on Origen, 61; his Epistles, 146; on luxury, 159; on Hilary, 227; on Pelagianism, 269; a scholar, 313; his character, 316.
Jerusalem, fall of, 6.
John the Faster, 248, 345, 348.
Jovian, 151.
Jules Simon, 52.
Julian, 137, 149, 150.
Justin Martyr, 2; on baptism, 40; on Lord's Supper, 42 his Apology, 50; compared with Origen, 66; on spread of the gospel, 92; his second Apology, 113; his suffering, 120.
Justina, 151.
Justinian, 154, 156, 158, 286.

Kaye, Bishop, 75, 144.
Ken, Thomas, 83.

Lactantius, 124.
Laurence, 329.
Leo the Great, 241; his sermon, 243; on the Atonement, 274, 347, 349.
Levvigild, 310.
Liberius, 239.
Lightfoot, Bishop, on elders, 26; on angels, 28; on forms of government, 30; on liturgies, 35; on Irenæus, 57; believers in Rome, 101.

Liturgies, 35, 281.
Lord's Day, 37, 286.
Lord's Divinity, 344.
Lord's Supper, 35, 39, 43, 45, 161, 235, 255, 280, 287.
Lucian, 115.
Lucias, King, 105.
Lucullus, 146.
Lupus of Troyes, 307.
Luther on justification, 276.

Macrina, 199, 204.
Maitland, Dr., 382.
Manicheism, 152, 263, 272.
Marcion, 76.
Marcus Aurelius, 112, 123.
Mariolatry, 161.
Martin of Tours, 153, 228, 230.
Mattidia, 16, 17.
Maurice, 372.
Maximinus, 97.
Melania, 313.
Melito, 58, 86.
Mello, 104.
Meropius, 353.
Milman, Dean, 96, 146.
Mohammedanism, 356, 357.
Montanism, 30.
Montanus, 73, 74.
Moorish schools, 357.

Narcissus, 58.
Natalius, 86.
Neale, 68, 167, 215.
Neander, 63.
Nepos, 70.
Nero, 111, 112.
Nestorianism, 215.
Nestorius, 165, 172, 177.
Newman, Dr., 74, 230.

Nicene Creed, 141, 143, 167, 193.
Nonna, 203.
Novatian sect, 161.

Oberlin, 321.
Ordination, 31.
Origen, 10; on angels, 28; in his *Contra Celsum*, 37; on Lord's Supper, 45; on Christian workers, 53; his learning, 61; on the Scriptures, 63, 260; philosophical, 65; character of, 67; on Christianity, 93; his creed, 264; his works, 349; compared with Augustine, 271.

Pædagogus, 59, 60.
Palladius, 238.
Palmer, 34.
Pantænus, 57.
Papias, 57, 58.
Patrick, St., 318.
Paul of Samosata, 133.
Paulinus, 284.
Pelagianism, 269.
Pelagius I., 176, 245, 268.
Perpetua, 122.
Philippus, 58.
Plato, 90, 349.
Plautus, 103.
Pliny, 33, 94, 98, 111.
Plotinus, 52.
Polycarp, 57; on Easter, 86; visited Rome, 87; martyrdom of, 117, 118.
Polycrates, 58.

Pontinus, 78.
Pothinus, 58.
Prætextatus, 147.
Praxeas, 88.
Predestination, 56.
Primus, 58.
Priscillian, 152, 153, 154, 230.
Pudens, 103.

Radegonda, 305.
Reccared, 310.
Recognitions of Clement, 15, 16.
Religious novels, 19, 20, 22.
Remigius, 307.
Robertson, Dr., 382.
Ruinart, 123.

Sabellianism, 143.
Sacraments, 44, 261.
Salvian, 303.
Schaff, Dr., 213, 262, 315.
Septimius Severus, 122.
Septuagint, 72, 313.
Serapion, 58.
Shepherd of Hermas, 14.
Simon Magus, 16.
Sisterhoods, 205.
Socrates, 65, 103, 108, 150, 280.
Sophocles, 65.
Soter, 57.
Southey, Dr., 67.
Sozomen, 103, 161.
Spyridion, 138.
Stoics, 104, 105.
Stromata, 59.
Stubbs, Dr., 145, 336, 338.
Sylvester, 239.
Synesius, 215.
Teaching of the Twelve, 39.

Tertullian, 2; on councils, 33; on baptism, 39; orthodox, 75; style, 77; followed by Cyprian, 83; on the Trinity, 88; on Christian influence, 92, 98; on the Millennium, 277.
Theodora, 154, 156.
Theodore, 151.
Theodoret, 103, 173, 205, 352.
Theodoric, 294.
Theodosius I., 151, 162, 185, 234.
Theodotus, 86, 89.
Theophilus, 218.
Tracts for the Times, 231.
Trajan, 98, 109.
Trinity, 68, 261.
Trypho, 50.

Ullman, 189.
Ulphilas, 292.

Valens, 151.
Valentine I., 151.
Valentinian II., 151.
Valerian, 113.
Vespasian, 147.
Vigilantius, 315.
Vigilius I., 245.
Vincentius Lirinensis, 231.
Virgin, images of, 164; name in prayer, 285; in Spain, 308.
Vitringa, 38.

Western theology, 259.
Whitsuntide, 286.
Wiltsch, 98, 99.

WORKS BY THE SAME AUTHOR.

Religion in England during the first half of

the Present Century : A History, with a Postscript on Subsequent Events. By JOHN STOUGHTON, D.D. In Two Vols., crown 8vo, 15*s*.

"The present book will long be the standard authority on the important subject of which it treats."—*Academy.*

History of Religion in England : from the

Opening of the Long Parliament to the End of the Eighteenth Century. Third Edition. In Six Vols., crown 8vo, 45*s*.

"A history conceived and written in the true historic spirit by a writer looking back upon the contests and disturbances of the past, and contemplating the battles upon which freedom was achieved with the calmness of posterity. The result is a book which the members of all churches may read with equal satisfaction and advantage."—*Daily News.*

Recollections of a Long Life.

Second Edition. Crown 8vo, cloth, 6*s*.

"The scenes he has witnessed, the men he has seen, come back to him in vivid mental pictures ; he sees old faces, and hears again the voices long ago silent. His reminiscences are therefore lively, and the pictures pass almost too rapidly before us."—*Daily News.*

"A volume of genial reminiscences. . . . Dr. Stoughton has led an active life, and has often been brought into contact with many of his most distinguished ecclesiastical contemporaries, of whom he writes with uniform good taste and good feeling."—*Times.*

"The interesting volume is full of most charming reminiscences."—*Record.*

The Daily Prayer Book, for the use of Families.

With Additional Prayers for Special Occasions. Edited by JOHN STOUGHTON, D.D. Crown 8vo, cloth, 3*s.* 6*d.*

" To those who, whilst believing with Dr. Stoughton that 'united prayer is the duty and privilege of every household,' do not conduct it extemporaneously, these prayers will be a reliable and treasured means of assistance."—*Christian.*

———

LONDON : HODDER & STOUGHTON, 27, PATERNOSTER ROW.

HODDER & STOUGHTON'S
NEW AND RECENT PUBLICATIONS.

The Life of John Cairns, D.D., LL.D.,
Principal of the United Presbyterian College, Edinburgh. Edited by the Rev. A. R. MacEwen, M.A., D.D. 8vo, cloth, 14s.

Andrew A. Bonar, D.D. Reminiscences and
Letters. Edited by his Daughter, MARJORY BONAR. With Portrait, Illustration, and Facsimile. Crown 8vo, cloth, 6s.

Andrew A. Bonar, D.D. Diary and Letters.
Transcribed and Edited by his Daughter, MARJORY BONAR. With Portrait. Seventh Thousand. Crown 8vo, cloth, 6s.

The Religions of Japan. From the Dawn of
History to the End of Méiji. By W. E. GRIFFIS, D.D., formerly of the Imperial University of Tokio. Crown 8vo, cloth, price 7s. 6d.

Studies in Theology. Lectures delivered in
Chicago Theological Seminary. By the Rev. JAMES DENNEY, D.D., Author of "The Epistles to the Thessalonians," etc. Fourth Edition. Crown 8vo, cloth, 5s.

"The most original and remarkable contribution to the literature of dogmatics that has been made by any of our younger theologians.... In his new book Dr. Denney proves himself more clearly than ever to be the legitimate successor of Dr. Dale.... It will be obvious to every competent critic that Dr. Denney has in rare combination the intellectual powers necessary for the fit discussion of his subjects, and he has a perfect comprehension of contemporary thought."—*British Weekly.*

LONDON: HODDER & STOUGHTON, 27, PATERNOSTER ROW.

WORKS BY THE
REV. PRINCIPAL FAIRBAIRN, D.D.

I.
Christ in Modern Theology.

By A. M. FAIRBAIRN, D.D., Principal of Mansfield College, Oxford. Sixth Edition. 8vo, cloth, 12s.

"His work is, without doubt, one of the most valuable and comprehensive contributions to theology that has been made during this generation."—*Spectator.*

"A more vivid summary of Church history has never been given. With its swift characterisation of schools and politics, with its subtle tracings of the development of various tendencies through the influence of their environment, of reaction, and of polemic; with its contrasts of different systems, philosophies, and races; with its portraits of men; with its sense of progress and revolt—this part of Dr. Fairbairn's book is no mere annal, but drama, vivid and full of motion, representative of the volume and sweep of Christianity through the centuries."—*Speaker.*

II.
Religion in History and in Modern Life;

Together with an Essay on the Church and the Working Classes. Ninth Thousand. Crown 8vo, cloth, 3s. 6d.

"One of the finest extant specimens of a historical argument for Christianity."—*Westminster Gazette.*

"A timely and weighty contribution to a subject which theologians but too seldom venture to grapple with."—*Scotsman.*

III.
The City of God. A Series of Discussions in

Religion. Fifth Edition. 8vo, cloth, 7s. 6d.

"We find in the discourses which form this volume much able statement and much vigorous thought, and an admirable comprehension of the great questions which are being discussed in our day with eagerness and bated breath."—*Scotsman.*

IV.
Studies in the Life of Christ.

Seventh Edition. Demy 8vo, 9s.

"There is ample room for Professor Fairbairn's thoughtful and brilliant sketches. Dr. Fairbairn's is not the base rhetoric often employed to hide want of thought or poverty of thought, but the noble rhetoric which is alive with thought and imagination to its utmost and finest extremities."—*Expositor.*

LONDON: HODDER & STOUGHTON, 27, PATERNOSTER ROW.

The Historical Geography of the Holy Land.

Especially in Relation to the History of Israel and of the Early Church. By GEORGE ADAM SMITH, D.D., LL.D, Professor of Hebrew and Old Testament Exegesis, Free Church College, Glasgow. Second Edition. 8vo, cloth, 15*s.* With Six Maps, specially prepared.

"It is not often that we have to review a book so thorough and so masterly, and at the same time written in a style which commands attention as well as admiration. . . . It contains and 'uses' the important parts of all the immense mass of modern research and discovery, enriched and illuminated by a mind of imagination and poetry, as well as scholarship."—*Saturday Review.*

The Church in the Roman Empire before A.D. 170.

By W. M. RAMSAY, M.A., Professor of Humanity in the University of Aberdeen. Fourth Edition, with Maps and Illustration. 8vo, cloth, 12*s.*

"The whole volume is full of freshness and originality. . . . I lay down his book with warm and sincere admiration. He has succeeded in investing a number of critical discussions with extraordinary vividness and reality. He has done so because he writes always 'with his eye upon the object,' and that an object seen in the light of knowledge which in its own special sphere (the geography of Asia Minor and Roman administration) is unrivalled."—Prof. W. SANDAY in *The Expositor.*

"This volume is the most important contribution to the study of early Church history which has been published in this country since the great work of Bishop Lightfoot on the Apostolic Fathers. It is, too, unless our memory fails us, without a rival in any foreign country. . . . Alike in its methods and conclusions its value is unique. . . . In the first portion, Professor Ramsay uses a wealth of topographical and antiquarian knowledge to illustrate the missionary journeyings of St. Paul, and succeeds, we believe, completely in demonstrating the thoroughly historical character of the account we possess. . . . He has reconstructed the cities and the city life of the past, and with this picture before his eyes he has examined every line and word of the original authorities."—*Guardian.*

LONDON: HODDER & STOUGHTON, 27, PATERNOSTER ROW.

WORKS BY
The late DR. R. W. DALE, of Birmingham.

Christian Doctrine. A Series of Discourses.
Fourth Thousand. Crown 8vo, cloth, 6s.

"Like everything that Dr. Dale writes, these discourses are eminently thoughtful and suggestive. Even when the topics discussed are thoroughly familiar, there is a freshness and originality in the treatment of them which makes the reader feel that he is well repaid for going over old ground. In days such as these, when loud voices are proclaiming that the doctrines of the Holy Trinity and Incarnation are metaphysical subtleties, 'sectarian' and 'denominational' dogmas, it is refreshing to note the powerful and outspoken vindication of them which is here set before us."—*Guardian*.

Fellowship with Christ and other Discourses
Delivered on Special Occasions. Fourth Thousand. Crown 8vo, cloth, 6s.

"These are certainly among the most massive, and, as a consequence, most impressive sermons of the day. Each is a sort of miniature theological treatise, but the theology is alive—as it were, heated through and through by the fires of a mighty conviction, which has become a passion to convince. . . . In these sermons there is a fine universalism; they might be addressed to any audience—academic, professional, commercial, artisan. And to hear them would be to feel that religion is a thing to be believed and obeyed."—*Speaker*.

The Living Christ and the Four Gospels.
Eighth Thousand. Crown 8vo, cloth, 6s.

"As a man of culture and eloquence he has put the case strongly and well, and it will not be surprising if his book, which is not written, he tells us, for Masters of Arts, but in the first instance for members of his own congregation, and then for all ordinary people who take an interest in such matters, should be the means of convincing many that the assumptions sometimes made about late origin of the Gospels, etc., are utterly unfounded."—*Scotsman*.

Laws of Christ for Common Life.
Seventh Thousand. Crown 8vo, cloth, 6s.

"Sound sense and wholesome Christian teaching conveyed in pure, idiomatic, and forcible English."—*Scotsman*.

"A storehouse of wise precepts, a repository of loving counsels—shrewd, practical, and fully cognisant of difficulties and drawbacks; but informed by such sympathy and a sense of Christian brotherhood as should do much to make it acceptable and effective."—*Nonconformist*.

LONDON : HODDER & STOUGHTON, 27, PATERNOSTER ROW.

DR. R. W. DALE'S WORKS—continued.

Nine Lectures on Preaching.

Seventh Edition. Crown 8vo, cloth, 6s.

"Admirable lectures, briefly written, earnest and practical."—*Literary Churchman.*

"Dr. Dale's lectures are full of practical wisdom and intense devotion."—*The Expositor.*

The Jewish Temple and the Christian Church.

A Series of Discourses on the Epistle to the Hebrews. Ninth Edition. Crown 8vo, cloth, 6s.

"Wholesomer sermons than these it is almost impossible to conceive. Mr. Dale's preaching has always been remarkable for moral energy and fervour, but here this characteristic rises to its highest power."—*Expositor.*

The Epistle to the Ephesians. Its Doctrines

and Ethics. Seventh Edition. Crown 8vo, cloth, 7s. 6d.

"The terse and vigorous style, rising on occasion into a manly and impressive eloquence, of which Mr. Dale is known to be a master, gives lucid expression to thought that is precise, courageous, and original."—*Spectator.*

Week-day Sermons.

Sixth Edition. Crown 8vo, cloth, 3s. 6d.

The Ten Commandments.

Sixth Edition. Crown 8vo, cloth, 5s.

"Full of thought and vigour."—*Spectator.*

Impressions of Australia.

Crown 8vo, cloth, 5s.

"Dr. Dale's articles . . . constitute one of the most sensible books about Australia. . . . The book is readable, and indeed excellent."—*Athenæum.*

The New Evangelicalism and the Old.

Cloth, 1s.

"It has more in it than many an elaborate treatise; it suggests by every sentence; it is throughout succinct, pregnant, masterly."—*British Weekly.*

LONDON: HODDER & STOUGHTON, 27, PATERNOSTER ROW.

www.ingramcontent.com/pod-product-compliance
Lightning Source LLC
Chambersburg PA
CBHW050845300426
44111CB00010B/1129